CHELTENHAM
&
GLOUCESTER
College of Higher Education

# THE
# BIG BROTHER
# SOCIETY

# THE
# BIG BROTHER
# SOCIETY

## IAN WILL

**HARRAP** **LONDON**

*First published in Great Britain* 1983
*by* HARRAP LIMITED
19-23 Ludgate Hill, London EC4M 7PD

©*Ian McLean Will* 1983

ISBN 0 245-53924-7


Designed by Michael R. Carter

Printed and bound in Great Britain
by Mackays of Chatham Ltd

For my family
who suffered while I wrote this book,
and for Simon Dally
who commissioned it

# Contents

1   Recognizing 'Big Brother'    9
2   Legal Niceties    32
3   Servants above their Station    52
4   Security through the Looking-glass    76
5   Soldiers of the Queen    100
6   Computers — to Serve Them
    All Our Days    123
7   The Technology of Tyranny    148
8   Thin Trees with High Foliage    168
9   Re-addressing a 'Post' Society    187
    Index    217

# 1
# Recognizing 'Big Brother'

The conflict between the liberty of the individual and the remorseless progress of state bureaucracy, constantly seeking to direct and control our lives, has been extensively documented and discussed. Excessive repetition of expressions such as 'inalienable rights' and 'freedom', associated with concepts of liberty, has tended to obscure just how fragile is the base upon which these concepts are constructed. The parameters of individual liberty have naturally always been constrained by contact and interaction with the equally 'inalienable rights' of other individuals to exercise their own particular 'freedom'.

An overpopulated society of ever-increasing complexity imposes massive social and organizational demands on government. Faced with general expectations of more equitable sharing of the national wealth, and with inevitable changes in living, working and recreational patterns as a result of today's technologies, governments often appear to have the unenviable task of reconciling the irreconcilable. In undertaking the task, the principle of the greatest good for the greatest number holds obvious attractions. To some extent this has reduced, and will continue to reduce, the scope for individual expression of personal freedom; the danger is that personal liberty may become totally submerged in a rising tide of collectivism. As the parameters of liberty contract, it is important for the individual to maintain the integrity of any remaining freedom against the intrusion of the state and other organizations.

In a speech in 1864, Abraham Lincoln addressed himself to the meaning of liberty:

We all declare for liberty: but in using the same word we do not mean the same thing. With some the word liberty may mean for each man to do as he pleases with himself and the product of his labours; while with others the same word may mean for some men to do as they please with other men and the product of other men's labour. Here are two, not only different, but incompatible things, called by the same name, liberty. And it follows that each of the things is by the respective parties called by two different and incompatible names, liberty and tyranny. The shepherd drives the wolf from the sheep's throat for which the sheep thanks the shepherd as his (sic) liberator, while the wolf denounces him for the same . . . Plainly the sheep and the wolf are not agreed upon a definition of liberty.

The third element of the story is the role of the shepherd. In protecting the liberty of the sheep to live it was being defended against the tyranny of the wolf. The sheep was being protected, however, only in order for the shepherd to cut its throat at a more convenient time. What was being defended was not the sheep but the shepherd's power to decide when it should be turned into the family joint: something the shepherd would defend as his personal liberty.

Whether torn apart and digested raw by the wolf, or roasted, garnished and served up on a silver platter for the delectation of the shepherd, the sheep remains the only true victim. In the context of human society the message is apposite: in seeking protection from the wolfish predator, be wary of those who offer safeguarding services no matter how benign they may appear.

A political party which offered the British electorate free choice to elect a form of government clearly defined as one which would impose upon the country a totalitarian dictatorship would be unlikely to gain popular support. The problem is, however, that tyrannies do not identify themselves to an electorate in these terms; and those tyrannies are unlikely to see themselves as tyrannical. Tyranny is a subjective concept, as Abraham Lincoln illustrated.

There is always a danger of concentrating too much on extreme examples and overstating the case. Hitler and Stalin were outrageously extreme in their views and for that reason are difficult to see as relevant analogies in the context of modern trends in British society, when one considers the extent of human slaughter and terror associated with their leaderships. It seems inconceivable that any regime could emerge in Britain to approach the horror of that of Hitler in pursuit of his 'Thousand Year Reich', or Stalin's with his highly specialized version of a 'Dictatorship of the Proletariat'. Tyranny on a lesser scale, however, could be equally oppressive and, moreover, more difficult to identify.

Tyrannies become identified with leaders, as in the cases of Hitler and Stalin. In attempting to comprehend the full magnitude of evil perpetrated in their names it is possible to ignore an integral element of their power: leaders can conceive, create and mould their regimes, but they cannot possibly administer them without support. Without an effective, supportive administrative machine tyrants can neither gain nor retain power. One of the central questions asked in this book is whether such an apparatus could succeed, if not already in embryonic existence, in British society.

It may seem fanciful to imagine a stable British democratic system being set aside in favour of some form of totalitarian regime, whether of the Right or Left, however well its ultimate intentions were disguised. It is important, therefore, to establish the validity of the question in the context of current British society.

The traditional electoral system of 'first past the post', with no provision for proportional representation, clearly demonstrates that Britain can allow itself to be governed by a party which does not enjoy majority support. There is no reason to suppose that a totalitarian regime would find itself impotent by its failure to achieve the majority mandate that many democratically elected governments have similarly failed to secure in the past.

It is generally acknowledged by parliamentary observers that the negative vote, cast as an expression of opposition to the other party rather than as a declaration of support for the favoured candidate, is a significant factor in every election. A potentially totalitarian regime emerging from within the traditional structures of the existing major parties could unquestionably count on some degree of similar support. This negative factor is an important element in the proposition that totalitarianism could emerge in Britain in the foreseeable future. It demonstrates the deep-rooted suspicion which already exists in society about the ultimate goals of opposing political parties either of the Left or the Right. More importantly, it demonstrates that this traditional, ingrained suspicion held by one side of the other is a potent political weapon. However misconceived the suspicion may be, properly manipulated it can be used, on the one hand, to create distrust of benignly intended actions by the opposition and, on the other hand, engender support for questionable acts by the aligned party. In short, under the influence of traditional suspicions and party allegiance, a significant section of society can be induced to ignore an unpalatable reality.

Provided that an emergent totalitarian regime can be made to appear to have its roots within one of the traditional parties of British government, it is perfectly feasible that it could secure substantial public support. That does not in itself explain how such a regime could emerge in a country with a long history of relative social and political stability. The question is, however, how stable is Britain now? The question has to be addressed in three parts: in terms of political, economic and social stability, since each will significantly influence the attraction, or rejection, of totalitarianism in Britain.

Paradoxically, the popular belief in the opening years of the 1980s that successive governments had failed to meet the material aspirations of society had the effect of enhancing the credibility of both extremes of the political spectrum at the expense of the forces of moderation. Hardliners on both sides argued that what had failed was the 'soft centre's' ineffectual attempts to apply Conservative socialism, or Socialist conservatism, depending on the political affinities of the critic concerned.

Both political extremes were unanimous in the view that Britain was witnessing the inevitable collapse of a mixed economy of free enterprise and state-assisted industry: a view which to some extent appeared to be supported by post-war experience. The divergence between Right and Left naturally produced opposed political interpretations of what had gone wrong.

According to the Right, the economy had failed to perform adequately because successive governments had replaced the market economics of true capitalism with placebo remedies. Instead of forcing the public to swallow the bitter pill of economic realism, sugar-coated measures had been substituted to humour the voting population while encouraging the economic disease. Restrictive trades union practices leading to overmanning, excessive wage demands, low production and inefficiency were cited as factors which led to Britain being uncompetitive as a nation.

Nowhere were these things more in evidence, it was claimed, than in the nationalized industries and government bureaucracy. Responsible investment to encourage entrepreneurial skills in the wealth creating sectors of commerce and industry had been sacrificed. These funds had instead been dissipated on a massive scale by being ploughed into unprofitable state-owned industry, a burgeoning civil service, and open-ended expansion of social services which could be neither controlled nor sustained. In the eyes of the political Right capitalism had not failed, it had simply not been applied.

At the other end of the political scale, the hard Left saw the progressive decline of the mixed economy, and the pressures that decline imposed on employment and the social services, as the long predicted and eagerly anticipated death throes of an iniquitous capitalism. No less important in their eyes, it could also be convincingly portrayed as irrefutable evidence of the political futility of watered-down socialism. They pointed to three million plus unemployed, a disaffected youth, escalating crime and civil disorder, all of which provided the social chemistry to enhance left-wing credibility and the attractions of a Marxist society as an alternative to the impotence of successive indecisive governments.

The most tangible evidence of the emergence of Marxist militants from the political wilderness was revealed when penetration of the Labour Party's internal structure forced the resignation in 1981 from the party of large numbers of moderate social democrats.

The infiltration of the Labour Party by the militant left, and the retreat of the moderates, vested militant socialism with political respectability it could probably never have achieved by electoral means. What had been generally regarded as the lunatic fringe of British politics was granted a certificate of sanity.

Having surreptitiously penetrated the party machinery the Left took control of the administrative reins of policy-making at grass roots and party level. The impeccable democratic credentials of Labour Party membership housed them in the party traditionally regarded by the working class voters as their party of government. Once installed it was not difficult for the new 'labour' activists to exploit the tensions which had always existed in the party between the apparatchiks of the party machine and the parliamentary representatives.

In a time of recession, social turbulence and technological change, fundamentalist messages of total state control and radical redistribution of wealth from their own party held obvious attractions for the traditional Labour supporter. Suddenly, it was the forces of moderation in the Labour Party who found themselves being moved to the periphery of politics. Moderates found themselves being assaulted by the accusation that they were the political deviationists attempting to resuscitate the pink froth of centrism instead of drinking deep from the cup of red-blooded Socialism. The hard left argued : Socialism had not failed, it had simply never been tried.

The current political scene sees the extremes of left and right poised in classical confrontation. The new element is that both are conscious of their own, and each other's, proximity to the levers of government power. Moderation – both Conservative and Socialist – which has hitherto restrained the application of extreme policies, has suffered the inevitable consequences of failing to perform over the lives of successive parliaments to the satisfaction of large sections of the British population.

The centre of British politics is in turmoil. Moderate Conservatives and Socialists are increasingly discovering more in common with their moderate opposite numbers than with hardliners in their own parties. Attempts at realignment of the political centre become complicated by traditional allegiance to party divisions: entrenched attitudes demand the formulation of alternative and distinguishable party policies rather than inter-party consensus agreement. While political moderates annihilate each other in an internecine battle of doctrinal semantics, only the extremists appear capable of winning the war. It is the extremists who seem most able to provide clearcut alternatives which, regardless of any fundamental evils attached to them, attract the electorate with a deceptive clarity and certainty.

With the political centre in disarray a power vacuum has been created in British politics. This vacuum faces both extremes with the most critical and urgent decisions which they may consider too dangerous to delay for long.

Many political commentators believe that the fate of Capitalism in Britain will be decided in the 1980s. Industrial development in third world countries, the evolution of high technology, and the increasing competitiveness of other industrial nations have all added up to contracting markets. British management has increasingly come to seek, and to rely on, state support. In the view of Capitalist purists this state support has made a mockery of the concept of free enterprise and market economics which dictate that any business which cannot undertake its own profitability goes to the wall. If capitalism is to survive, it has been said, there has to be a return to its free enterprise roots and an end to state support for ailing industries.

Substantial public investment has been absorbed by industry: investment both in new technology and more efficient business methods. Overmanning in industry has had to stop. Above all, if business was to obtain the investment required, industry had to be relieved of the burden of taxation. In order to do this it was necessary for government to reduce, or control, its own expenditure by shedding unprofitable nationalized industries, curtailing spending on state bureaucracy and halting the unrestrained expansion of social services, all of which were draining the country's resources. To revitalize the economy and reverse the political, economic and social trends of some forty years, it had to be accepted that some pain would have to be inflicted. This begged two crucial questions: who was to suffer and how willing would they be to bear the pain?

Whatever the definition of monetarism, as it was applied by Margaret Thatcher's government from 1979, it became identified as a return to capitalist fundamentalism. State-owned industries were hived off, aid to ailing industries was cut off or severely curtailed, and strenuous attempts made to reduce the state bureaucratic machinery. Wholesale surgery was carried out and, as the scalpel began to slice into local government spending, education, health and the social services, the anticipated pain began to be felt.

By 1982 the first of the two questions had been answered: the major suffering was to be borne by 3½ million unemployed – untold thousands of the country's youth facing the prospect of never being gainfully employed – and the most disadvantaged elements of society. That the suffering was not always the direct result of government policies did not make the pain less intense. The second question – how willing would they be to bear the pain? – has not yet been answered. Racial unrest and street rioting, youth disaffection, rising crime figures and general social unease suggest to many that they are very unwilling indeed.

The 1980s appear to hold out three possibilities for the political right. The first possibility is that the Conservatism of Mrs Thatcher will be successful and that the fruits of applied capitalism will quickly prove attractive to the great mass of the British public, and, moreover, within their reach. The second possibility is that the tentative realignment of political moderates, started in the 1980s with the SDP/Liberal Alliance, will solidify into a coherent force, retaining elements both of economic realism and of social concern for the disadvantaged. The third possibility is that there will be a resurgence of Socialism under a Labour Party, heavily influenced by left-wing militant extremists, determined to implement policies which will not only reverse the trends of Mrs Thatcher's government but destroy any prospect of their future revival.

The hard right would find the first prospect ideal; the second they could accommodate; the third possibility would be anathema.

It is not only the extreme right who are conscious of the dangers of the emergence of a Labour government heavily dependent on support from the extreme left. The scope for militant penetration of the established infrastructure of state power in the forms of the security agencies, police, judiciary and military services would be of unprecedented scale. Having seen the impact of sustained publicity campaigns funded by the resources of the Greater London Council, under the leadership of Kenneth Livingstone, it needs little imagination to envisage what a media conscious militant left could achieve with central government funded information services at their disposal. There are many people of all political shades who could not be expected to view the overall prospect with equanimity.

In the solid traditions of a long established parliamentary democracy the outcome will be decided by the electorate at the ballot box. That fact in itself, however, does not totally reassure the extreme right. There may be no other democratic options, but that does not mean there are no other options.

If the closing years of the twentieth century are critical for the extreme right, they are no less critical for the extreme left. Successful penetration of the Labour Party has brought the revolutionary Marxist left closer to real political power than ever before in Britain. Having achieved a degree of influence in a credible party of government, the theoreticians of the militant left must decide whether to consolidate their gains or press on regardless.

By keeping a low profile and submerging themselves in the broad mainstream of Labour party socialism there is a great deal they can achieve, not least political respectability. A number of factors exist in their favour. They have a situation where the moderate centre is splintered across the entire political centre which enhances the influence they can exert within the Labour Party. The ruling elements of the Conservative Party are pursuing economic policies which have a built-in acceptance of massive unemployment, which many consider will be irreversible. At the same time their social policies are viewed by many as a fierce attack on the concept of the Welfare State and a return to the jungle law of the survival of the fittest.

When militant penetration of the Labour Party was discovered, there were signs of reaction by the orthodox party moderates. There are already signs that moderate resurgence based on consensus policies and the individual expulsions of the most extremist subversives will in time return them to the political wilderness. If that happens, they will have peaked too soon with little prospect of re-establishing themselves in the Labour Party in the foreseeable future. Equally dangerous for the extreme left is the prospect of an effective force emerging from a realignment of the political centre outside the Labour Party. This could be by the Conservative Party drawing back from their existing hardline policies or by a new grouping such as the SDP/Liberal Alliance. This could mean not only political oblivion for the militants but for the Labour Party itself.

The militants must also face one other unpalatable possibility. When Mrs Thatcher coined the expression There Is No Alternative she referred to her monetarist policies. Few people accepted that proposition in its entirety. In the wake of the Falklands adventure the acronym TINA underwent a subtle change. The emphasis came to be placed less on TINA policies and more on Mrs Thatcher. With the prospect of a dramatic lurch towards left-wing totalitarianism under a future Labour government, a great number of Britons who scorned the first TINA might just embrace the second.

In some ways this may not be as bad for the revolutionary or militant left as it initially appears. One lesson that the extreme left have learned is that the British people cannot be persuaded to identify with extreme policies in any significant numbers. In recognition of this, the militant strategy for some years has concentrated on forming alliances with the sections of society with genuine grievances, even though the causes espoused may lack any roots in Marxism. Since many of Thatcher's most loyal supporters are identified with the hard right of the Conservative Party, revolutionary theoreticians welcome the prospect of right-wing domination of the Conservative Party and the resulting potential for alienation of the people.

Although they may be necessary to the economy, financial policies which are implemented without regard to social consequences alienate vast numbers of people and swell the ranks of protest. There is a very narrow line between strong measures to enforce law and order, and oppression. The most vigorous and vociferous champions of law and order do not always attach the same meanings to the words as others do, as former President Richard Nixon and Vice-President Spiro Agnew of the United States have demonstrated. It is not enough for government policies to be theoretically sound. When opposition to policies within society reaches a certain level they have to be changed regardless of financial cost if society is to retain its basic stability. The alternative is to create a state apparatus capable of suppressing the opposition. The more obdurate the opposition the more oppressive the apparatus.

It is in such a scenario that the Marxist left sees the opportunity for future power: the implementation of hard right political, social and economic policies will generate widespread revulsion and opposition which, in turn, will provoke oppressive totalitarian countermeasures. In such a situation the opposition would not be united in favour of an alternative: they would be united against the status quo. It is the belief of the extreme left, with its trained, organized and politically committed cadres, that in such a union it would be the Marxist alternative which would inevitably emerge as the dominant force.

The early 1980s, perhaps for the first time, sees a considerable number of moderates and politically uncommitted citizens looking more fearfully towards the right wing of the Conservative Party, which is in power, than to the left wing of politics which is not. Rightly or wrongly they detect a hardening of attitudes and the eclipse, however temporary, of the caring conservative. Tolerance, moderation and conciliation appear to be in retreat from the policies of confrontation. The extreme left has rarely, if ever, been in a stronger position to turn its united opposition into reality. If it fails to take advantage of its present position, a similar opportunity in the future may not arise – particularly if the political moderates regain their former influence.

The question remains: how stable is Britain politically? Given the country's long democratic tradition, and the fact that the parliamentary election system is still in operation, Britain must on one level be considered politically stable. When the two political extremes are each so close to the levers of government power, however, it seems fair to regard it as a precarious stability. That stability depends largely on economic and social factors.

Since the Industrial Revolution, in common with every other industrialized nation, the material expectations of the British people have been
conditioned by a belief in continuing economic growth, fuelled by full
employment provided by the industrialized society. The clearest message
received, if not acknowledged, by the industrialized nations in the
opening years of the 1980s was that the traditional concept of the
'industrial' society had been overtaken by the advance of high technology.
The unresolved question for millions of ordinary people is: will there
be a place for them in a post-industrial society?

For the first time in post-war Britain, people are confronting the
prospect of mass unemployment and real cuts in living standards for
millions as permanent features of their future existence. A generation of
the nation's youth has emerged from educational institutions at all levels
with little hope of employment. Not only do they face a contracting
labour market, but also the accusation that their educational attainment
is irrelevant in the context of society's requirements.

At the other end of the age spectrum lies a substantial element of
skilled workers and management discarded en masse because their skills,
or even industries, have become outmoded by the advance of technology.
Young enough to harbour personal ambition and too young to retire,
they are at an age when the acquisition of new skills is difficult.
Even when the transition is attempted they sometimes find themselves
disadvantaged in competition with younger staff. In addition to coping
with reduced personal status and financial circumstances, they have the
additional handicap of offering a limited working life in return for
training investment by any prospective employer.

The effects of unemployment are clearly disruptive to a nation's
internal stability even when applied to only one section of the community
for a relatively short time. The present prospect is one of continuing
unemployment crossing traditional working class divisions. The political
and social consequences of this for the future are incalculable.

The prospect is no longer that of periodic bouts of unemployment
being the inevitable lot of an uneducated and inarticulate proletariat.
What is being held out is the sustained erosion of present and future
living standards and aspirations of skilled working and managerial
elements of society who are educated, articulate and politically aware.
Many of today's unemployed are familiar with the mechanics of power
in the modern state.

Given the inherent stability of the British system of government, the
state will be able to mitigate the divisive social effects of widespread
unemployment for some time to come – assuming that the government
of the day has the political will to heal divisions. It is also conceivable
that a general upturn in world trading and international commerce will

create fresh opportunities for a lean, efficient and competitive British manufacturing industry to become a leading exporter once again. This could, in the view of some economists, gradually reduce unemployment figures. This in itself, however, will not solve the underlying dilemma of modern society.

Technological and scientific progress are rapidly overtaking society's capacity to adjust to the enforced changes. Technological and scientific advances require, essentially, reduced human participation. This applies to industry, agriculture, commerce and management. Nineteenth-century Luddites acted on vague fears about industrial technology, the implications of which were difficult for them to conceive. Modern Luddites are concerned with the predictable consequences of technology which, in many ways, are understood only too well. The modern Luddite has the advantage over his predecessor of having historical precedent and contemporary example to justify his fears.

There is a view that the search for knowledge and the interests of scientific advancement provide their own irrefutable justification transcending conventional morality: that science and technology are surrounded by an intellectual purity which protects practitioners from any responsibility for their discoveries. Buttressed by this conviction, scientists and technologists have produced weaponry which can destroy the world many times over; chemicals have been created for the express purpose of extermination; and psychological techniques developed for the purpose of brainwashing.

Those who live under the shadow of the technology of mutual destruction have not yet been able to devise a failsafe means of control. There is no certainty that they ever will, but that has not prevented the search for yet more sophisticated technologies of even greater terror. Is there any reason to suppose that greater restraint will be exercised in the area of economics where the consequences of technology and its impact on the future social fabric are uncertain? Advanced technology has created a new dimension to the economics of wealth distribution, and this raises an even more fundamental question.

Technology is rapidly advancing to the state where it will eventually become largely self-sustaining. As it advances, society may increasingly see itself being divided into three functional classes. There will be those who control technology, those who service technology, and those who service those who control and service technology. In addition, there will be one non-functional class of society: a class which will serve no functional purpose other than to exist. They will be the successor of the working class: now dispossessed of the work function to become the non-working class.

The contribution of the non-working class to the national economy will be minimal, their numbers huge and their degree of self-sufficiency small. The question of unemployment is, therefore, only one factor in the economic dilemma of the future.

An élite is in the process of evolving which will not only control the wealth produced and its distribution, but for the first time it will be capable of creating wealth. No longer will there be conflict between those who control but do not create and those who create but do not control. The economic struggle of the future may be between the technological monopoly who create, control and distribute wealth and those who contribute nothing to the creation process and yet make endless demands for an increasing share on those who do. It is comforting to think that in a civilized society the economic problems of the post-industrial society will be overcome by a united determination to maintain belief in the innate dignity of the individual.

Less comforting are the historical precedents which illustrate the reluctance of those who have to share generously with those who have not. Even less comforting is the analogous contemporary example of Western developed nations with stores bulging at the seams with rotting grain, meat and butter mountains, while millions of people starve to death each year throughout the world. In essence, there is no precedent to suggest that the producers will support the non-producers.

The economic stability of Britain seems then to be no less precarious than its political stability. Since both factors are interrelated that suggests the dangers of destabilization are increased. There is, however, a third factor to be considered before the question, 'How stable is Britain?' can be answered.

Politics and economics alone do not determine the cohesion of a nation. British society has remained intact in the face of political and economic crises in the past. The scale of crises in the future may be greater than those previously experienced but, given social stability, there is no reason why the resilience of the national character should not triumph in the face of adversity as before. That, of course, depends on having a stable society to begin with.

In George Orwell's book, *1984*, it is suggested that the composition of the leadership of the emergent 'Big Brother' regime had been entirely predictable long before it gained power.

The new aristocracy was made up for the most part of bureaucrats, scientists, technicians, trade-union organisers, publicity experts, sociologists, teachers, journalists and professional politicians. These people, whose origins lay in the salaried middle class and the upper grades of the working class, had been shaped and brought together by the barren world of monopoly industry and centralised government. As compared with their opposite numbers in past ages, they were less avaricious, less tempted by luxury, hungrier for pure power, and, above all, more conscious of what they were doing and more intent on crushing opposition. The last difference was cardinal.

In ways which might have surprised Orwell more than others, the composition of the social élite he predicted for his 'Big Brother' regime has largely stood the test of time.

The growth and expanding appetites of central and local government administrative bureaucracies have been matched by the security of tenure they have achieved. Their permanence has forged them into a lethal weapon poised over the jugular vein of parliamentary democracy. The faceless Establishment exercises its influence along its private corridors of power. By virtue of being an administrative monopoly, reinforced by its hierarchy, and operating in almost impenetrable secrecy, it has created a greater concentration of power than is theoretically possible under the aegis of a parliamentary system of government. While elected governments come and go, the hidden government lives on.

Despite the self-evident concentration of power in the hands of the Establishment executive – power which influences the security services, the law, police and military – it appears to be immune to change and protected from public scrutiny. There are signs of growing political militancy in its ranks, and yet, with an ability to strangle the implementation and administration of government policy, the civil service retains the right to strike. An entrenched Establishment, largely unaccountable, exercising executive power in secret, capable by perfectly legal means of emasculating elected government, all adds up to a highly potent mixture. In a time of political crisis would government be allowed to rest with accountable, elected representatives or with the self-elected Establishment?

The role of scientists and technicians envisaged by Orwell in a 'Big Brother' state remains irrefutable. There has been no horror yet known which has caused science to withdraw regardless of the consequences for mankind. There is no reason to believe that the prospect of totalitarianism would deter the march of science and technology any more than the prospect of annihilation.

Trade union officials like Arthur Scargill openly advocate the concept of a one-party socialist state. What makes the participation of trade union organizers in a one-party totalitarian state of the future more likely, should one emerge in Britain, is the changing base of their collective power. As technology increasingly replaces human labour so the power base of union membership may find itself more threatened by the material demands of the more numerous non-working class than by the ruling élite.

How much social concern trade union organizers would be allowed to demonstrate under such circumstances would depend on the willingness of the rank and file membership to share their wealth with those who have made no tangible contribution to the creative process. There are many who fear that the trades unions exercise a disproportionate influence on the affairs of state. Paradoxical as it may seem, it is conceivable in the foreseeable future that the British Labour Party, which was a child of the trades union movement, may have more to fear from the movement than from any government of right wing persuasion. Some indication of future trends in trades unions' social concern may be gained from the consistent failure of the heavy battalions to support weaker union brethren in the lower paid sector.

The mass media can be regarded as a wholesale distributor of information and as a primary source for the general public. By curtailing the supply of information the media can restrict the public's knowledge. In the same way, fed with false information by the media, the public may consider themselves knowledgeable about events when, in reality, they may be in a state of ignorance.

Orwell's 'publicity experts', the adman and PR man, have evolved into a unique social species: 'media man'. These are the uncommitted mercenaries of industry, commerce and politics: social freebooters for whom there is no end other than the message and the sale. For them the means are the end. Media man alone has the access and the ability to satisfy the colossal appetite of instant communications systems for instant messages. This ability reduces philosophy to captions, politics to slogans, and reflective consideration to 45-second comment at peak viewing time.

With the aid of 'media man' political parties and policies are sold to the public like an anodyne: quick to assuage pain, mentally soothing, and painless to take. In common with other consumer products, packaging and presentation are more important than content. With the advent of multi-channel television, made possible by satellite and cable, the already well-established role of 'media man' will be further enhanced. If society succumbs without active resistance to the projected future of human contact being replaced by communication technology interaction, the distinction between reality and fantasy, truth and falsehood, substance and image will become increasingly obscure. Media man is an image-maker. In a world given over to images, the image-maker will play a supreme role. Clearly Orwell's 'publicity experts' have a niche in any emerging totalitarian regime.

As the evolution of the modern mass media has advanced the influence of 'publicity experts', so developments in education have achieved the same thing for sociologists and teachers. Education has always been recognized as a powerful influence within the state; an instrument capable, on the one hand, of reinforcing the mores of the established order, and, on the other, of subverting and undermining them. The second half of the twentieth century has seen a number of trends in schools which have had a revolutionary effect on teaching attitudes. In due course these trends may have an even more revolutionary effect on British society.

Reduced emphasis on the importance of the three Rs as the staple educational diet for school children, and increased emphasis on instilling a wider social awareness, more or less coincided with the emergence of politically active teachers, committed to far-reaching social changes. In the hands of politically militant ideologues, sociology has come to be seen as a classic weapon of revolutionary agitprop. With the three Rs, the veracity of the subject material, the quality of teaching, and the standards of student learning can each be examined and assessed. This is less true with sociology.

Sociology is an inexact science which lends itself to subjective interpretation. When the wisdom being imparted to the young is the inescapable product drawn from objective sociological study it can expand the social consciousness of the nation's youth. When the conclusions being invited merely conform to the conventional wisdom of committed political activists, sociology becomes an instrument of political indoctrination and propaganda. This is particularly true when aimed at impressionable and immature schoolchildren at the lower end of the academic scale.

A nation's youth converted to the state's basic principles will help sustain the stability of the state. Alternatively, a subverted youth can lead to its destruction. These are two fundamental revolutionary principles. As the political left moves towards the abolition of private education and the right moves to dismantle the comprehensive system, the basic issues have become increasingly politicized and polarized. The current debate is less about teaching students how to reason and reach their own conclusions and more about teaching them what to think.

Without question an adequately funded state comprehensive system offers all the youth of Britain the best prospects for equal opportunities in education. At the same time, a total state monopoly of schools and education would cede a degree of power to government; and to an educational bureaucracy, which many find unacceptable and could advance Britain towards totalitarianism. The freedom of a parent in a free society to choose the best education, however, is a basic right. At the same time, public schools in Britain have had a divisive social effect in creating and perpetrating an elitist system of class privilege, based on personal wealth and denied to the less affluent. In the struggle between those who favour one system or the other there can be no outright victory by either side which does not involve a suppression of what is fair about the other view.

Mutual compromise could bridge the divisions without sacrificing principle. Insistence on absolute victory by either side must end in bitter confrontation. Regardless of these predictable consequences, one good and one potentially disastrous, the political protagonists in the education debate opt for absolutism. Attitudes are hardening as the left call for total abolition of private education and the right, under Margaret Thatcher, move to introduce a new system of educational funding which in time would completely sabotage the concept of state funded comprehensive education. As the prospect of confrontation approaches, the prospect for social consensus recedes. It seems there are no costs to be counted in the march to victory whatever the issue.

Any signs of social and political intolerance are disturbing. Such signs become critical when they threaten the stability of the nation's educational system for political ends. It is a measure of the distrust and divisions that currently exist in British society that political intolerance has been allowed to become an increasing feature of contemporary education. Sociologists and teachers have successfully introduced polit- ical controversy into the nation's classrooms. Where they will take it from there is anyone's guess. George Orwell, for one, seemed to have no doubts.

In Orwell's *1984* all journalism was centralized under the control of the 'Ministry of Truth' or 'Minitrue' as it was known in Newspeak, the language of Big Brother. Every form of publication and all elements of the mass media were scripted by Minitrue to reflect the truth proclaimed by Big Brother. The underlying principle was simple. Big Brother was infallible and what he said was true. Since what Big Brother holds true today may not be what he held true yesterday or will hold true tomorrow, it follows that while Big Brother's truth remains constant the words used to express it are variable. In this way not only is what Big Brother says the truth, so also is what he claims to have said whether he has said it or not. This form of omniscience is the dream of every politician and political party.

One advantage of a free press and journalistic independence is the protection it affords the public against truth becoming too flexible an instrument in the mouths of politicians. This is one reason for censorship being such an important weapon in a tyranny's armoury. Censorship, however, assumes many forms and can be applied in many ways.

A totalitarian regime is often more threatened by the absence of an identifiable opposition than by the existence of one, providing it can be controlled. Without an opposition on which to focus public attention, a totalitarian regime will eventually turn on itself since there will be no one else to blame for its own shortcomings. Stalin, for example, dealt with this problem by systematically creating his own opposition, identifying individual members to the public in show trials, and destroying them. This achieved two things: it prevented any effective opposition evolving by removing anyone remotely capable of forming one; and it kept alive the idea of the state being under threat from dangerous and subversive factions. In this way repression could be justified in the interests of state security.

State monopoly censorship is only one way of manipulating the media. There is some justice in the assertion often made by the left wing that the British media does not enjoy entirely uncensored journalistic freedom. A number of mass circulation journals, all owned by capitalist proprietors, can censor freedom of expression just as effectively as a state-controlled journal. The left makes the point that in a capitalist society, capitalist-owned papers are sustained by capitalist advertising. Owners appoint editors who decide the content and its form of expression. Editors who campaign against capitalism and advertising are unlikely to receive gold watches for long and meritorious service.

There is a tendency in the popular media to ignore the fact that there are two forms of freedom involved in the concept of a free press. One is the freedom of journalists to express independent views, and the other is the freedom of the readership to receive factual information free from preconceived opinion. The words, 'Workers go on strike – Management closes factory', conveys factual information to the reader. Given a text which sets out the underlying issues, the reader is free to reach an opinion without preconditioning by the writer. That form of journalism allows the two freedoms to co-exist without one impinging on the other. All too often, however, this is not the case.

In the same way that different words can be used to say the same things, the same words can also be used to say different things. The two phrases, 'Workers on strike force management to close factory', and, 'Management force workers on strike to close factory', use exactly the same words. Both are journalistic judgments. Equally, both are an infringement of the public's basic freedom to receive objective news without having it moulded by journalistic prejudice. Trivializing important issues or sensationalizing unimportant ones are other accusations which can be levelled against the British media. The diversity of the media, however, tends to mitigate the validity of the criticism. The freedom of choice and the range of opinion available compensate for instances of irresponsibility.

The principal commitment of independent journalism must be to the concept of an open society. In such a society, however, it is important to distinguish between information which is legitimately public and that which belongs to the individual and is not public. When an individual's privacy is invaded by the press it is an act of tyranny. When journalism colludes with political figures and public institutions to veil what might be considered unacceptable features from the public, the resultant censorship is no less malign by virtue of being self-imposed. To err on the side of individual privacy is to act responsibly: to err on the side of secrecy in public affairs is the highest form of journalistic irresponsibility. There must always be social dangers when journalism fails to reflect the private views of politicians and public institutions when they differ significantly from those uttered in public.

Implicit in any concept of journalistic freedom of expression must be the freedom, if not the duty, to air subjects and views which may be abhorrent to many, providing comment remains within the bounds of the law. From the mid-1960s the sensitive issue of how to achieve an integrated multi-racial society was allowed to fester virtually unaired beneath the surface of British political and social affairs. Few major issues capable of arousing public passions have ever been so successfully relegated to the wings of the public stage as the controversy over race prior to the 1980s. No other issue has backfired with such dramatic impact – a timely reminder to reinforce the principle of open political and journalistic debate in a free society on public issues, however sensitive.

When Enoch Powell hit the headlines with apocalyptic visions of the 'Tiber flowing with blood', he incurred the united wrath of the political and journalistic establishment. Unnecessarily intemperate though the tenor of the views may have been, they reflected the private fears of many political contemporaries of all political persuasions. Despite this, Powell was publicly castigated as a dangerous political demagogue indulging in self-fulfilling prophecies for his own ends. Ignoring the underlying reality of the issues, the mass media reacted with an outpouring of liberal revulsion: incensed by the words and unmoved by the message.

By the 1980s immigrant ghettos had become entrenched in the inner wastelands of Britain's major cities and produced a culturally and economically alienated black youth. In 1981 they announced spectacularly their alienation from a society complacently determined to maintain a façade of multi-racial homogeneity. The colour of the Tiber may not have changed significantly but the skies over the Thames and the Mersey became tinged with an ominous red. More than property came to be consumed in the flames of rioting and petrol bombs. Also consumed was the idea that serious social problems will evaporate merely by drawing a veil of political and media discretion over them. The media share a considerable part of the responsibility for allowing the veil to be drawn for so long.

Conventional wisdom has it that street crime and inner city unrest was, and is, a reaction to poverty, unemployment, educational and social deprivation, and, in the case of the immigrant communities, racial discrimination in all these areas. The undeniable predominance of black youths in muggings over the years in Brixton is identified as the inarticulate voice of black protest. If this is so, then journalistic restraint, which for so long suppressed evidence of black youths' involvement in escalating violence in Brixton and elsewhere, merely throttled that expression of protest. By being denied a forum the problems were ignored. It was not only the ethnic minority who were socially abandoned by this process.

Political and journalistic indifference produced a climate of artificiality in British society. The vast majority of the British population do not live in, and have no contact with, the areas affected by large-scale immigration. This unaffected majority were deluded into believing the myth of a tolerant Britain evolving painlessly towards an integrated multi-racial society. They drew gratification by vicarious association from the illusion of British societal maturity, stability and tolerance suggested by the journalistic and political comment of the time. This uninvolved majority accepted the principle of integration as a worthwhile goal and considered it was laudable that those who had to do it were getting on with it.

The minority of the indigenous population directly in contact with the reality were not so sanguine. To the indigenous minority what was being portrayed as integration appeared to be disintegration. Freedom under the law was being interpreted by gangs of marauding black youths as freedom from the law. More bewildering to them was the lack of political concern and media interest in the phenomenon. Levels of violent street crime which, in other areas, would have provoked a public outcry barely excited comment in 'responsible' circles of society. These circles did not have to live with the problem, or so it seemed.

In 1981, the flames in Brixton, Toxteth, Manchester and other inner city areas brought new vision to the uninvolved mass of the British population. The establishment of ethnic fortresses in strategic urban areas of the country was providing haven for significant elements of society prepared to use serious violence as a means of proclaiming their social disaffection. The true significance of the fortress phenomenon was not just the ethnic composition of the areas. Serious though that was, even more serious was the potential within those areas for exploitation by more dangerous social elements capable of fanning the violence into political and social disorder.

Rioting and public disorder have not been uncommon features of life in mainland Britain during the twentieth century. Issues as diverse as the emancipation of women, unemployment, industrial disputes, fascism, Vietnam and Ulster have all brought violence to British cities. Setting aside the largely black ethnic identity of the majority of participants in the riots, rioting in 1981 was unique. In that year,it erupted spontaneously without any specific bond, cause or reason to provide the unity which usually characterizes rioters. These spontaneous riots in places as far removed from each other as Bristol, London, Liverpool and Manchester, with all their gratuitous violence, destruction and looting, were simply major dramatized productions of cameo incidents which had come to form part of daily life in some inner city areas.

If, as most observers agree, the riots were a protest against social deprivation and economic inequality, the riots did more than identify an ethnic presence in urban areas. They inadvertently reflected the growing divisions within the national community by placing them in the symbolic context of black and white.

Most social observers believe that the real blackness was less one of skin than of despair: the black despair of those who are always destined to be the sacrificial lambs on the altar of economic progress; the people for whom the time is never right to make demands. In times of relative economic prosperity their demands for education, housing and welfare hold back the realization of the aspirations of others, who have these things, to achieve greater wealth. In times of recession their demands threaten the wealth and social conditions the others have already achieved.

If the observers who make these claims are wrong, then Britain will still face the immediate problem of neutralizing the social dangers of having alienated ethnic enclaves strategically located in society. The threat they pose will always be there as long as they exist in their present form. One danger arising from the threat posed can be seen in the response the authorities made to the riots of 1981. This response has involved a major change of emphasis in the British police service towards confrontational policing strategies: increased riot training, contingency deployment of police resources to respond to riots, and the envisaged use of such anti-riot equipment as CS gas. The police themselves are conscious that the more emphasis there is in the service on confrontational policing, the more likelihood there will be of confrontation. Equally, there is no guarantee that such confrontation will be limited to certain areas. The inherent dangers are infinitely increased if the observers are right in their analysis of the social condition.

If the 1981 riots are a symptom of much wider political, economic and social despair, they suggest a latent violence in British society which augurs ill for the stability of the country. This is reinforced by evidence of increasing criminal violence. There are, however, even more ominous signs of violence at the margins of British society. The Irish question, which has plagued successive British governments, has still not been answered. The problem is no nearer solution now than it ever was. The only certainty is that it will not go away. By any standards the choices available appear stark.

One British option is to continue to maintain the position that Ulster is an integral part of the United Kingdom and could no more be ceded by a British government than Texas could be ceded to Mexico by the United States government. This policy option presents Britain with two alternatives. The first is for the British security forces to destroy a Republican movement in Ulster which is constantly rejuvenated with fresh recruits committed to the cause, and which is gaining increasing support from international revolutionary movements. In the process of destroying the Republican terrorists, the measures necessary could irreparably damage relations with Eire and provoke a counter-productive backlash: the alienation of over a million Irish people in mainland Britain with all the security implications that would entail; and the inevitable escalation of terrorist violence on the mainland. The second alternative under this option would be to continue to accept as before a degree of violence, death and destruction in Ulster which elsewhere in the United Kingdom would be regarded as total anarchy.

Another British option would be to impose a solution on Ulster which would relinquish all British claims to the province, either by creating the framework for an Ulster union with Eire, or allowing an independent Ulster to evolve. In either case the result would be regarded by millions as the disenfranchisement of over a million Ulster loyalists from British citizenship. The predictable violence this would unleash would be horrendous and would not be confined to Ulster. This in itself would create a massive security problem for Britain.

Whether British governments continue as before or take the initiative to impose a political solution on a reluctant Ulster, the British people will remain hostages to fortune in the context of Irish inspired violence. There are, however, lessons being learned from the Ulster crisis which have application in other parts of Britain.

There are more geographical divisions in the United Kingdom than the one between Ulster and the mainland. In both Wales and Scotland there are separatist movements. Their importance and potential for disruption cannot be discounted on the grounds of insignificant numbers or that only a minority of even those small numbers are prepared to engage in violence to achieve their ends. The sound of detonating explosives has an effect which reaches far beyond the immediate area of blast. The sounds of bombs with Scottish and Welsh connections are already reverberating in Britain. Exploding bombs demand a government security reaction. The logic behind the bombs is that the security reaction will prove offensive to those who are being defended. The process is by now a familiar one: action to create reaction which will, in turn, prompt counter-action.

Underlying all social grievance is one central thread: politically, socially and economically there has been a movement away from the centre of national consensus. Politics have achieved domination over economics and social interaction, and have come to be dominated by professional politicians, some of whom are elected and others who have no ambition or prospect of being elected by a free electorate. In this way professional politicians have justified their inclusion in Orwell's 'new aristocracy' of totalitarianism.

Under the influence of professional politicians the current trend is towards fundamentalism – politically, economically and socially. The confrontation of problems is consistently misrepresented as the means of solution. The art of compromise, which is widely recognized as the only civilized means of reconciling fundamental opposites and providing acceptable solutions, is derided as weakness or 'wetness'. Fundamentalism is the stalking ground of extremism: extremism subscribes to confrontation; and confrontation without compromise ends in violence. There have always been divisions in British society. They have never been permitted in the past, however, to become so deep or so wide that they have threatened the unity of the people. If such unity is to be retained it calls for the building of bridges, not security barricades.

The internal security of the nation cannot be ignored, of course. Britain is a parliamentary democracy and the inviolability of the parliamentary system has to be guarded. The question is how is it to be guarded? To answer that it is necessary to decide who it is to be guarded against and who is doing the guarding. In the context of Abraham Lincoln's parable: who is the wolf, who are the shepherds and what do the shepherds have in mind for the sheep?

The remaining chapters of this book are predicated on a number of assumptions, some of which the reader may reject. There are two, however, which are fundamental. The first is that an open society and a secret government are a contradiction in terms. If democracy cannot be sustained by open means with the knowledge of the people, then democracy has failed and will not be revived by any security measures. Secondly, if it proves necessary to introduce measures of security which grossly infringe the rights of the individual to privacy, personal liberty and freedom, then again democracy will have failed and is not worth preserving. The struggle that democracy faces in Britain involves a battle on two fronts. One battle will be to prevent confrontational political, economic and social policies degenerating into violent insurrection. The other will be to ensure that specious calls for measures of increased security, and the application of security technology, do not achieve by an erosion of liberty what insurrection would seek to achieve by violence. Totalitarianism would be the inevitable consequence of losing either battle.

# 2
# Legal Niceties

Few British institutions in the second half of the twentieth century have fallen from grace so rapidly and so surprisingly as the police. Shifts in the social structure and movements across traditional class lines presented the police with an identity crisis. Social progress, increasing permissiveness and a growth of anti-authoritarianism have made it more difficult for the police to distinguish between friend and enemy.

Police were created in the nineteenth century by, and for, a social Establishment imbued with a reverence for 'natural authority' and respect for property and its ownership. This reverence was embodied in the laws the police were entrusted to enforce. Instead of a more enlightened and better educated public supporting and reinforcing traditional social mores, the reaction was quite different. Increased social awareness and political nous led to a questioning of conventional values. The growing pervasiveness of the law, and thus the state, in almost every feature of daily life was challenged. Scepticism about the reality of any strong relationship between law and justice led not only to calls for law reform but for reform in the means of enforcement.

A general decline in the influence of the church removed the imprimatur of heavenly values from the law, leaving it to stand unaided: an imperfect instrument of fallible man. Viewed in this light the law could be interpreted as corrupt, corrupting and corruptible. It was seen by many to be bound up in artifice, social expediency and power. For these and other reasons, not least the recognition that social inequalities played a significant part in establishing criminal behaviour patterns, British society largely rejected the convention of unquestioning obedience to authority. This rejection was reflected in social attitudes to the police who were both the symbol and the enforcers of that authority.

The test for any society's police, its laws and any form of authority can be found in the words of the seventeenth-century writer, Blaise

Pascal: 'Justice without strength is helpless, strength without justice is tyrannical . . . Unable to make what is just strong, we have made what is strong just.'

It is said that the public gets the police it deserves; but who is to decide what the public deserve? Human rights in a democracy are not divisible between those entitled to have them and those who are not – all men are equal before the law. This applies to the police as much as to any other section of society.

One of the benefits of living in a parliamentary democracy is the knowledge that unjust laws can be changed. It also has to be recognized, however, that just laws which are unjustly administered create as much injustice as unjust laws. The rights of a majority cannot be protected democratically by abrogating the rights of a minority.

Just laws cannot suffice: they must also be justly administered and enforced. To paraphrase Pascal: society has to strive to make what is just strong and not what is strong just. In a police context this means establishing a service which may be better than some elements of society deserve.

The word 'service' is crucial. As the police in Britain have evolved professionally, the dividing line between servant and master has become increasingly blurred. Part of the crisis in the police service has been a growing tendency for police to see themselves more as master than servant. Increasingly, police have come to see themselves in the role of social leaders rather than as public servants responsive to the demands of a changing society.

As with any servant-master relationship, there are limits beyond which the police cannot be allowed to define their own function. There are even stricter limits on the extent to which they can be permitted to be the final arbiters of their own standards of integrity, competence and efficiency. Although a degree of operational freedom and flexibility is essential if any servant is to perform adequately, the standards necessary can only be those which the master finds acceptable.

The relationship between police and public is complicated in that the police are, in effect, appointed to exercise supervision and restraint over their own masters. It is not difficult under those circumstances for police to forget their essentially subordinate social role. In the absence of adequate public supervision and control, it is as natural for the police as for any other servant to fulfil their function according to their own perceptions of the service required. The alternative, if the public are not to be wholly reliant on police self-appraisal, is for the public to maintain an established independent body capable of scrutinizing the internal mechanics of police law enforcement and peace-keeping.

Any idea of a servant police being a truly accountable public service, in the absence of an independent machinery for police scrutiny, is a dangerous nonsense. Yet, by the early 1980s, it had become increasingly clear to growing numbers of the British public that the police service had been permitted to evolve with no such machinery in existence. This is more the fault of the public than the police. Serious questions were raised about how well the public were being served in the light of a body of disturbing evidence.

Changing social patterns and attitudes call for changes in policing. Whether policing was reflecting the social changes which had taken place seemed questionable. Financial corruption and instances of institutionalized malpractice have surfaced repeatedly despite police assurances that they are not representative. Police recruitment itself has raised doubts about the extent to which the police are representative of the society they serve. Questions have been raised about operational policing strategies, inefficiency, incompetence and, more significantly, about the increasing autonomy of Chief Officers of police. All these aspects of concern about the police, and more, prompted the view that greater external scrutiny and control were necessary. The view was reinforced by the intransigent resistance of influential elements in the police to calls for independent investigation of allegations of serious police misconduct.

As these various aspects of policing are examined, it is important that they be looked at in the context of Chapter 1. The operational deployment of the police will be an important factor in determining the nature of British society in the future. The question of who will deploy them is as important as how they will be deployed. They can either be deployed to build bridges across new and existing social divisions, or deployed in social confrontation. They can either be a social adhesive strengthening the structural cohesion necessary to meet future challenges, or an abrasive influence capable of creating further divisions or exacerbating existing ones. Whatever powers the police are to be given will be based on one or other of two social strategies. Either they will be designed to make 'what is just strong', or to make 'what is strong just'.

The social attitudes reflected in anti-authoritarian trends, declining reverence for property ownership embodied in the law, and the rejection of unquestioning obedience to an established authority, clearly have all had profound effects on the relationship between police and public. In a society conditioned to accept and obey established authority, the question of policing with the public's consent does not arise to any significant degree. As part of the established authority, the order the police impose is the order of their own authority. In a more liberated society, which does not accept automatically the decrees of an established order which the police seek to impose, these decrees can only be imposed with the consent of the public.

The lower social classes have traditionally been regarded as the natural home of the criminal fraternity. It is not unreasonable to assume that the greatest threat to property will come from those who have no property of their own. If a little knowledge is a dangerous thing, then the enlightenment of the better educated lower class brought dangers to the police in their relationship with the hitherto educationally disadvantaged. The problem is twofold. At its heart lies the irony that both police and criminal share a common class origin.

One element of the problem is that it requires very little educational stimulus for the lower orders to question what they are conditioned to regard as the natural order in society. In time, even the most disadvantaged in society re-evaluate the implications of their particular station in life in the context of their relations with police. This group became increasingly aware in the early 1980s that the social obligations which their class cousins, the police, were constantly drawing to their attention – sometimes conventionally, sometimes forcibly – reflected only one aspect of the law. The other side of the coin revealed a whole range of rights rarely, if ever, alluded to by the police and then only obliquely. This was no surprise in itself, for no other section of society had such first-hand experience of the vast gulf between the private reality of law enforcement and its public image. It began to dawn, however, on the collective consciousness of the lower orders that, in their relations with the police, what was sauce for the goose was also sauce for the gander. This growing awareness applied to the criminal and non-criminal public alike. In the case of the general public, a little knowledge had opened up a pandora's box of newly discovered rights and privileges.

Closely bound to the lower, working class by shared background and association, with all the familiarity that implied, the police were privy to the same degree of knowledge. There is a difference, however, between those who have authority imposed upon them and those who seek to impose authority on others. The lower class police officer had made the transition from the former to the latter. Instead of experiencing intellectual liberation from the little knowledge they had acquired, however, they discovered the constraints. The basic education they had acquired ill equipped them for the task of enforcing law on a public who had to consent to its enforcement and were insistent that the law the police sought to apply to others also applied to them. In Chaucer's *Canterbury Tales* in the 'Man of Law's Tale' is expressed the sentiment: 'Laws are for all, and he who seeks to lay them/ On others should by rights himself obey them.' The newly enlightened may not have been familiar with Chaucer, but certainly the sentiments were well understood.

Partly as a result of the increased enlightenment of the less socially advantaged, class lines became diffused. 'Pop' culture produced a young, affluent, self-assertive, anti-authoritarian and classless strata in society. They symbolized everything an ordered, disciplined and authoritarian police service found repugnant. A social clash between the two was as predictable as it was inevitable.

Another influential element in the police crisis was created by the need to enforce laws which crossed conventional class boundaries. The social sub-culture which evolved around prohibited drugs was the most significant factor. Here the police were drawn into conflict with large sections of people from every social class, many of whom would otherwise have been regarded by the police as their natural allies. The drugs sub-culture crossed all class divisions. Its membership included aristocratic, wealthy, academic, professional, managerial, entrepreneurial and Establishment figures in addition to the nouveaux riches of the pop world, criminals and the young working class.

Whatever the merits of the arguments against the decriminalization of drug abuse, one thing is clear: law enforcement measures are fighting a losing battle. However convinced the police and the majority of the British public may be that drugs are a corrupting and socially destructive influence, they have been unable to marshall a case capable of persuading hundreds of thousands of intelligent and articulate fellow citizens that this is so. That fact poses a serious question mark over the social wisdom of using criminal legislation to combat the private habits of individuals in the community and placing the enforcement of such legislation in the hands of the police.

All these factors had a traumatic effect on the police. They had been trained to deal with criminal opponents drawn largely from one recognizable, non property-owning, working-class fraternity – a criminal fraternity which shared with the police a perception of the natural social order. Rules for both conflict and co-operation were understood and accepted by both. Both accepted that the law itself had little part to play in these rules. Offenders accepted the belief that crime and punishment went hand in hand. Whether punishment was administered by police, courts, or both was a matter of indifference. The law was about punishment and the police enforced the law. Any protection afforded by the law was conditional on the individual remaining within the offender-police rules of conduct.

This perception, however, changed for the offender with the realization that the breaking of one law did not necessarily mean that the protection afforded by other laws was forfeited.

However unpalatable it might be, the police might have come to terms with this had it not been for other new factors. With the breakdown of class barriers in criminality under the influence of the pop and drugs sub-cultures, the police were confronted by an even more pernicious phenomenon. Here the police were faced by people who were reluctant to cede authority over their private lives to the law, far less power of authority or rights of censure to the police. The police now found themselves dealing with intelligent, well-educated and articulate offenders who evinced neither guilt nor remorse. Such offenders, moreover, had the means and social standing to reverse the roles being played by taking the police to task for their own shortcomings. It was a unique and unwelcome new experience for police officers to find themselves being judged and sometimes intellectually and morally patronized by their own prisoners.

There was another equally unpleasant aspect of the situation for the police. A more enlightened lower class began to rebel against traditional police methods and law enforcement. With the exposure of significant numbers of the middle and upper classes to the same procedures, most sections of society gained a knowledge that had previously been restricted almost exclusively to those at the bottom end of the social ladder. As a more intimate knowledge of police methods began to permeate society the reaction was predictably mixed.

In some quarters the knowledge merely reinforced existing suspicions. In others the reception was one of scepticism. A not uncommon reaction was for the evidence to be regarded as isolated and unrepresentative examples of police behaviour or an indication of falling police standards. These reactions were totally misconceived. Police standards, their methods, procedures and practices had remained more or less constant. Corruption and malpractice have been endemic in the police service since its inception, just as they have in every other section of society.

The misconception arose from the British Establishment's long tradition of never allowing reality to tarnish the projected image of public institutions. It may seem ironic but there is strong evidence to show that the outlawing of pornography and drugs, for example, did more to corrupt the police than to stamp out either pornography or drugs. This, however, would have come as no surprise to anyone who had taken the trouble to research the effect of other laws, which the police had to enforce, that attempted to regulate forms of social behaviour considered acceptable by many citizens. Before controlled gambling, for example, became legal, street betting and illegal gambling, particularly in the major cities, both enjoyed a degree of police patronage.

Few forms of human activity attract the application of dual standards more than bribery and corruption, and this is also true in the police service. The expenditure of £20 on a lunch for a police officer would usually be regarded as normal business entertainment. To present the officer at Christmas with a bottle of wine costing £20 would be considered by most as an unexceptional seasonal gratuity. Placing the same £20 in an envelope and handing it to a police officer in a pub toilet would be to invite prosecution for bribery.

In a free market economy there is a fine line between acceptable enterprise and corrupt practice. Police officers often find more difficulty than most in distinguishing when they have crossed the line from one form of conduct to the other. It is, of course, arguable that any form of ex-officio consideration made to an officer is corrupting. Corrupt practices, however, do not always involve financial considerations, and even when they do they are not always the most serious form of corruption.

A rural officer sitting down to a salmon or pheasant donated by the local poacher is unlikely to choke at the idea of dining on the proceeds of crime. The same officer, however, might look askance at the big city police coroner driving a new car bought with commissions from favoured undertakers. Officers drinking after hours in a friendly local hostelry will have few qualms about aiding the licensee to contravene the licensing regulations. These same officers might not condone the practice of traffic patrol officers who accept considerations from garages they call to the scenes of accidents, or similar rewards by crime prevention officers received from private security companies grateful for having their products plugged to the exclusion of their competitors.

A senior officer, exercising his discretion not to prosecute the son of a local dignitary, would not see his actions in the same light as those of the detective officer who accepts cash from a criminal to approve bail, when knowing full well that that bail would be granted by the magistrate whether he objected or not.

Some more serious forms of police malpractice invite universal condemnation: police officers aiding criminals to commit serious crimes; blackmailing innocent people by threatening prosecution if payment is not made; allowing criminals to escape prosecution in exchange for financial rewards; planting incriminating evidence on innocent people to gain a conviction; fabricating a false case against an innocent person. Even the most tolerant find such cases unacceptable. Unacceptable, that is, unless these things are being done 'in the public interest'. When the public interest is involved, the unacceptable tends to become acceptable.

All are said to be innocent until proven guilty, yet it is a fact of life that some must be considered less innocent than others. The use of informers, in order to arrest criminals, is a long-established custom in police forces worldwide. An informer must not become an agent provocateur to incite, or induce, crimes which might not otherwise take place but, nevertheless, most of them do sometimes and some of them do always. It is standard practice to blackmail arrested prisoners with threats of more severe consequences, either to themselves or their families, if they fail to co-operate. It has been traditional in the police for deals to be struck allowing criminals immunity from prosecution in exchange for assistance, although with official sanction in the case of Supergrasses this reached unprecedented peaks. Although the planting and fabricating of incriminating evidence have never been officially sanctioned, they have in varying degrees long played a significant part in judicial procedures, only causing concern when they were revealed to be so blatant that some response had to be made.

Police corruption and malpractice divide into two forms, therefore. The most serious is malpractice in which the individual officer gains financial reward, or does to an innocent person what might be excusable if that person were guilty. The less serious form is where the same things are done without financial gain and without making mistakes in the choice of person. The dilemma for any police service has always been to discriminate satisfactorily between misconduct, which the service and the public consider altruistically inspired because it is in the public interest, and misconduct which is not so inspired.

In 1972 when Sir Robert Mark became Commissioner of the Metropolitan Police he made public his view that the force's Criminal Investigation Department 'had long been the most routinely corrupt organisation in London'. It was his conclusion that the situation had arisen because, by a constitutional quirk, the CID had been left to investigate complaints and allegations of their own wrongdoing. Sir Robert laid less emphasis, however, on the fact that the CID had also been responsible for investigating allegations of criminal misconduct of uniformed officers too.

The failure to lay equal emphasis on both areas of CID responsibility was seriously misleading in two major respects. It was misleading because it suggested that less stringent standards of investigation were applied to allegations of CID malpractice than to other forms. This was untrue. The same standards, or lack of them as the case may be, were applied to complaints regardless of the branch of the service they concerned. It was also misleading in that it appeared to contain the implicit assumption that the form of financial corruption associated with major CID scandals was the most significant factor in police misconduct, which reinforced to some degree the principle of two forms of corruption and malpractice: misconduct that was acceptable and misconduct that was not. This obscured the reality that other forms of institutionalized police misconduct were, in fact, more influential in determining their overall relations with the public than corruption in the CID.

Based on his conclusions, Sir Robert instituted two major changes in the Metropolitan police. One was a new format for internal investigation of serious complaints against police and this was placed under the control of uniformed officers. The other was to integrate the entire CID into the uniform Area and Divisional command structure, breaking up what had been a single, cohesive entity into a number of barely related parts. The first measure was portrayed as an acceptable alternative to the creation of a totally separate investigative body independent of police control. The second measure was justified on the basis that it brought the largest professional investigation department in the United Kingdom into line with provincial police forces throughout the country, in the expectation that it would prevent the emergence of the forms of financial corruption identified with various CID scandals.

Any reader of the former Commissioner's autobiography, *In the Office of Constable*, could be forgiven for forming the impression that the measures largely succeeded in purging the force of corruption. In the event, as critics at the time foretold, and subsequent events proved, the new system for internal investigations was merely cosmetic.

Some ten years after the new investigation system was implemented, the assertion that allegations of serious police misconduct could be left to an internal enquiry was sensationally rebutted by the Countryman affair. This was a massive enquiry, handled by constabulary officers from outside London, into allegations of widespread corruption amongst London police officers. The one notable achievement this produced was to highlight the fundamental flaw in the internal system: the credibility factor.

Arthur Hambledon, who as Chief Constable of Dorset had been heavily involved in the direction of the Countryman enquiry, made a series of startling allegations. He accused senior officers of the Metropolitan Police of having sabotaged the enquiries by obstructing the investigators. The Director of Public Prosecutions was accused of demanding too great a weight of evidence before giving authority to prosecute suspected officers. It was claimed that evidence had been elicited which would have justified criminal charges being laid against more than twenty officers. The corruption alleged to have been revealed was said to extend to all but the top echelons of the Metropolitan Police which, if true, suggested a situation as serious as any identified by Sir Robert Mark. By implication, Hambledon was also saying that subordinating the CID to the uniformed commanders, interchanging officers between branches, and the creation of a new complaints department, had achieved nothing in terms of wiping out police corruption. These allegations were all vigorously denied.

Predictably, the accusations arising from the Countryman fiasco generated a counter-attack from senior London police officers, the DPP, the Attorney-General Sir Michael Havers, and others. In essence, the counter-claims pointed to the conspicuous lack of any significant number of directly related prosecutions resulting from the enormous investigative effort expended. Costing somewhere in the region of £2 million, and lasting over two years, the investigation was justifiably derided by its critics as a monumental shambles. Its manifest failures were described as a disastrous combination of professional bungling, arrogance and indiscretion bordering on total incompetence.

Clearly, Operation Countryman was an unmitigated public relations disaster for the police service. It generally increased or confirmed fears that corruption in the police was as widespread as ever it had been before Sir Robert Mark had implemented his much vaunted reform measures. More particularly, it highlighted the problems associated with drafting officers from one force to investigate misconduct among police officers of another. These fears were not engendered by uninformed, anti-police critics. It was police officers themselves who made the claim that London police were riddled with serious corruption, and it was police officers who accused the hundred or so police officers from provincial forces of professional incompetence. Both these police opinions cannot be wrong. The public are entitled to take the view that both are right to the extent that they demand independent investigation of serious police misconduct. The police service, however, still successfully resists independent examination.

In his autobiography, with a lack of guile and a frankness many found refreshing in a top cop, Sir Robert touched on some instances of police brutality in the pre-war and immediate post-war era. He made the comment: 'Before and immediately after the war, there was a willingness by the police to use violence against the hardened criminal which I believe now to be rare indeed, and perhaps more important, strongly disapproved of by most policemen if ever it did occur.'

Mark described how in the late 1930s he had broken a bone in the leg of a struggling drunk by striking him with an unofficial type of truncheon. The truncheon was carried because police experience had shown it could inflict more damage than the official type. It was not clear whether or not the drunk had been a 'hardened criminal'.

In another example Mark described the interrogation technique adopted by a successful and senior Manchester detective for dealing with unco-operative prisoners. This involved a number of officers upending the prisoner, inserting his head in a lavatory bowl and repeatedly flushing it. This procedure was continued until the prisoner indicated by waving his feet in the air that, whatever else he may have taken aboard, he was now filled with a desire to co-operate. The prisoner would then presumably make a 'voluntary statement of admission'.

The main issue is how much faith can be placed in Sir Robert's belief that the incidents described are irrelevant in the context of a modern police force. The disapproval of 'most policemen', referred to by Mark, is not something from which the general public can take much comfort. The reality is that the majority of police officers are rarely, if ever, directly involved in arresting anyone, as the current crime statistics show only too clearly.

The police service is divided into two basic groups of officers: non-operational and operational, and in the view of many officers there are too many of the former. The latter group is further subdivided between those who are operationally active and those who are largely inactive to the extent that they might as well be classified as non-operational. It is not the disapproval of 'most policemen' which is the influential factor in the question of violence therefore; it is the attitudes of the minority of active, usually forceful, operational police officers. The examples quoted by Sir Robert, safely placed in the 1930s, appear to be merely past indiscretions.

The unofficial truncheon carried by Sir Robert was not an unofficial police implement peculiar to a past era. In the wake of the Southall riots of 23/24 April 1979, an investigation was carried out into the death of Blair Peach. In the course of the investigation the lockers of officers of the Metropolitan Police Special Patrol Group were searched and a list of items found therein was subsequently published. The list included: one brass handle; one leather encased truncheon, approximately one foot long with a knotted thong at the end; one metal truncheon encased in leather of about eight inches in length with a very flexible handle and a lead weight in the end; one wooden pickaxe handle; one sledgehammer; one American-type beat truncheon almost two feet in length; one leather whip; two case openers or jemmies; one white bone-handled knife with a long blade case; one crowbar about three feet in length and two inches in diameter; and one further crowbar.

These items were totally unconnected with the death of Blair Peach. All of them, despite their sinister connotations, may have had perfectly innocent explanations attached to them. Some may have been souvenirs, curiosity objects, or, in some cases, retained for use to force entry into locked premises in the execution of search warrants.

The fact remains that throughout Sir Robert Mark's tenure as Commissioner there were few stations in the Metropolitan Police area which did not harbour a similar array of implements. It is true to say that these implements were not always retained to be used offensively or to be planted on prisoners who could then be charged with possession. It is also true that they were available to be used for such purposes if operational officers decided such a course of action was warranted, and inevitably such occasions did arise from time to time.

Unconventional forms of interrogation did not die out in the early days of Sir Robert's career in the police service. In 1963, for example, it was revealed that 'rhino' whips had been used as an aid to interrogation by Sheffield police officers. Much later than that, however, unusual means of interrogation were employed in London. Occasionally, for example, West Indian immigrants with a rather rudimentary grasp of the British judicial process were subjected to mock trials at the police station. On at least two of these occasions it was reputed in police circles in West London that, after elaborate pseudo-judicial trials, death sentences had been passed. In one the 'convicted' prisoner had been led under a noose in the charge-room. In the other an empty police revolver had been placed to the condemned man's head.

Such charades were certainly conducted: the sentences and the means of execution may, or may not, be apocryphal. Certainly the sentences were not carried out and they were never intended to be carried out. It is not clear whether the prisoners always appreciated the distinction. In any event voluntary confessions were obtained which qualified them for more orthodox legal processes.

Not all unconventional interrogation methods and techniques are quite so esoteric and neither are they always totally effective in eliciting a confession. Technical hitches sometimes occurred, and no doubt still do occur, due to the obduracy of prisoners whose apparently unreasonable reluctance to confess was due to their innocence. The problem is that what is demonstrably true to the suspect is not always convincing to a suspicious interrogator. Innocence in itself should never be regarded as a shield from police errors. Three examples illustrate the type of error that can be made and they are by no means exhaustive.

It is a well-established basic principle of interrogation that the interrogator should impose his authority on a suspect at an early stage. Acting on this, one experienced investigator summoned to interrogate a suspect detained by other officers at the police station made a dramatic entrance by walking in and striking his man before speaking. Unfortunately the interrogative effect was lost on the suspect since he was elsewhere at the time and the person struck was the original victim of the crime being investigated.

On another occasion a youth found in possession of a radio, with wires still hanging from it, vehemently disclaimed having stolen or dishonestly received the radio. The radio matched in every detail one recently stolen locally, down to a broken third button on the radio face. Frustrated by the obduracy of an unrepentant youth, the police interrogator gave him what is commonly referred to in police parlance as 'a smack'. The youth was still trying to stem the blood flowing from his nose when the owner of the stolen radio arrived to point out that the broken button on his radio had been the third one from the left and not, as in the one held by police, the third button from the right.

Social position and professional status sometimes provide no more protection than innocence under such circumstances. A lawyer who had patronized one of London's West End nightclubs until the early hours aroused the suspicions of the staff when he tendered a cheque with a signature which appeared at odds with the name printed on the cheque. When questioned by police he proved to be arrogant, dismissive and under the influence of drink. The injuries he sustained en route and at the police station, while they may have been consistent with those an arrogant, dismissive and drunk fraud might have accepted, were not those expected by a lawyer – particularly when under the bright lights in the police station the signature on the cheque could be seen to be authentic. The matter was 'satisfactorily' resolved by the lawyer being convicted of assaulting the arresting officers, despite the disparity between the visible injuries he had sustained and the lack of any apparent injury on the assaulted officers.

The exercise of force is something which can never be removed from law enforcement. Ultimately, the police service has to stand for the will of a society to survive. It must be the symbol of society's determination, if all else fails, to meet internal aggression with overwhelming force. The central question for society, however, is who is to decide how, when and against whom the force is to be applied. For many years that decision has been largely left to the police and it is not one which they are reluctant to make. The public should understand, however, that the answer to that question determines to a significant extent the nature of the society they are to live in.

There are two tests which can be applied to police malpractice: quantitative and qualitative. These are not necessarily mutually exclusive. In resisting calls for independent investigation of complaints of serious police misconduct, Chief Officers of police rely heavily on the quantitative approach. By this assessment it is quite properly claimed that gross misconduct is not truly representative of the police generally. Since only a minority of police are operational, the real question is how representative it is of the active minority.

In the three examples given of innocent people being subjected to varying degrees of violence it can be said unequivocally that they represent only a minority. They were not the only ones, they were not the first and neither will they be the last. They are, however, only a minority of people who suffer violent treatment at the hands of the police. Many more people who are guilty suffer such treatment than those who are innocent. Whether that makes the practice more acceptable depends largely on whether the standards applied are quantitative or qualitative and whether they are applied by the police or the public. It also depends on which element of the police the standards are applied to.

There is often a wide gulf between the public's perception of policing and the police view of their own role. Perhaps more significantly, there is an equally wide gulf between police practice as seen by operational police officers and their non-operational colleagues. These divisions were identified by Sir Robert Mark who, throughout his long and distinguished police career, performed very little active operational work in the criminal field.

In his autobiography, commenting on the rare occasions when he had direct experience of operational work, he wrote: 'I admit quite frankly that there were some occasions on which my hair stood on end when I discovered the difference between theory and practice in applying the rules governing police interrogation.' Emphasizing that the fault lay with society for its reluctance to 'define police powers', he stated: '. . . let me make it clear that I am one of those who believe that if the criminal law and the procedures relating to it were applied strictly according to the book, as a means of protecting society it would collapse in a few days'. In the context of the detention of IRA suspects for four days before charging, he said: 'The NCCL [National Council for Civil Liberties] were quite right in assuming that we [the police] would not let any legal niceties prevent us from dealing with terrorism . . .' These three statements are at the heart of the policing dilemma.

The first identifies the fallacy of the public being reassured by claims of misconduct being unrepresentative of the majority of police officers. It is the attitudes and practices of the minority of active operational officers which are a more accurate reflection of policing than the views of the majority. It is on these that the quality of the police service has to be judged, and not on the utterances of senior or administrative officers.

The 'criminal law and the procedures relating to it . . . as a means of protecting society' have not collapsed. Whether this is entirely due to the police disregarding the rules is not as clear to everyone as it appears to be to Sir Robert. If so, the avoidance of collapse has had a price for the law, police and society. This price has been reflected in criminal courts which have been turned into music-hall palaces of variety where farces have been performed daily by participants who each produce their own scripts to conform to legal parameters in which few of them believe. The police, too, have had to pay a price which has been met from their reserves of social credibility, which they are finding increasingly difficult to sustain.

It is not just in the context of IRA terrorism that the police refused to let 'legal niceties' inhibit their freedom of action. The refusal to be bound by the rules has led the police to taking it upon themselves to interpret the rules according to their own perceptions of society. In the best Establishment tradition of maintaining the public illusion regardless of private reality, courts have been applying a code the police have largely rejected. Doing one thing and being compelled to say another, in the police, leads to perjury – often technical, sometimes full-blooded – becoming an institutionalized, routine police procedure.

Each new challenge presented by the police hierarchy, in response to bouts of public or official disquiet, merely generated a further stimulus to the ingenuity of operational officers. The mythical importance of pocket books, contemporaneously recorded notes of interview, notes of times, cautions and the like, merely added a spice of danger. This, however, was amply compensated for by the certain knowledge that society was being protected from its own folly and that, in the main, it was the guilty who suffered.

The problem associated with contemporaneously recording conversations which were purported to have been exchanged between officer and prisoner has probably introduced more black comedy into British criminal courts than any other single factor. Only notes made at the time of an interview, or made so shortly afterwards that the actual words used can be recalled almost verbatim, are technically admissible as a means of refreshing a witness's memory about events long past. Factional accounts sometimes have to contend with submerged reefs when being constructed some time after the events. Attempts made to have these notes conform to times shown in a miscellany of official police records can lead to problems when trying to confer authenticity upon them. Reasonable care, attention to detail and experience of where the hidden reefs in cross-examination are located usually ensure that sensible officers sail along navigable channels with little risk of being holed below the water-line. Sometimes, of course, corrective measures are necessary.

'Authenticity' was conferred on one officer's notes, which through unavoidable circumstances would only be acceptable in court if they were made in a moving vehicle, by the officer writing the notes while being rocked backwards and forwards in an office chair to simulate the movement of a car. Another officer, belatedly discovering that his writing hand would have had to have travelled at the speed of light to have completed the notes in the allotted time, had to take more courageous evasive action. Correctly anticipating a request from defending counsel to test the speed of his writing by practical demonstration, the officer duly arrived in the witness box with his writing arm in a sling. It says much for the officer's personal fortitude that the contingency planning had included the infliction of an injury in the event of an examination being requested. Whether the charade actually fooled anyone in court is debatable. It did, however, prevent the officer having to provide an unconvincing explanation for his inability to repeat the writing speed necessary to have recorded the notes in the time claimed. Perhaps not many, but more officers than might be expected, over the years have had to give explanations for notes ostensibly recorded at the time of interviews appearing in notebooks out of chronological order. Thankfully for some officers, the introduction of Incident Report Books which relate to only one incident offer protection from this form of self-incrimination.

Incidents of corruption, violence and the other forms of institutional-ized police misconduct have been commonplace ever since the force's formation, including the period when Sir Robert Mark was the Metropol-itan Commissioner. Much of it was confined to the minority of operation-ally active officers upon whom the service almost exclusively depends for such positive results as are achieved. Certainly there were few officers at the lower end of the rank structure who were unaware of misconduct, and any at the top who may have been unaware of the situation were in that position because they chose to be so.

Many police officers share the views expressed by Sir Robert that the police force cannot allow themselves to be bound by the book in administering criminal law, or be constrained by 'legal niceties'. There is a strong belief in the police service that society never allows the police the powers they feel they need to get the job done. This is married to a paternalistic, authoritarian belief that the police service truly represents the views of society and, therefore, any failure to conform to police perceptions is necessarily antisocial. It is these deep-rooted beliefs which lead to the rejection of 'the book' and provide the self-justification for misconduct in the general, if unspoken, public interest.

These beliefs create the fundamental anomaly of two forms of police malpractice: conduct which, although improper if not criminal, tends to be unofficially sanctioned because it is considered to be free from self-interest; and conduct which is seen to be motivated by individual self-interest and is therefore unacceptable. The problem faced by police officers engaged in internal investigations is how to distinguish satisfacto-rily between one form and the other when allegations of serious misconduct are made. The threat posed to the police service by proposals to employ external independent investigators is that no attempt will be made to discriminate between the two forms of misconduct.

Society should not underestimate the reality of the threat posed to the police by an independent investigative body, or the traumatic consequences it would have for the police service generally. It is not a step which society can take lightly. The alternative to taking that step, however, may have far worse implications for society.

If criminal law is to remain a credible instrument for ensuring the continuance of a civilized society, the proposition that the police should be allowed to ignore it, and the procedures which relate to its administration, is socially unacceptable. The idea that leaving the police to be a 'law unto themselves' as a realistic option for defeating crime is a dangerous fallacy. Despite counter-claims by some police officers, there is no evidence that any increase of police powers short of the imposition of tyranny will have any significant effect on curbing serious crime violent or non-violent.

The rationale that giving the police increased powers to stop and search people will significantly increase detection rates is untenable. There is no credible evidence to support the view that large numbers of criminals actively engaged in crime have escaped arrest because the police have had insufficient powers to stop and search them. Proposals to extend the period police can detain suspects in custody before charging or bringing them to court are equally questionable, except in the most serious and complex of cases. If the powers of detention are introduced without adequate external supervision they may prove marginally effective in numerical terms, but the cost in terms of individual liberty will eventually prove to be unacceptable to the public. If an effective system of external monitoring is implemented some of the advantages of detention will disappear; one has to appreciate the attractions for the police of powers to detain without charging.

All powers vested in the police are inevitably pushed to their legal limits and on occasions beyond. Since the 1960s there has been a subtle but discernible change in the law enforcement process. Two particular trends have played a significant role in this change. One has been a reduced emphasis on the importance of 'reasonable suspicion' being based on something more tangible than an officer's personal whim or uncertainty about the extent of his powers in particular circumstances. The other has been the growth of an artificial distinction between arrest and detention.

With a weakening of the test of 'reasonable suspicion' and the replacementof formal arrest by a form of detention with little formality, gradually but perceptibly police stations have become places of first resort for officers with 'suspects' instead of places of last resort. The procedural requirement that the exercise of a power of arrest should almost certainly be followed by a charge was relaxed to a large extent. Over the years this form of de facto detention without charge has become more common even when 'legal niceties' and 'the book' suggested that arbitrary police detention did not carry the force of law. This was one form of 'legal nicety' referred to by Sir Robert Mark in connection with the detention of IRA terrorists.

It is, however, misleading to consider detention solely in the context of IRA criminals. It is applied to a whole range of other suspects, most of whom are suspected of serious crime, others who are not. One practical problem is that the word 'serious' is incapable of being legally defined in the context of the gravity of criminal offences. To steal a bottle of milk from a doorstep is theft: stealing an Old Master from an art gallery is also theft. Most people would consider the first offence less serious than the latter. In between the two extremes, however, there is an infinite range of possibilities which are capable of being regarded quite differently by one officer and another.

There is no dispute about the importance of the power of detention in the police armoury. It provides an opportunity which might not otherwise exist for extensive questioning and careful inquiries to be carried out into the events under investigation. As often as not, however, that will not be its prime function. In some cases detention can be used simply as a form of inconvenience which can be imposed on objectionable members of the public. In many more cases, however, the objective will be much more responsible, although the means may be questionable to libertarians.

Few who have not had direct experience of the phenomenon, either as a suspect or as an interrogator, can realistically appreciate the disorientating effect on a suspect created by being locked up in a police cell. More people are now aware of the term sensory deprivation. Although the effect will vary from individual to individual, it is a powerfully persuasive interrogation technique, particularly when accompanied by a subtle blend of questions and threats. Obviously, it tends to be more productive when applied to those who are guilty of something rather than those who are innocent. The guilt need not, however, be related to the immediate reason for the suspect's detention.

One bewildered youth was arrested on information provided by an informant which related to a vicious gang of active armed robbers. Along with others arrested he was taken to the police station where, after initial questioning, the interrogating officers were as bewildered as the youth himself about his presence at the station. After two days of solitary confinement interrupted only by meals and a few visits from interrogating officers, the youth duly confessed to a burglary of a few thousand pounds' worth of zip fasteners: a comparatively minor burglary of which the officers had no knowledge and which was totally unrelated to the issues in hand. The youth was quite relieved when he was charged with the admitted offence and was subsequently sentenced to a year's imprisonment.

Before any free society concedes more powers to the police it must decide what these powers are intended to achieve and the relevance of the proposed powers to the achievement of the objective. The first question must always be whether any failure in law enforcement is due to the inadequacy of the powers police have, or to the professional inadequacy of those who exercise these powers. Above all, it has to be borne in mind that there are no police powers which apply only to the guilty to the exclusion of the innocent. Even measures which prove effective as a means of dealing with a society's criminals will ultimately prove to be counter-productive if they threaten or punish the innocent.

The British police service is not entirely corrupt, nor brutal, and it is not operated with a complete disregard for the law. The service is basically honest, benign, tolerant and responsible. Its high reputation is justified and, in relative terms, it stands favourable comparison with any police service in the world. Those commendable attributes, however, must not blind society to aspects of the police service which are equally true.

It is in the nature of every police force to crave more power. It is in the nature of police officers to extend their powers beyond the parameters of those envisaged by unwary legislators and a complacent public. Corrupt practices, varying degrees of brutality and disregard for the law are not the most representative features of the police. They are, however, features which have played a significant role in policing over the years. Furthermore, they are features which have been tolerated or they could not otherwise have existed. Whether or not this tolerance was inspired by a police view of a wider public interest, it is clear that police perceptions do not always coincide with the highest principles and aspirations of the society they serve. For that reason alone it is essential that they are not left to be the judges of their own case and that independent means be available to the public to examine the operational mores of the police.

A society can disintegrate if it permits its police to become emasculated, and a society can also suffer by allowing its police to become too powerful. There is, however, one vital difference. In the face of the former danger, a free democratic society can take steps to redress the balance before disintegration takes place. In the event of the latter, the democratic option may be closed. Orwell's 1984 portrayed a totalitarian tyranny: a police state. It seems self-evident that a police state holds fewer terrors for a police service than for most other citizens of a free society. In the context of the police, society must decide how deeply it is committed to the principle:

Laws are for all, and he who seeks to lay them
On others should by rights himself obey them.

In a wider context, as an increasingly divided society moves towards the twenty-first century, it becomes more important to examine other underlying trends in policing. It is important to look at the composition and structure of the police, and at those who speak for them and at what they are saying.

# 3
# Servants above their Station

Sir Robert Mark did more than any previous Commissioner to foster the view that chief officers of police could safely engage in public debate on controversial law and order issues and, at the same time, maintain their political independence and their professional autonomy. In his autobiography he said: 'There can be no doubt at all of the freedom of a chief officer of police to express opinions publicly about matters within his sphere of responsibility. The difficulty in the past has been that some have been intellectually or otherwise incapable of doing so, some have thought their own personal interests might be adversely affected, and some have been content to draw their pay and not stray outside the limits of management.' Unfortunately, Sir Robert did not define how far the 'sphere of responsibility' extended, and not everyone agrees that the intellectual capability of chief officers of police has significantly changed for the better.

In January 1982, five years after the publication of the autobiography, Eldon Griffiths, MP and parliamentary advisor to the Police Federation, launched a series of attacks on chief constables. In an article in the *Daily Express* he wrote: 'Too many of our chief constables are men of great personal vanity, ill prepared for the awesome tasks our increasingly turbulent society imposes on their forces.'

From a speech made at Bury St Edmunds, Eldon Griffiths was quoted in *Police Review* as saying that, although there were a number of able chief constables'. . . there are also second raters, men who cannot stand criticism, who surround themselves with toadies, who do not read enough, whose temperament and training no longer fit them to carry the heavy duties or handle the complexities of late twentieth century Britain'.

All of that begs the question, where are such men or women to come from? Are they to come from inside or outside the service? One thing is certain: if the present composition, structure and deployment of society's policing system is irrelevant to the problems in society, the intellectual capabilities, or lack of such qualities, in chief officers will make little or no impact.

A fascinating exercise recommended for anyone attempting to assess the qualities of police leadership is to ponder not on who are or have been chief officers, but to consider those who are not and never could be. The composition of the police service is such that a large proportion of society is barred from serving because of their physical attributes. This means that a whole variety of human talent is excluded from the hierarchy for reasons which have nothing to do with intrinsic ability. Those excluded from the police have, in other fields, produced leaders, military commanders, entrepreneurs, managers and efficiency experts: those who are too short; lame or otherwise physically handicapped; too fat or too thin; homosexuals; sexual deviates; the promiscuous and the adulterous. Although the service does not openly operate a policy of discrimination, it does not generally recruit too many who are artistic, cultured and sensitive, or specially talented members of society. There are relatively few graduates with good degrees. Academics and recruits with top management experience or a proven track record of success outside the police service are as common as penny blacks.

Clearly, while competition to reach the top in the police may be tough, and the infighting fierce, the scope of the competition and the calibre of competitors is not all that it could be. The relationship between a society and its police is not determined solely by standards of police leadership. Reflection on those who are excluded from police service must make one doubt police officers' claims that, 'the police are now a meritocracy truly representative of all the people they serve'. The police are quite unrepresentative of vast numbers of the people they 'police'; and the question is how much do the views of the people they serve reflect our society? The answer may be less than we think.

The majority of police are recruited from the upper working and lower middle classes; recruits are unlikely to come from a family background of political militancy or of highly progressive radical attitudes. They tend to have an innate respect for conventional authority and to see the police service as the traditional instrument of that authority. Many will see the service as the guardian of the established social order and the embodiment of public morality. Subscribing largely to such views, recruits then become a subordinate part of a hierarchical structure closed to the public: a closed society which tolerates few nonconformist views within its ranks, and an organization which equates status with rank, order with enforced discipline and law enforcement with authoritarianism. Chief constables, the pyramid rank structure and the social recruitment of the police must then be permeated with social attitudes which do not always accurately reflect the whole of society. These entrenched attitudes, moreover, go back to a time when both police and public shared a common perception of the nature of desirable policing. There have been many changes since then.

Police forces are no longer directly accountable or subject to the control of local authorities. From the amalgamations of town, borough, city and county police forces into giant conglomerates there emerged a new breed of chief constable exercising autonomous operational powers, usually from headquarters remote from local community life. At the same time, there has been a massive, yet unco-ordinated process of police diversification into such social roles as juvenile crime prevention; new social perceptions have emerged concurrently which gain less currency with the police than some sections of society. The expansion of the police role to encompass ever more esoteric, complex and sophisticated views of the police function has all but submerged traditional concepts of conventional policing. Demarcation lines defining the relative responsibilities between the police executive and elected community representatives have become so obscure as to be virtually unintelligible to police and public alike.

The amalgamation of small police forces into larger formations changed the face of policing in Britain. It transformed a community based police service into an inter-community police service with disastrous consequences for police and public alike. It was conceived on artificial considerations which ignored police operational realities and community requirements. Created by bureaucrats for bureaucrats, the policy severed police links with local communities without in any way strengthening the national cohesion of the police service.

The amalgamation policy was fatally flawed from its inception by the assumption that the policing requirements of individual communities could be made to conform to artificial administrative boundaries, and police rank and organizational structures, unrelated to the communities being served. This ignored the reality that police structures, like communities, evolve without regard to boundaries, either administrative or geographical. The effectiveness of community policing will largely be determined by the evolution in concert of police and community, and this joint identity cannot be achieved by one evolving separately from the other.

The separate development of a police service with an operational structure separated from each of the communities being policed meant that police officers no longer had their careers linked to a community but to an organization and internal hierarchy. As the ability of local communities to influence the nature of policing priorities in their own areas waned, so the power and autonomy of chief officers of police grew. In theory answerable to the community, in practice chief officers of police were answerable to no one. What was achieved instead was a bastardized form of police service, neither a 'community' police nor 'national' police service. As this flaw came to be recognized within and outside the service, it produced diametrically opposed views. Some police elements identified a need to return the service to its community roots. Others supported the amalgamation process to its ultimate conclusion: the creation of a single National Police Force. Both views, by implication, acknowledged the irrelevance of the existing police structures to the problems of local communities and society as a whole.

Both views recognize a central truth about policing. There are two dimensions to policing in Britain: at one level there is the need to provide policing which is sensitive to local needs and will ensure stability within individual communities; on another level there is the need to preserve the integrity and stability of the state. The two are not always compatible or complementary. A West Indian or Asian community, for example, may decide to adopt social standards which it may consider acceptable for itself, but which are so alien to other communities as to create a disruptive effect on the state. The problem the police are wrestling with is how to reconcile the two conflicting functions of local and national responsibilities within one police structure, while retaining the autonomy they have come to enjoy as a product of force amalgamations. There is no way this can be satisfactorily achieved in practice.

The failure of the present structure, together with a combination of social and political factors, means that the service must change. These social and political factors clearly indicate that a fullblooded return to community policing, and its attendant small forces, will considerably diminish the power and autonomy of chief officers of police. Community policing, therefore, holds few attractions for police chiefs anxious for national stature. This natural aversion to any restriction upon their autonomy is strengthened by venomous attacks on the police by the extreme Left in the opening years of the 1980s.

Throughout the country, and more particularly after the local government elections of 1981, left-wing activists found themselves in a uniquely powerful position to launch destructive broadsides at their traditional police enemies. The situation was exemplified by the creation of a GLC Police Committee in London by the Leftist dominated Labour majority group. The stated aim of the committee was to have the 26,000 strong Metropolitan Police brought under the control of local authorities in London instead of being, as it had traditionally been, answerable only to the Home Secretary. As the one force in the country which had always operated free from local political influence, the suggestion was greeted by police with minimal enthusiasm. The proposal was made even less attractive by the appointment of Paul Boateng, a London solicitor, as chairman of the committee. Judging by the bias shown in his public utterances about the police, Boateng appeared to subscribe to the view that virtually every crime committed in London could be attributed to the police more than to the actual offender.

In March 1982, Pat Wall, a prospective Labour candidate for the constituency of Bradford North and publicly linked to the aims of Militant Tendency, a group since outlawed by the Labour Party, also set out his views on the police. In a well-reported speech he made it clear that one of the top priorities of any future Labour government should be to sack the chief constables and put the police service under whatever passed in his mind for democratic control. Despite the furore created by the speech, there was nothing particularly new in its content. What was new in the eyes of the police at least was that, for once, there appeared to be a real possibility of a Labour government making moves in that direction, with pressure from the militant Left under its new found cloak of respectability.

The concept of community policing had in the 1980s become generally synonymous with the views of John Alderson, who until 1982 had been Chief Constable of Devon and Cornwall. The fears of serving chief constables and other police officers were in no way allayed when, shortly after his retirement, John Alderson announced his intention to seek parliamentary election as a Liberal candidate. In the eyes of many officers who identify the problems of the nation as being a direct consequence of a surfeit of liberalism, the distinction between the Liberal Party and the extreme left is so fine as to be academic.

It is not surprising, consequently, that senior police officers have increasingly exercised themselves with the search for an alternative to community policing which would represent change from the status quo, while allowing them to retain their autonomy and power. Neither is it surprising that more of them should see the possibility of a single National Police Force as a solution which would not only consolidate their autonomy, but strengthen their position immeasurably. A society can have a form of 'community' policing, or it can have a monolithic National Police Force. What it cannot have is community policing in its true sense operating within a monolithic national force managed by a pyramid rank structure. Since a national force of the sort envisaged by senior police officers is merely an extension and escalation of the amalgamation policy, which has proved to be disastrous, any extension of the process requires careful scrutiny.

The larger any organization becomes, the more important it is to produce a management and administration structure which has a direct bearing on its operational role. The first problem in any attempt to reach a balanced appraisal of the effectiveness of police management is that of drawing relevant comparisons. There are no production norms; the police are relatively free from financial constraints; and the intangible nature of most forms of police work does not lend itself to convenient equations of cost effectiveness or returns on investment.

The bulk of day to day operational decision-taking and action in critical situations is undertaken by the most junior officers in the service without any form of direct supervision or management presence. This, of course, argues for the need to improve the quality and increase the numbers of officers undertaking these responsibilities. Despite the widely acknowledged need to improve the quality of officers on the ground, the police recruitment and promotion system is geared to removing the most promising and able officers from the streets with the utmost speed. The result over the years has been consistently to weaken the quality of the operational police force. The rapid promotion of young officers beyond any probable level of experience or competence has similarly weakened the ranks of management generally and line management in particular.

There is no distinction drawn in the service between functions which require technical, professional or administrative expertise or skills, and those which demand supervisory or managerial qualities. Although these functions are not synonymous or capable of being performed equally well by all officers, they are treated as if it were so by an inflexible salary structure, which makes no provision for rewarding skill and professional ability other than by promotion to a higher rank. The result of this confusion of functions and individual attributes has been to produce a rank structure overburdened with proficient technicians who have become incompetent administrators and skilled administrators who have become operational liabilities.

This was probably true of the police before any amalgamations took place; in smaller forces, however, the scope for monumental incompetence and inefficiency to exist undetected by the public is far less than in conglomerate forces which perform diverse functions on an inter-community basis. In varying degrees, police amalgamations have produced bureaucratic monstrosities obsessed with rank structures, an indestructible and acquisitive administration, and burgeoning, esoteric policing concepts which defy any rational appraisal in terms of social relevance. Although it is impossible to quantify the social effects of this or the impact on overall police efficiency, some indications can be seen in particular examples.

Something in excess of one in four police officers hold ranks above that of constable. Figures published in *Police Review*, researched by

Graham Marsden and J. Mervyn-Jones, produced an analysis of certain trends in the police service between 1970 and 1979. In that period the service had a net gain of 14,227 officers from increased recruitment. During that period the service rank structure was increased by 4699, a figure which accounted for a third of the entire net gain from the service's recruitment figure. The question was whether this distribution truly reflected the needs of society or the personal ambitions of officers for status. One thing was clear – the ratio of promoted officers was grossly in excess of anything required to advance sensible supervision and management. It does accord, however, with the police concept of leadership by instruction and efficiency by retrospective supervision with an emphasis on talking heads rather than active bodies.

One feature of the lack of discrimination in the salary scales between tasks which justify particular recognition and those which do not is the anomalies produced. Not the least of these is the obvious iniquity of fully operational officers, contending with the rigours of shift work, unsocial hours and on occasions personal danger, being paid the same as their administrative colleagues who share neither the hazards nor the inconvenience. This has produced an indefinable number of often sub-standard officers performing routine, undemanding clerical duties at salaries far in excess of anything which could realistically be expected for performing comparable work in almost any other field. This anomaly extends into the rank structure where, while senior officers are absorbed checking records of past events, junior officers are engaged in less exalted functions such as the investigation of rape, robbery and burglary or in the prevention of these and other crimes.

Regardless of spurious arguments to the contrary, police ranks too often have nothing to do with management responsibilities. Of 3212 officers in the Metropolitan Police CID in 1979, for example, 1764 carried the rank of sergeant or above, while 1448, less than half, were constables. Clearly the ratio had no bearing on the distribution of executive responsibility, and, ironically, neither does it reflect a recognition of the importance of specialist skills or expertise. The mere suggestion that it should is anathema within the police service which, disregarding logic and common sense, clings to the view that police skills are interchangeable. According to this view, the only difference between the traffic patrol officer, the mounted branch officer and the detective officer is that one rides a motor cycle, one rides a horse and the other a chair.

The policy of routine interchange of police officers between different departments, which often require quite different individual skills, is based on the principle that specialist aptitudes and expertise acquired by work experience are unnecessary for officers to hold detective ranks. This was the principle applied by Sir Robert Mark when he destroyed the CID as an entity staffed entirely with officers dedicated and trained to be detective specialists. The system of accelerated promotion for young officers passing examinations is predicated on the belief that not only is it unnecessary to have specialist aptitude or work experience, it is unnecessary to have relevant experience of any kind to hold or assume detective ranks.

By 1981/82, some ten years after the introduction of these policies to the Metropolitan Police CID, London crime rates have reached what many consider to be epidemic proportions. Crime rates were rising before the CID was broken up by Sir Robert, as they were in the country generally, where police forces have always operated the form of interchange more recently introduced to the London force. What is significant about the crime phenomenon in the Metropolitan Police, however, is that the numbers arrested since the CID were placed under uniformed and non-specialist control have progressively decreased. At a time when the Metropolitan Police, over 26,000 strong by 1981, had more police officers available than ever before, and when there was more crime in London than ever before, the revamped detective branch proved itself incapable of maintaining the previous levels of detection let alone improving on them.

It was not only in the Metropolitan Police that the deep-rooted police service antipathy to specialization was called into question. The farcical Countryman inquiry, although carried out in London, was conducted by provincial detectives. The woeful degree of professional inadequacy displayed was hardly surprising given the lack of experience of many of the officers engaged. In 1982 the Home Secretary, William Whitelaw, revealed that similar serious defects had been revealed by an enquiry into the investigation by the West Yorkshire Police of the infamous 'Ripper' murders. These are merely symptoms, however, of a general malaise.

Contemporary research suggests that serious fraud accounts for £5-9000 million being misappropriated from the British economy. Despite the national scandal which this staggering sum represents, the police service deploys very few resources on the investigation of fraud. The position has deteriorated to the extent that fraud squads and prosecuting authorities have introduced artificial and antisocial criteria to decide which frauds will or will not be investigated and prosecuted. Regardless of the intrinsic criminality of frauds, decisions are taken on the basis of the predetermined likelihood of detection of offenders, the anticipated costs of prosecution, and the probability of securing a conviction. Since successful detection is the essential first step in the process, the professional ability and expertise of the investigating officers is crucial. For many years grave misgivings have circulated about the general quality of police officers deputed to investigate serious fraud. This was the case in London when the premier fraud squad in the country, the Metropolitan Police and City Company Fraud Squad, drew its investigators from a criminal investigation department staffed exclusively by professional detectives. The concern expressed then is even more valid now that investigators are drawn from a CID subject to routine interchange, in a service where specialization is regarded as a positive handicap for officers ambitious to achieve high rank. Standards of case preparation and presentation of evidence in courts have fallen abysmally due to the lack of general CID experience and professional expertise applied to investigation, and are attracting increasing adverse comment from judges, magistrates, lawyers and clerks to criminal courts. Such low standards provide a partial explanation for apparently perverse acquittals in criminal trials. Nowhere is this more relevant than in complex frauds which demand the highest standards of preparation and presentation.

The public scandal attached to the investigation of fraud identifies a more fundamental weakness in the police service than its attitude to specialization. It highlights the question of whether some forms of investigation should remain wedded to the police structure or whether they are so inimical to police moves that they should be separated from the police completely. The controversy over the question of independent investigation of serious police complaints reinforces the urgency of the situation.

The whole emphasis of police detection is orientated towards the apprehension of offenders who have committed a crime. In practice, however, a police investigation is considered unsuccessful if it fails to secure the conviction of an offender. The adversary judicial system, where the police are de facto prosecutors, places the police in opposition to defendants. The system in effect charges them with the task of proving guilt, and this not unnaturally conditions police investigators to approach investigations subjectively. It may be desirable to have police officers who can remain impartial as to a suspect's guilt or innocence, but, in practice, this would require police who were prepared to subject even the people they believed to be innocent to a process in which innocence would not ensure immunity from conviction. Whatever the flaws of the present British system, it must surely be preferable to this. The essence of conventional policing in Britain, therefore, is to prevent crime where possible and to identify and prosecute offenders when prevention has failed. That, however, leaves a massive gap in society's defences against crime.

Corruption and fraud are examples of antisocial activities which are immune to conventional police prevention techniques. Although there are exceptions, most corrupt and fraudulent practices are devised on the assumption that the identity of the offender will not be disclosed because the criminal act itself will not be detected, if not forever, at least until escape is assured. Alternatively, the fraud is so devised that, even if revealed, it will not be readily apparent that the action is in itself criminal. For those reasons such matters call for a high degree of objectivity both in discovering the crime and pinpointing the offender. This form of investigation has to be approached as a voyage of discovery with no preconceived ideas. Success is not determined by having individuals arraigned in a criminal court and found guilty. The public interest is equally served, and the investigation successful, if it is shown that no criminal offence has been committed and the individuals' innocence proven. It is self-evident that, in a society where revealed crimes are rampant and increasing, the police service cannot afford itself the luxury of too many investigations merely to find out whether hidden forms of crime are being committed.

In the specific context of corruption and fraud, however, an open democratic society is better served by knowing the extent to which these are influential factors in the society than merely having the guilt of a relatively few individuals established in court. The case for independent investigation of serious police misconduct is not that it will convict more errant officers. The case is that it would establish the extent corruption and malpractice may, or may not, influence the policing of society. This holds true for every public body, not merely the police and probably even less for the police than many others.

This fact was reinforced in the 1980s which saw recurring financial scandals erupting in Lloyds Insurance in the City of London, hitherto regarded as a bastion of the British Establishment, exemplifying standards of probity and integrity. These scandals revealed that corruption and fraud had been a feature of this financial holy of holies for many years. Clearly, the partial disclosures of institutionalized malpractice called for investigation with a view to prosecuting the crooked financiers directly involved. A more important priority was to establish how representative their conduct was of the system. Fraud Squad officers were assigned to investigate the scandals which surfaced, but the question remained of who was to investigate the scandals which had not been revealed. Police investigators linked to the conventional police apparatus cannot undertake the task.

The city itself demonstrably cannot be allowed to undertake the task, and arguments advanced by city interests to the contrary are based on the same spurious foundations as those advanced to justify the police investigating and dealing with their own incidents of serious internal misconduct. Society therefore finds itself in the position of suspecting the presence of a contagious disease. It has a police investigation body which can only deal with visible symptoms; a city patient that cannot be trusted to disclose the extent of the disease; and no independent investigative body capable of determining whether or not the disease has reached epidemic proportions.

The point which emerges is that British society has been badly served by over-reliance on police investigation in such areas. At best the relationship between investigation and conventional policing has been that of an uneasy alliance. The two primary police objectives of crime prevention, and detection and prosecution of offenders do not always coincide with the primary requirements of society and the primary functions of investigation which are revelation and disclosure.

Police-orientated investigation concentrates, quite properly, on issues which police and society both clearly see as wrong: burglaries, robberies and the like. It is right that a service which has a mainly preventative social role should concentrate on the forms of street crime it was created to deal with. An open democratic society, however, demands more sophisticated information than police investigation can provide. Objective investigation is an essential prerequisite if a truly open society is considered preferable to one in which the public faces of institutions and government are set to conceal secretive, and often, unacceptable realities. The police monopoly of criminal investigation never did and, under the existing police structure, never could reflect the division between subjective investigation, inextricably linked to prosecution, and objective investigation, where the end product is not determined in advance. The subordinate role of investigation in the conventional police structure has had two major defects. It has had the effect of inhibiting the development of professional investigators, and prevented the evolution of investigation into a cohesive and coherent professional process capable of responding to social demands for more objective knowledge of the mechanics of society.

Police recruitment and training standards have little or no relevance to the production of skilled investigators. An investigator's physique and physical prowess, for example, are rarely influential in determining the successful outcome of a complex investigation. Knowledge of traffic laws, procedures for dealing with stray dogs and familiarity with laws governing the movement of cattle are unlikely to assist in the investigation of fraud or corruption.

Conventional police ranks relate in the main to the deployment of larger organized bodies being orchestrated to perform in concert. These ranks have no relevance to investigative work which largely demands qualities of individual skill and personal initiative. Promotion examinations based on an interdepartmental police syllabus, and selection procedures which stress interdepartmental experience, are counter-productive as a means of producing skilled specialist investigators.

Although serious crime and matters of grave public concern can happen anywhere, crime patterns are not evenly distributed throughout the country. Consequently, investigative experience and expertise are not universally consistent throughout all police forces. Geographical police boundaries, the autonomy of individual chief constables within their own forces, inter-force and interdepartmental rivalries all militate against any public guarantee that the best investigative expertise available nationally will be applied to particular incidents, regardless of geographical location.

All these factors have had a major influence in preventing the logical evolution of investigation in the United Kingdom as a function which does not conform to conventional policing perceptions. Concern over the standards of investigation applied to the Yorkshire Ripper and Countryman enquiries underlines the practical implications of this for society.

Criminal investigation is merely one example of conflicting functions being uneasily housed in the police service. The effect of police force amalgamations was to merge too many diverse and disparate responsibilities into a managerial framework, which was incapable of responding coherently to the conflicting pressures. A strong police service and a well-policed society are not the same thing. What the amalgamations produced was a strong police service which was not structurally or managerially designed to meet the exigencies of a complex society and the conflicting policing demands made by such a society.

One justification advanced for the force amalgamation policy was the increased mobility of professional criminals. This overlooked the fact that the overwhelming bulk of all crime was, and still is, community-based. The amalgamations weakened the capability of the police to respond to community-based crime, without significantly increasing their capacity to respond to inter-community crime and mobile criminals. The subsequent formation of inter-force Regional Crime Squads acknowledged this, without acknowledging that such squads could equally have been formed with a co-operative effort by smaller forces which had retained their community roots.

Community-based crime, organized crime which has no geographical boundaries, crime prevention, crime detection and crime investigation all compete with each other for management attention and resources from the same pool. In the same way, these competing crime interests jointly compete and conflict with road traffic demands. In turn, localized community traffic problems compete for police resources with the demands of national arterial motor routes which require a degree of national co-ordination and specialized skills which, by virtue of their professional insularity, police are ill-suited to provide. All these policing demands are important. They are certainly all important enough to justify the development of specialized management and professional skills. At the same time, the skills required are so different that there are no rational grounds for assuming police recruiting, training and management are designed to provide these skills. There are, however, grounds for suspecting that, in attempting to reconcile the irreconcilable, the police service is failing to do justice to any of its tasks.

No one can question the importance of policing traffic in a modern society where the emphasis is on high speed transport and communication. The role of the traffic patrol officer has become increasingly technical. The problems created by mechanically defective vehicles, laws relating to transcontinental juggernauts, multiple vehicle accidents and determining responsibility, coping with urban and motorway traffic flow, and many other high priority functions all call for intensive training and experience. In the main, however, the skills called for are not ones which police recruitment and training foster to any significant degree.

The need to maintain police autonomy limits any association with other directly involved organizations and authorities, who have a major role to play in planning and traffic administration, to liaison and consultation. This, together with the subordination of traffic regulation and enforcement to overall police priorities, has restricted the scope for technical innovations in traffic management. Many of the professional qualities ideally required by a traffic patrol officer are technical and mechanical ones which are more evident in Automobile Association Patrols and Department of Transport vehicle examiners than in police officers. At the same time physical and training instruction standards set for police are almost totally irrelevant to the traffic role. Removing traffic from the managerial umbrella of conventional policing and integrating a new formation into a rationalized traffic structure could provide significant benefits for society.

Conventional police wisdom would have it that divorcing some forms of criminal investigation and traffic responsibilities from the present police structure would be tantamount to breaking up the police. A less emotive and more rational reaction by police and public would be to regard the proposals as a process of logical restructuring which would leave police in a stronger position to concentrate on the problems of conventional policing. At the same time this would allow the separated functions to evolve sensibly in response to the needs of society.

In the meantime, however, senior police ranks continue to be based on a theory of non-specialist interchangeability. When viewed together with the professional insularity of the police service the process makes for farcical contradictions. The police service, for instance, which sees nothing questionable about appointing a police traffic specialist to take command of a criminal investigation department or a career detective to preside over its traffic division, would energetically resist the appointment of an outside expert to either of those positions.

The Customs and Excise drugs investigation unit has often achieved considerably more success against major drugs dealers than police drugs squads. A notable feature of that success up to and including 1982 was that it was not accompanied by the same degree of scandal as the successes achieved by some police squads. Indeed, occasional clashes have arisen when C & E investigators discovered close links between police and drugs pedlars which they considered inexplicable. Despite the expertise of Customs Officers, any senior and experienced Customs officer wishing to apply for a position of comparable seniority in a police drugs squad would not be considered by police authorities, while a police traffic officer would.

The process of transferring square pegs into round holes will continue as long as the conglomerate functions created by amalgamations remain under the pyramid rank structure. It is a process which demeans the relative importance of all branches of the service, while massaging the ego of a police hierarchy hungry for advancement and incapable of admitting that there just might be limits to the extent of their personal qualities of leadership and specialized skills.

Police amalgamations produced large and cumbersome organizations of enormous complexity. These large new formations were created in a service already insular by tradition and convention. The lack of professional cross-fertilization of management between the service and other industrial, commercial or social disciplines has produced a structure which reflects this traditional insularity and one ill-suited to the cost-effective and efficient running of such large and complex formations. These factors, together with the minimal intellectual and academic qualifications required to hold senior police rank, have ensured too often that internal policies on command, police strategies, tactics and social philosophy are primarily service orientated. All these features are evident in the emergence of esoteric police functions in pursuit of questionable social objectives. Of all the mysterious functions undertaken by police, none has had more questionable social objectives than those ascribed to the Crime Prevention role.

Since the late 1960s increasing police resources have been misguidedly given over to what were misleadingly described as Crime Prevention departments with Crime Prevention Officers and Crime Prevention Campaigns. The investment of the resources allocated was misguided, as officers who were critical at the time claimed and subsequent events have demonstrated: there was not a shred of evidence to show that the investment had any relevance to police operational objectives. Similarly, the term Crime Prevention was misleading because it was not a term understood by many CPOs in its true sense.

From its inception, the prevention of crime has been one of the founding principles of the British police service. If all police officers are not crime prevention officers their relevance to society becomes indeed obscure. Social evolution, however, has altered perceptions of crime prevention from the days when the police were formed. These revised perceptions have created a more subtle, sophisticated and complex appreciation of the many elements of social interaction involved in the crime prevention process.

The product of these more advanced perceptions has been the recognition that effective crime prevention in society is determined by a synthesis of political tolerance, economic egalitarianism, social equality and individual freedom. Since individual freedom can only be protected by laws enforced by police, it is in this area that police make the most direct contribution to crime prevention. Sensitively managed and effectively structured, they can also form part of a co-ordinated local community framework to advance the social consensus implicit in the other areas mentioned. In other words, crime prevention in its true form requires the integration of police into the community working jointly towards the removal of the social causes of crime.

Instead of that, police practice, with a travesty of reason, turned crime prevention into a mechanical game for professional halfwits. Like wide-eyed children delighted with Christmas train sets, police officers seized on locks, bolts, alarms and an endless array of mechanical junk willingly provided by commercial manufacturers of devices. Flattered by professional salesmen, betrayed by their own technical ignorance of all things mechanical, and occasionally seduced by payment of retainers, CPOs have foisted the idea on the public that these devices and security measures can be equated with crime prevention. In fact, it has amounted to a scandalous waste of police resources and represented a disgraceful betrayal of fundamental police principles.

Acting in all but name as sales representatives for private security gadgetry, police officers do the public no service when they present the sale of these commercial products as a coherent social crime prevention policy. There is nothing wrong with encouraging the public to take sensible precautions to protect their personal property, but to pretend that security devices will make a significant impact on levels of crime in society will, at best, encourage a costly social myth and, at worst, create dangerous social divisions.

The vast majority of crime is committed by opportunist criminals who do little or no pre-planning and without the aid of any sophisticated implements. It is true that an open door or window is more inviting and provides easier access to premises than those which are locked. Strong locks on doors and windows, however, will add nothing to the strength of wood in the door, or its surrounds, or to the resistance of glass to force. Only the most expensive and sophisticated security precautions provide any real defence against a determined attack by any but the most incompetent, opportunist criminal. The security precautions available to the average member of the public have no deterrent effect whatsoever on the casual criminal. It must also be borne in mind that criminals soon become competent to the extent that security systems which may initially deter become less daunting. Some degree of security may indeed deter ineffectual criminals from a particular project. Faced with an unacceptable level of security at one premises, for example, a burglar may be deterred and turn away. This is speciously presented as crime prevention. What the burglar does, however, is to turn away in favour of an easier target. The result, therefore, is not a crime prevented, merely a change of criminal venue.

Belatedly, in 1982, Home Office research into the effects of crime prevention campaigns began to raise doubts about their validity. This research, by implication, indicated the financial and social futility of a policy practised by police for over twelve years at a colossal cost. Far more fundamental and important social issues were involved than merely money, however.

Security technology can never be relied upon as an effective form of crime prevention. At best it merely treats particular symptoms of a deep-seated disease with drugs to which the disease quickly forms a natural immunity. As reliance on security technology increases, the scale of the criminal response escalates. New points of vulnerability are identified and the degree of force applied to either property or person is increased. Security technology in general makes society more dangerous, not more secure.

It is a form of crime prevention basically contrary to everything for which a responsible community police should stand, representing as it does a departure from the values of a free and open society. The theory advanced that protection from criminal attack depends on an individual's financial means devalues society and is socially divisive. The policy represents, too, a major retreat from the concept that individuals and communities should look to government, law and the police for their protection in society, regardless of wealth or social standing.

In effect, the police policy of advocating private security measures represents the relinquishment of their social responsibility for the preservation of community stability. This is underlined by an associated trend in policing of discontinuing the investigation of burglaries and other forms of street crimes. The inevitable consequence of this council of despair, and perhaps an indication of worse things to come, was provided when, in 1982, it was revealed that major insurance companies were refusing to give burglary cover to homes in certain parts of the United Kingdom.

The composition, policies and performance of the British police forces since the introduction of force amalgamations hardly inspire public confidence in the service as a whole. It may be that some contemporary chief constables are better technically qualified than their predecessors. Apart from blind faith, however, there appear to be no objective grounds for assuming they have the qualities necessary to make sound judgments on the disposition of police resources. More significantly, considerable caution has to be exercised before attributing to them the qualities of social awareness demanded by their extension into social roles.

One officer who took Sir Robert Mark at his word when propounding the right of chief officers of police to speak out publicly was James Anderton, Chief Constable of Greater Manchester. It is important, however, for the public to bear in mind that there are few police views which are universally held by the police. There is a common tendency to ignore powerful bodies of dissentient views which exist within the service. Too often these dissentient views are muted as a result of a hierarchical system which limits public debate to the conventional wisdom of senior self-publicist officers who have unlimited access to the media. In this they are supported by a sophisticated public relations apparatus which ensures them a public forum available to few politicians. The degree of support in the police, therefore, for Anderton's views is unknown: that they represent the views of a significant and influential element of the service is beyond doubt.

On 22 April 1980, in a prepared speech to the International Fire, Security and Safety Exhibition and Conference, at London's Olympia Hall, Anderton presented a chilling spectre of society as he saw it. He claimed the views expressed were his own and not necessarily those of the police service: 'Penal reforms, sloppy leadership, and judicial weakness have become the enemies of public safety.' There is, he claimed, a 'quiet but hardly bloodless revolution' in progress worldwide. Sinister evidence can be seen in 'pressure' which is being 'brought to bear for more open government, freedom of information and the elimination of secrecy'.

Anderton averred that it was the police service and 'other disciplined and established institutions which embody commonly accepted values and stability' and that it was to those bodies that we had to look to if 'disorientation and ultimate totalitarianism' was to be avoided. Attempts to find out how we are governed is only one dangerous trend identified by Anderton. 'Questions on the work of Special Branch; qualms about police accountability and the power of chief constables; doubts about police investigation of their own alleged malpractices; and inference of widespread police corruption' are all identified as insidious trends.

Anderton ignored the fact that there is considerable support inside the police for an independent investigative body to examine the most serious allegations of police malpractice. Neither did he address himself to Sir Robert Mark's belief that the 3000-strong Metropolitan Police CID had long been 'the most routinely corrupt organization in London' or to the evidence which suggests police malpractice to be as prevalent elsewhere as in the capital.

He said, 'There have been times in the past when police have appeared to act *both locally and nationally* [author's italics] according to the wishes of the dominant political party or in the interests of persons with power, and there certainly have been times when individual chief constables could have done more to assert their professional autonomy and integrity against partisan political pressure. Thankfully the days when chief constables were perhaps a little too ready to comply with biased requests from the local town hall have surely disappeared.'

If ever a chief constable issued a unilateral declaration of independence from the constitutional machinery of government in Britain, this would appear to be it. The cumbersome term, 'dominant political party', cannot disguise that it was the wishes of government, local and national, which were being referred to and that, as a chief constable, Anderton did not consider himself bound by them.

He continued, '... the public, that huge indescribable mass of humanity with no single mind of its own, is the most disorganized body imaginable. Each man has his own feelings and expectations and can relate them to whomsoever and whatsoever he chooses. The public are always primed for persuasion if not revolution and it is, therefore, imperative for the police urgently to identify the public more strongly with the police task.'

The question is whose perceptions of the 'police task' are the public expected to identify with if not those of elected government? Implicitly, the perceptions of chief constables seem to be the choice. But what if the undisciplined rabble of a public rejects the perceptions of chief constables in favour of their own? Anderton's view is illuminating: 'Sometimes the only alternative with an undisciplined and crime-ridden community is to force it to conform and obey.' 'Conform' to what and 'obey' whom? Since, according to Anderton, elected government is clearly suspect, 'penal reforms, sloppy leadership and judicial weakness' are the enemies of public safety, and the public are obviously a complete shower, what are the alternatives? Where is the leadership so clearly needed to come from?

'The police are now a meritocracy truly representative of all the people they serve. They are now entering a new era in which frank and open contact with the public will promote real accountability and end the *silent and subservient police force* [author's italics] its opponents would like to retain.'

There we have it: who needs elected government, penal reforms and a judiciary when we have a ready made 'meritocracy' ready and willing to step into the breach? Of course, we must accept less open government, restricted information and more secrecy. We must stop asking about Special Branch and trying to curb the powers of chief constables. There has to be an end to criticism of police internal investigations and worries about police corruption and malpractice. After all, meritocracies should know what they are about, should they not?

The problems of creating a more orderly and disciplined society are really rather simple, according to Anderton. It merely requires that'... emphasis should be put upon what gives the innocent and law-abiding the best possible protection against the criminal classes [?], and what gives the whole community peace of mind and a belief that the nation cares for them, even if it means the reintroduction of measures previously rejected as being too costly or repressive. I firmly believe that crime can only be dealt with on the basis of what gives immediate protection and relief.' In other words, social principles should not interfere with expediency. If this is so, it would be socially expedient to round up the 'criminal classes'...

In addition to the reintroduction of measures previously rejected as too costly and repressive, Anderton also advocates a National Police structure. To achieve this it would be sensible to '... create about ten Regional Police Forces whose chief officers would form a Commissioners Standing Committee – *a cabal of police top-liners more likely to speak with one voice* [author's italics] – to devise operational policies and police strategies against crime'.

In a prepared speech with words presumably carefully chosen, it is instructive that he should choose to define the word 'committee', for those who may not understand it, as 'a cabal'. It is instructive because a cabal is a particularly sinister form of committee. The word is an acronym of the surnames of a secret seventeenth-century cabinet of ministers governing England in the days of Charles II. The word is apt in the context of a society governed from behind closed doors, where information is restricted and secrecy is the guiding principle.

One advantage offered by the proposed new police structure, we are told, is that: 'The opportunities in emergency for the immediate and urgent unification of police effort in the national interest would be readily apparent.' No doubt it would if the nature of the emergency had been specified, or by whom and how. This is important since the national interest is rarely something which attracts unanimity of political and social views. Neither does the chief constable hazard a guess as to which single voice would emerge from the 'Cabal of Ten', and, holding itself aloof from elected government, to whom the voice would be answerable. James Anderton is an important police voice. As Chief Constable of Greater Manchester, he was operating as an autonomous commander of one of the largest and most powerful police forces in the United Kingdom and it would be fatuous to dismiss his appraisal of British society as generally unrepresentative of the police service.

His voice reflects the innately paternalistic and authoritarian police attitudes already discussed: the overweening self-esteem of an element of the service which sees itself as the repository of all proper social values, contemptuous of suggestions that its internal affairs should be scrutinized; public servants who no longer regard themselves as instruments of government, the law and society. It is an element which instead sees itself as independent of government, not bound by the 'niceties of the law', as the meritocratic leaders of a 'disorganized', 'undisciplined' and 'crime-ridden' society. The vision of communities being forced to 'conform and obey', 'criminal classes', and a return to 'costly and repressive measures', all reflect the traditional views, nurtured by an insular service, which, through its recruitment strategies and a lack of cross-fertilization, cannot be truly representative of the society it polices. It is a closed environment, strengthened by the amalgamation process, leading to the progressive isolation of the service from its community roots, and which will become increasingly isolated if the amalgamation process is carried to its ultimate conclusion.

The clearest possible evidence that the creation of a single national police force is not merely Anderton's pipedream was provided by Col. Sir Eric St Johnston, once a chief constable and a former HM Inspector of Constabulary. In *The Guardian*, 10 August 1981, the Colonel argued the case for a single national police force. More significantly he revealed: 'Within the police force during the past ten years, particularly amongst those attending the senior command course at the National Police College, opinion has moved significantly towards the establishment of a national police force taking administrative control away from local authorities and placing it in the hands of the Home Secretary.'

In the same article Eric St Johnston also identified the real power-base of chief constable autonomy when he pointed out: '. . . there is no way a chief of police can be removed [from office] unless he is found unfit for his appointment as a result of disciplinary proceedings'. It is from this base that, over the years, chief officers of police have constantly been redefining the limits of their professional autonomy in amalgamated formations, free from the restraints of direct accountability to individual communities. It is in that context that the movement towards a monolithic police service has to be assessed.

James Anderton made it clear, whatever his intentions, that chief constables are fast becoming capable of being rogue elephants in the British social and political scene. So unassailable have they become by virtue of acquired autonomy, they can, and do, exercise power and influence free from independent scrutiny by the public and with little or no real accountability to elected government. Instead of explaining their manifest failure to preserve law and order, chief constables have increasingly used sophisticated press and public relations facilities to attack government and the judiciary, thus evading their own direct responsibility for many police failures. In too many cases, far from fighting an overwhelming flood of crime, chief constables have been presiding over grotesquely inflated rank structures, bloated and maladministered bureaucracies, and a dissipation of effort by misguided policies and managerial incompetence.

At a time when crime is rising and civil disorder is endemic, James Anderton sees the police as the last bastion of democratic freedom: the Spartans of Britain determined to fight to the death to deny passage to the ungodly hordes of 'criminal classes' threatening to pour through the Thermopylaen passes of local police committees and subjugate the nation. Who the latter day Leonidas will be is left to the imagination: that he will arise from the ranks of chief constables seems certain for, according to Anderton, they are the ultimate guardians of our traditional social values. But, in rejecting the authority of elected government over the police, Anderton also denies the truth of the words:

> Laws are for all, and he who seeks to lay them
> On others should by rights himself obey them.

If this does not hold true for police why should it hold true for others?

Repression and justice make strange bedfellows. No one has ever seriously suggested that democratic principles make for easy living. However expedient, draconian measures can sometimes misfire. On 18 June 1981, £65,000 was paid to three youths held to have been wrongly convicted of the 'Confait' murder in London. On 19 June 1981 a man was released from Edinburgh's Saughton Prison, his sentence quashed by the Scottish High Court after he had served eight years of a life sentence for murder. In March 1982, against the wishes of many police officers, the Police Federation spent £30,000 advertising to encourage a return to capital punishment.

There is in the police, and elsewhere in British society, a genuine fear that a left-wing, Marxist dictatorship could emerge. In that context, there is a superficial attraction in the idea of a powerful, unified police force. On 15 March 1982, identifying the threat of a nationally orchestrated left-wing conspiracy, Anderton reiterated that the defence of democracy against 'the dream of a Marxist totalitarian state in this country' rested on the ability of the police alone to stand against terrorism, crime and social disorder. It is his belief that 'an uncompromising deterrent will be necessary' to meet those threats.

The extreme right has an affinity with aggressive chief constables and welcomes a movement which calls for a re-establishment of traditional social values and authoritarian concepts of law and order. Confused moderates, fearful of society being plunged into anarchy by terrorism, crime and racial and urban unrest may be tempted to draw comfort from the deceptive certainties of a powerful police force, ostensibly committed to the preservation of social stability and democratic freedoms. On all counts the right and the moderates could be proved wrong.

In order to sustain a totalitarian state, power has to be concentrated. Uncontrolled and uncontrollable power poses as much threat to the forces of totalitarianism as it does to their enemies. Once welded into a single monolithic structure, under a cabalistic committee of chief officers, free from external investigation, the police would become an awesome instrument of concentrated power. Capture the head of this structure, and the instrument is as adaptable for use by a totalitarian left as by a dictatorial right. Order, discipline, uncompromising deterrence, and the power of the state to impose its authority on the individual regardless of natural justice are just as vital for ensuring the stability of a Marxist dictatorship as any other.

An Orwellian state is a totalitarian state is a police state. What do the police have to fear from that? To paraphrase Pascal, if it proves difficult to make what is just strong, are we to believe the police would flinch from a society which sets out to make what is strong just? Police practices have encompassed such esoteric indulgences as up-ending people into lavatory bowls, stimulating suspects with 'rhino whips', mocking up trials and execution preliminaries and similar diversions. That these and other widespread forms of misconduct took place without the approval of the majority of police officers and without the direct sanction of the state did not prevent their occurrence. Who can say what imaginative projects would materialize under a more powerful regime.

It is not known if the revolutionary left have succeeded in infiltrating the Association of Chief Police Officers; if not, the influence of Anderton and likeminded colleagues could serve their purpose admirably. One of the best established precepts of revolutionary strategy is that Marxist militancy is advanced when right-wing opponents are provoked into postures of intolerance, the suspension of individual liberties, and social confrontation. Policies of enforced conformity, unquestioning obedience to authority, repression, and uncompromising deterrence are the weapons of tyranny not democracy.

It is not the united might of a monolithic police structure which can ensure the continuance of British democracy but the collective will of a united society. The future stability of democracy will be determined only by the ability of society to sustain political, economic and social consensus in the face of mounting confrontational extremism. Social tolerance and compromise are the strengths, not the weaknesses of democracy. The effort to achieve social consensus in these fields is not simply to pursue idealistic social dreams: efforts in those directions form the basis of the only practical internal security strategy available to a free democratic society. The opening years of the 1980s have seen a concerted effort on both sides of the political spectrum to denigrate the concept of a consensus.

Orwell intended that *1984* should be remarkable for the nightmarish qualities of the society he portrayed. There are some who would see Orwell's society as nothing more sinister than one which was properly disciplined and orderly, and one which had a due regard for authority. It is also important to remember that, in the new technological age, a steady erosion of individual freedom and personal liberties can achieve a state of tyranny as effectively and certainly as revolutionary insurrection.

In his speech to IFSSEC in 1980, Anderton said:

The completed study has now been approved and work is now going ahead to plan the first phase of computer-aided policing in Greater Manchester. It will involve four major initiatives:

(i) The introduction of a comprehensive modern system for computer-aided despatching (Command and Control) covering the force area

(ii) The conversion of Manchester Criminal Records Office (Mancro) from manual to computer-based operation

(iii) The provision of computer-driven information support facilities to enable operational policemen to make full and effective use of the criminal records system, the Police National Computer, *and other information sources which become available in the future* [author's italics]; and

(iv) The provision of management information systems covering all aspects of force operations.

With apparently unconscious irony the Chief Constable concluded his remarks with the comment:

'I am hoping this will be fully operational in 1984.'

# 4

# Security through
# the Looking-glass

Power exercised without public scrutiny cannot be truly held accountable and is more likely to be abused than any form of power wielded openly. The truth of this is readily illustrated by the relative attitudes adopted by totalitarian, as opposed to democratic, states towards power and public accountability. Totalitarianism functions by concentrating power and by maintaining the secrecy of that power. The protective veil can be drawn over what reflects badly on the regime and parted only to reveal what is favourable. In this way any stupidity, incompetence and malpractice in the bureaucratic machinery poses little threat to the stability of the regime. Totalitarianism also recognizes that personal freedoms are forms of power which could inevitably create a challenge to its authority.

A democracy operates on precisely the opposite premises, in theory at least. Democracy is based on a principle of open government, in which the powers of the executive and government are defined and regularly scrutinized. Personal freedom and individual liberties are seen as the most effective guarantee against tyranny. Even in a democracy, however, it must be recognized that the state will come under threat at some time and that these threats may be internal or external. The state, therefore, must maintain the capacity to defend itself and preserve its democratic principles. The role of state security institutions is to enable society to respond to those who seek to act unlawfully to destroy the state and the principles on which it is founded. To be effective, state security organizations have to be vested with some degree of authority and power which, in the wider public interest, may occasionally conflict with individual rights and freedoms. Specifically, security organizations of state need the operational capacity to identify potential enemies and the means to neutralize those enemies.

Under totalitarianism, those who do not support the regime are the natural enemies of the state and thus targets for the security agencies. Things are not that simple in a democracy: the freedom to dissent from existing mores and the conventional wisdom of the day is built into British democracy. From the National Front on the extreme right to the extremes of Marxism on the left, the broad spectrum of politics demonstrates the problems confronting security services attempting to define and identify enemies of British democracy. The problem is simple: it is a perfectly legitimate aim for political activists of any political persuasion to work towards the destruction of parliamentary democracy, and its institutions, providing they do not break the law as it stands at any given time.

Given the diversity of political views in British politics, governments, subject to the vagaries of the ballot box, are inconstant and inconsistent in their judgment and appreciation of security objectives. Does the spy who discloses the disposition of Britain's nuclear defences pose a greater, or lesser, threat to the nation's security than the opposition defence spokesman determined to get rid of nuclear defences altogether? What criteria are the security agencies to use when the law respects the rights of individuals and organizations dedicated to overthrowing state institutions such as the monarchy, and regards efforts to that end as legitimate political activity? In a society predicated on principles of social and political change, with whom are the security services to align themselves?

Security services have to rely largely on their own perceptions of who, or what, constitutes a threat to the state. Given that the law is widely identified as ineffective, it would be remarkable if the security agencies did not regard it as an insubstantial crutch, and pay it little more than lip service.

Operational police officers, unofficially, have adopted a pragmatic approach to the administration of the law. On innumerable occasions, protective measures inspired by society's concern for the rights of individuals have been found wanting. Deciding, in the main, that these measures were either inoperable or incompatible with police objectives, operational police officers proceeded to disregard what they considered to be 'niceties of the law'. This has always been known. The scales of justice probably found themselves reasonably well balanced, if undue weight was not placed on the occasional innocent unexpectedly ensnared. Providing that the public were not made overly conscious of police unorthodoxy there was no great social impetus towards reform. This is a feature of British public affairs which is not unique to the police. It is a form of authoritarian paternalism endemic in most areas of Establishment thinking – paternalism which, in varying degrees, subscribes to the view that it is not in the interests of the public to be aware of more than is good for their peace of mind about the mechanics of power in society.

Nowhere is this paternalism more evident – and, the Establishment argue, more appropriate – than in the labyrinthine affairs of internal security. There is an obvious danger, however, that, in extending this principle too far, blind faith may replace reason and breed misplaced public complacency. Another problem is that the veil of secrecy, drawn over the affairs of police and security in the normal course of events, leaves the public only with periodic revelations of sensational misconduct, and monumental incompetence, upon which to judge the propriety and efficacy of these institutions of state. In the light of startling disclosures which emerged from the security services in the 1970-80s, the public could be forgiven for asking what they had achieved and for whom.

Before looking at some of those revelations in detail, it is important to see the security services, similarly the police, in the context of a society under pressure from resurgent political extremism, in the context of a society where political, economic and social divisions are likely to deepen and where the movement away from a consensus threatens the cohesion of the nation. The operational role of the security services has to face conflicting pressures externally and internally. Externally, they have the problem of pursuing even-handed security policies which, if they do not conflict with those of the government of the day, will almost certainly clash with those of politicians who may form the government of tomorrow. Internally, they have to contend with conflicting professional perceptions based on differing views of the divisions in society.

The basic dilemma which confronts the security agencies is whether or not it is possible to formulate a coherent, and yet impartial, strategy of national security. The dilemma for society is whether or not the security agencies can be safely left to wrestle with this problem and reach their own conclusions unsupervised. The Establishment, not unnaturally, argue they should, and that the involvement of the public would effectively emasculate the security apparatus. Before accepting this, there are a number of factors which the public should consider. Security agencies, which should fill a crucial role in defending the democratic way of life, have least to lose in the event of totalitarianism either of right or left emerging in Britain. A police state cannot exist without a strong police. In the same way, no other form of regime relies more heavily on its security apparatus than a totalitarian one which, unable to rely on the support of the people, is determined to survive regardless. The most persuasive reason for rejecting the Establishment view, however, is because it is fundamentally false.

It is axiomatic that some degree of secrecy and confidentiality are necessary in security and intelligence work, but other factors have to be accommodated. Organizations overprotected by secrecy, who conduct their affairs away from the public gaze, do not have the same incentive to re-examine their long-standing perceptions as those who have to face public examination. The strategic security objectives in a democracy are a far cry from those which operate in a totalitarian regime and do not conform to the conventional wisdom of professional security assumptions. The security of democracy depends on the openness of society and the involvement of the public in the running of society's affairs, while a totalitarian regime depends heavily on secrecy and the exclusion of the public from affairs of state. The British security services have been left too long to their own devices with the inevitable result that these fundamental differences have become obscured.

Security scandals are merely the tip of an iceberg, highlighting four basic areas for public concern: how accountable are the British security services for errors of professional judgment? Have they been penetrated to the extent that only the British public are kept in the dark about their activities? Has their traditional autonomy and anonymity cloaked inefficiency and incompetence? And, finally, how can any of these issues be satisfactorily resolved unless they are regularly subjected to independent public scrutiny and appraisal? Appraisal requires a full knowledge of the subject, but few have experience of the security world, and they are in any case denied information. Such is the lack of authoritative official information released, as far as the mass of the general British public are concerned, that there can be little certainty that the security and intelligence services even exist. The sensational breaches of internal security which surfaced in 1982 and earlier, coupled with government failure to anticipate the Argentine invasion of the Falkland Islands, could suggest to some that they do not.

There are three basic elements to the Secret Services: the Secret Intelligence Service (SIS), formerly MI6; the Security Service, formerly MI5; and the police Special Branch. Although, technically, the titles MI6 and MI5 are reminders of links with Military Intelligence long since severed, they remain apposite in that undisclosed government funding for both agencies is laundered through the Department of Defence budget. Special Branch funds are similarly disguised within police allocations.

Three distinct elements of national security have to be recognized in the security apparatus. Over the centuries, the conflicting territorial, military and ideological interests of sovereign nations have imposed the need for each nation to acquire intelligence about the intentions of the others. The more diverse and widespread the global interests of a nation, the more extensive the intelligence network required. The less compatible the interests of one nation with those of another, the greater the need for one to have intelligence about the other's intentions, and the more likelihood there will be that the intelligence will have to be acquired through covert activities, without the knowledge or approval of the target nation. MI6 reflects the need for Britain to have intelligence agents in other countries and MI5 is intended to counter the efforts of other countries to engage in similar activities in Britain. Special Branch, on the other hand, evolved from a recognition that Britain could also be threatened internally by political and ideological groups which, unable to achieve their aims through the conventional electoral process, were prepared to engage in unconventional or illegal means.

Although in principle the three basic elements of national security still hold true, various national and international trends have tended to blur the lines between the services in Britain as elsewhere. Ideologies which recognize no national or geographical boundaries have produced movements not directly linked to sovereign governments. These movements have found military expression through the medium of terrorist organizations dedicated to violence for their own ends and prepared to form bloody marriages of convenience with other movements, even when their eventual goals may be unconnected. Under those conditions, in an era of international terrorism, fine distinctions between spheres of responsibility between foreign espionage and internal security, or one form of security and another, become hazy. Although MI6 may not technically be an arm of internal security, events have conspired to give it a direct relevance to the subject.

Although known to the intelligence agencies of every foreign country and major terrorist organization in the world, the British public are not allowed to know the identities of the Directors of their own security agencies. The location of security establishments, the numbers and, less remarkably, the identities of personnel and their operational functions are all veiled from the public gaze. Yet it is known that the USSR government have maintained representatives in the organizations for years and almost certainly still do. A former Director and Deputy Director of MI5, Sir Roger Hollis and Graham Mitchell respectively, were both suspected by security officers of having been Russian agents. In the minds of some these suspicions have not been totally allayed. If either suspicion is well founded, there can be no doubt that the current head of the KGB will influence the running of the British security services.

It is known that there is a Joint Intelligence Committee which processes raw intelligence for the benefit of the Prime Minister, and that the Foreign Secretary and Home Secretary are the other ministers most closely involved with intelligence and security matters on behalf of the British government. The degree of control they exercise on overall strategy is speculative and their knowledge of the day to day operational activities of the services is at best limited. What is certain is that Parliament has no control or knowledge and, more significantly, no constitutional means to acquire either up to the end of 1982, although various moves are afoot to institute changes.

Scrutiny of the security services in the early 1980s was in the domain of a standing Security Commission, routinely presided over by an eminent judge, such as Lord Diplock, which, with monotonous regularity over a period of years, carried out investigations into serious security lapses and procedures within the services concerned. Equally monotonously, the Commission produced reports, the contents of which were never fully disclosed to Parliament or the public. What was released were consistently bland and unrevealing generalities which were, too often, overtaken by fresh scandals before they could be swallowed by the public.

It has to be accepted that no security organization can work effectively if it is to have every operational project, and the minutiae of its day to day work, subjected to external scrutiny and supervision. By the same token, no public organization can possibly be held to be truly accountable unless their strategic objectives are clearly understood by the public's elected representatives, in order that objectives and results can be compared. The British Parliament is not openly provided with information about the objectives of the security agencies, and without that information MPs have no real knowledge. In the absence of knowledge their understanding may be limited, their reasoning suspect, and their conclusions nonsense.

If the services were accountable for errors of professional judgment, it would, claims the Establishment, emasculate the operational efficiency of the services. Even if the security services are not strictly accountable in a conventional democratic sense, if they are free from major errors of professional judgment then there is no significant benefit to be derived from accountability. Every organization is entitled to be judged by a balanced appraisal of success and failure. One effect of the excessive secrecy which surrounds the Security Services, however, is that the only standards by which they can be publicly judged are their failures.

The real importance of security lapses is not that they have happened, but what they reveal about the areas in which the services operate and the implications for society of their strategic and tactical policies in those areas. At the heart of these issues is the question of the proper function of security in a democratic society.

The Security Services operate in both a passive and active role. The passive role involves the gathering, collation and dissemination of information to the government of the day. In their active role they become an instrument for influencing the course certain events will take, or a catalyst for making things happen which might not otherwise do so. In a time of war it is not too difficult to identify what a nation wishes to happen. Strategic objectives are clear and operational tactics can be tailored to achieve those ends. Under those conditions a tactical sacrifice of social principles may be a small price to pay to ensure ultimate strategic victory. Peacetime objectives are less clear and often defy definition by government, far less by the executive branches of government which include the security services.

In war the law and legal services of the country become an integrated part of the united cause against the enemy. Under those circumstances the law becomes subservient to government and, within defined limits, even to the executive. In peacetime, however, if the law is to retain any credibility it must be divorced from government and its executive branches, and it is those which occupy the subordinate role. Unless this is the case the law becomes impotent as a means of protecting the rights of the individual in society against the forces most likely to usurp them. There can be no moral or physical distinction between a totalitarian society and one in which the law can be disregarded or manipulated by government or its executives. It is in that context, therefore, that revealed security lapses have to be considered; and it is in that context the social implications of errors of judgment by the security services have to be assessed and questions of accountability raised.

In 1973 two British subjects, brothers named Littlejohn, who had been arrested in Eire for bank robberies committed in Dublin, were tried and convicted. During the course of the trial, and subsequently, it was revealed by one of the brothers, Kenneth, that he had been recruited by British security to infiltrate the IRA in Eire and encouraged to participate in bank robberies to gain acceptance. It was eventually confirmed that Littlejohn had links with the British authorities. It is important to stress that, in this context, 'agent' means no more than a casual mercenary and not an established security official.

The circumstances of the Littlejohn affair conform to the classic security scenario for attempted penetration of a terrorist organization, which in this case happens to be in Eire. The fact of disclosure does not prove failure or that the objective was misguided. It does, however, raise fundamental questions about means and ends. It also places a question mark over the quality and degree of professional security and governmental judgment brought to bear on the project. (Although incidental in this particular context, it is worth noting that Kenneth

Littlejohn's introduction to the intelligence/security world was alleged to have been through the medium of a junior Conservative minister.)

The conviction of Dennis Howard Marks on 16 February 1982 at the Old Bailey in London for drugs offences hopefully also concluded a long-running and embarrassing affair for British officialdom. It is, of course, in the nature of intelligence and security matters that truth and facts are rarely introduced into the public arena unless they are calculated to deceive; and so it may be with the bizarre case of Howard Marks who may still be a deep-cover agent for British intelligence. If this is the case Marks was provided with an almost incredible cover story. Whatever the truth of the Marks' affair, one thing is clear: like Kenneth Littlejohn, Marks was run by British Intelligence and in much the same way. Given his other activities, some concern is justifiable.

While an undergraduate at Balliol College, Oxford, and subsequently while living in the Oxford area, Marks had been an active participant in the local drugs scene. Active as both a user and dealer, he was known to the Thames Valley Police as someone who was in constant possession and use of cannabis in his Oxford cottage. In 1972 Marks was recruited to covert security work by a former undergraduate friend with the Foreign Office. The 'Foreign Office' is the standard cover for some career Intelligence officials.

Marks was recruited ostensibly to infiltrate an IRA arms procurement and distribution network, financed by drugs dealing and centred on the continent. Marks then went to Amsterdam where he became involved with a notorious international figure in the arms and drugs smuggling world who also had IRA connections, a man named James McCann. According to British official sources, alarm over Marks' extra-curricular activities led to links being severed in 1973. Marks did not agree that his services to British security had been dispensed with at the time claimed by the authorities. Whether by coincidence or not, it was at this same period that the Littlejohn affair was becoming public knowledge.

Marks was arrested in November 1973 and charged by British Customs officials with the first of a series of drugs offences. The value of drugs involved was considerable and it is unusual under these circumstances for bail to be granted. It is particularly unusual for someone who was in the habit of travelling extensively abroad. In a remarkable departure from standard practice, Marks was bailed and promptly left the country. From 1973 until 1980 Marks circulated freely on the continent and in Britain with the aid of false passports.

In May 1980 he was again arrested, this time in Suffolk on charges relating to the illegal importation of 15 tons of cannabis with a reported street value in excess of £20 million. He was also charged with passport offences. At his trial in November 1981 he was acquitted on the drugs offences. His defence hinged on his work for the British security services. Although the prosecution formally repudiated this defence, his acquittal indicated that the jury were not convinced by the official repudiation. Marks received two years' imprisonment for the passport offences. On 16 February 1982, Marks appeared charged with the drugs offences for which he had been granted bail in 1973 and pleaded guilty, for which he received a three-year sentence. Since the sentence was to run concurrently with his two-year sentence, the new sentence added little to his period of incarceration.

On 5 January 1982, ITV screened a documentary film, made by Anthony Thomas, entitled *The most dangerous man in the world*. This film exposed the activities of a former CIA agent, Frank Terpil, who, having left the CIA, had been marketing his professional services round the world on a freelance basis. He specialized in the supply of arms, explosives and the most sophisticated technology of terror available. His list of customers read like a *Who's Who* of the moral and social pariahs of modern times.

Terpil had supplied the regime of the former Shah of Iran. He had been a major weapons quartermaster, close personal friend and advisor to the monstrous Idi Amin of Uganda. From his experience in this role he was able to give explicit, first-hand details of the eating habits of a starving rat when trapped on the stomach of a prisoner: with only one source of food available and nowhere else to go, it seems that the rat does the obvious thing. Colonel Gaddafi was another valued customer for whom Terpil, in addition to terror technology, supplied American Special Forces personnel to assist in the training of international terrorists in Libya. At least one of the 'specialists' employed claimed to have received official leave of absence from his unit to undertake the assignment. What made the documentary of particular interest to British viewers was the revelation that the base for many of Terpil's activities had been the United Kingdom.

A substantial part of the programme centred on a meeting between Terpil and two New York police officers posing as Caribbean revolutionaries in the market for automatic weapons. Unknown to Terpil, the hotel-room meeting was secretly filmed and subsequently provided evidence in court where he was sentenced to 53 years' imprisonment. He did not serve the sentence, through the simple expedient of fleeing the country while on bail with the connivance, and some would say to the relief, of some American security services.

Terpil had lived in the United Kingdom in the 1970s. With his American partner, Edward Wilson, he had operated his affairs of terror with apparent immunity from British security. This was attributed to his contacts in these circles: one of these was a security official referred to only as the 'Baby-Sitter' but identified to Anthony Thomas by Terpil, and the other a high-ranking Special Branch officer. The automatic weapons required by the 'Caribbean revolutionaries' were to be supplied under arrangements made with a British based arms company. British officials in the pay of Terpil, in accordance with precedent, would be bribed to produce a phoney 'End User Arms Certificate' showing the destination of the arms as the Philippine Government, thus avoiding any interference from less sympathetic British officials.

Following up Terpil's information, the documentary reporter, Anthony Thomas, claimed to have interviewed the official named as Baby-Sitter, who had confirmed what Terpil had said. The official added one important rider, Thomas claimed: should Thomas reveal his identity, Thomas would find himself 'under a bush in Surrey'. The Baby-Sitter's identity was not revealed and it is not clear what official position he occupies.

In furtherance of Russian foreign policy, KGB intelligence operations are concealed by what appears to be a 'wilderness of mirrors', according to James Angleton, a former CIA senior counter-intelligence expert. Peering through the 'wilderness of mirrors', reality and illusion merge in an ever-shifting landscape where nothing is ever quite what it seems. The same description could equally well describe the public's appreciation of British security operations as revealed by the affairs of the Littlejohns, Howard Marks and Frank Terpil. The implications for British society range far beyond the particular individuals and events described.

Kenneth Littlejohn and Howard Marks were low-grade intelligence material from a professional point of view. They were, as far as is known, untrained as agents and they had identifiable criminal tendencies. They were used in situations where they could give free rein to their innate criminality for personal gain. The activities they were engaged in were unlawful in this and other countries. It has to be said that there is no absolute proof that the British authorities knew of, or encouraged, their participation in bank robberies and international drugs smuggling. The agents contend that the authorities did know and encouraged them to do precisely those things. In any event, such ignorance in controlling the activities of an operational agent must be an excuse of doubtful validity. While accepting that the events under review are being looked at through a wilderness of mirrors, and that it is sometimes necessary for those who protect us to get their hands dirty, the acid test of all these affairs must be whether the anticipated results could justify the means employed and the risks taken.

Only the most naive could realistically have expected low-grade, petty criminals like the Littlejohns to have penetrated the higher echelons of the IRA terrorist structure. Apart from anything else, their English background would have been a major hurdle. Intelligence provided by the Littlejohns could have been interesting and useful. At best, however, it would have had only a limited value in the overall campaign against the IRA. It was certain that if apprehended by the authorities in Eire the links with British intelligence services would emerge. It is true that a successful covert operation brings its own reward and tends to provide its own justification, but the Littlejohn venture was unsuccessful. Mounting it risked the central plank of the major British security strategy in the campaign against the IRA.

By any conceivable intelligence yardstick, maintaining good relations with the Republic of Ireland authorities rates as the overwhelming priority of the British security services in their efforts to defend Ulster and mainland Britain from IRA terrorism. Most of the success the British authorities have had is directly or indirectly attributable to unofficial and clandestine co-operation with their counterparts in Dublin. There is nothing which could conceivably have been gained from the Littlejohn connection that would have compensated for the possible damage to these relations by Irish revulsion at the idea of having armed British criminals acting as agents for British security in the streets of Dublin. One predictable consequence could have been a serious breakdown in inter-service co-operation. The effect of this could have been horrendous for Britain. How would the British people have reacted to the idea of having agents from Eire security indulging in bank robberies in London?

Similar issues arise from the Howard Marks affair. If published accounts are true, here again was an operative who lacked any of the restraint or professional motivation of a disciplined security body, or the operational caution inculcated by professional training. Marks was said to be a known drugs user/dealer/pusher who, under the aegis of British security, was encouraged to become involved in the murky waters of international terrorism, drugs and gunrunning – all this, it would seem, in the knowledge that criminal self-interest would almost certainly influence his actions and be a major consideration in any information provided. Like Littlejohn, Marks was more than a mere informant. He was allowed to become a catalyst in an unpredictable situation of extreme volatility and complexity, where the consequences of criminal activities could not be anticipated or controlled. The choice of agent seems bizarre: rather like letting an alcoholic loose in a distillery.

The Marks affair is significant in another, slightly different context. Although not all, and certainly not Marks, share concern about the harmful effects of cannabis, it remains illegal. Combating drugs abuse occupies the attention of large numbers of police and Customs officers.

Vast sums of money are generated by the criminal drugs industry and circulate in other criminal circles. It is generally accepted that the combination of drugs abuse and the financial consequences have a profoundly destabilizing effect on society. Nowhere is this more evident than in British inner city areas, where in 1981 civil disorder reached crisis proportions. The level of social disorder was of a greater order than anything achieved by IRA terrorism and bombings on the British mainland. Although only one of a number, drugs abuse and the enforcement of drugs laws was a significant factor.

Howard Marks, with or without the blessing of MI6, was reportedly involved in drugs offences valued at many millions of pounds in quantities of tons. He defended himself with the claim that he had been working for British Intelligence. If that was true, can working for the security services be a defence for a criminal charge? If it can, are then those services beyond the law. If they are beyond, and therefore not answerable to the law, to what or whom are they answerable? Certainly not to Parliament. To whom then are the faceless and nameless of the security establishment responsible to for errors of judgment? The question has added point when the Frank Terpil affair is considered.

Frank Terpil was known to the British security services as he was known to every other major intelligence agency in the world. Despite his unsavoury background, he and his partner, Ed Wilson, enjoyed an astonishing amount of freedom in Britain. Terpil used the country as a conduit to channel sophisticated weaponry technology and explosives to some of the most brutal regimes and terrorist organizations of the twentieth century, including apparently the IRA which has been responsible for hundreds of British deaths.

It is clear that Terpil enjoyed close contacts with members of the security services and government officials. Without active co-operation from these quarters he could not have conducted his operations successfully. Terpil claimed that this co-operation was obtained through bribery of corrupt officials. The Baby-Sitter was said to have been his protector. The same Baby-Sitter was said to have threatened the life of Anthony Thomas, television reporter. It may be that Terpil, like Kenneth Littlejohn and Howard Marks, was being used as an agent by the security services.

What conceivable intelligence could this self-confessed monster provide anyone which could outweigh his potential for universal harm? What moral criterion, national interest, intelligence priority or bureaucratic perception of British society could dictate that Terpil's presence and activities, in the United Kingdom would significantly advance the security and wellbeing of the nation? If a bureaucratic machinery exists in this country willing to plant people 'under a bush in Surrey', how could it decide that Anthony Thomas was the better victim than Terpil?

It may be that Anthony Thomas was mistaken and that no such threat was made to him. It may be he was the victim of a sick joke by the Baby-Sitter, or that the threat was uttered without official sanction. The British public are unlikely ever to know the answers to these questions. The questions and possibilities raised by the Littlejohn, Marks and Terpil affairs do make something clear, however.

The British security services are too remote from the influence of the law; they are not scrutinized by elected parliamentary representatives; in the absence of any properly constituted, independent and professional investigative body, their professional perceptions, procedures and practices cannot be challenged; and the inordinate degree of secrecy which often needlessly surrounds their activities cloaks major errors of professional judgment. Under those circumstances, not only are they not sufficiently accountable for any errors of professional judgment, but there is no way open to the public to make them accountable. Since the British people are denied knowledge of how their security services operate and what they do, it seems only reasonable that other countries are denied similar knowledge of British security affairs. The second question posed was not whether British security had been penetrated: it was whether they had been penetrated to the extent that only the British are in the dark about what they are doing?

From 1951, with the defection of Guy Burgess and Donald MacLean and subsequently in 1964 with the defection of Kim Philby, periodic revelations have surfaced which have amused, bewildered or shocked the British public depending on the individual. In many cases the public merely accepted the revelations as confirmation of long-held views about the 'spooks' who inhabit the twilight world of espionage and counter-espionage. Having one's own agents turned, or being penetrated by foreign agents, is an occupational hazard for every security service. Although it poses problems they are not necessarily terminal: you lose a few secrets and you gain a few.

The question for the British public by 1982 was no longer whether their security services had been penetrated: the question was whether the security services were still on the British side. Chapman Pincher, a former journalist specializing in defence and security matters, claimed that in the view of MI5 officers, whom he considered loyal, there was evidence to suggest that the penetration by the Russians of British intelligence and security not only neutralized but effectively ran the services. This view reinforced the evidence produced by authors Andrew Boyle and Nigel West, who had respectively exposed Anthony Blunt (then Sir) and Leo Long, both of whom had served with the security services and had spied for Russia.

Although the disclosures related, in the main, to matters prior to 1965, they nevertheless had direct relevance to the current activities of the British security services. What was revealed in the security services was not merely a few isolated traitors, or a cell of agents, subverted by greed or political conviction: there appeared to be a morally degenerate sub-culture forming a significant part of Britain's ruling bureaucratic Establishment and operating it as if it were a private members' club. Bound together by bonds of homosexuality, privilege, educational, intellectual and moral arrogance, they permeated the upper reaches of the secret services, the Foreign Office, Home Office and Treasury. This network of influence was manipulated to nurture and advance its own interests.

Guy Burgess: a marauding, drunken homosexual degenerate; who from youth had flaunted his sexual excesses and, in the process, attracted the patronage and protection of the high and the mighty of the Establishment. Donald MacLean: sexually ambivalent, intellectually and professionally brilliant and, prior to his defection, destined for the highest reaches of the diplomatic service; yet irresponsibly scandalous, violent, promiscuous and drunken. Tom Driberg, MP, later Lord Bradwell and one-time Chairman of the British Labour Party: an insatiable and compulsive homosexual prone to 'cottaging' in public urinals in search of 'rough trade', armed with a Special Branch number for use in the event of being apprehended by the police, as he once was, indulging in his extra-curricular activities; an agent for MI5, the KGB and/or Czechoslovakian intelligence – not necessarily in that order. Anthony Blunt: Cambridge don, homosexual aesthete, MI5 officer, Russian agent and appointed art expert to the Queen, given official immunity from prosecution despite admissions of treason.

The massive expansion of the security services prior to, and at, the outbreak of war in 1939 accounted for the relaxation of standards in recruitment. Academics and intellectuals of the thirties, beguiled by the ideals of Marxism, appeared blind to the harsh reality of the totalitarian, dictatorial and inhuman cruelty of Stalinist Russian communism. It had been the idealism, rather than the reality, which had been implanted in the minds of susceptible youth of the time. Coupled with this idealism had been the growing awareness of fascist expansionism crystallized in the territorial ambitions of Hitler and Mussolini and the threat they posed to democracy. Disillusioned by the inertia of western democracies and their failure to confront fascism, many sought the outlet of international communism in order to oppose fascism.

A brief flirtation with communism at university by privileged young elitists recruited to the security services merely established a chap's anti-fascist credentials. Fascism was the current threat and fascists the enemy. Under those circumstances, it was small wonder that the security services should prove vulnerable to infiltration when forced to react to events; from a base of few personnel, and an amateurish management structure, it expanded into a mammoth organization with wide-ranging and diverse responsibilities. Having identified the unique circumstances by which the security services had been subverted, the Establishment went on to explain why the public should have no further cause for concern.

Events after the war had opened the eyes of western democracies to the nature of communism and, more particularly, to the global appetites of Russian imperialism. In the aftermath of post-war defections and the exposure of Russian penetration of the west's security, policies were implemented to meet the threat. Internal measures were taken to increase security against Russian infiltration, to raise professional standards in the services by reducing the influence of the privileged 'old boy' network with its overtones of dilettante amateurism, and to widen the social base of personnel recruitment. Internal inquiries were carried out to establish the extent to which the services had been penetrated and to take counter-measures to minimize damage caused by breaches of security.

In 1966 an inter-service group named the Fluency Committee produced a report on a review of operations carried out by the security services. According to Chapman Pincher, the report had cited some 200 compromised operations, a number of which could not have been accounted for by the activities of the double agents already exposed. Some members of the Committee, admittedly a minority and on the flimsiest of circumstantial evidence if Pincher's evidence was all that existed, concluded that Sir Roger Hollis, Director General of MI5 until 1965, had probably been a Russian agent for some thirty years. Considerable suspicion had also been voiced by other officers about his Deputy, Graham Mitchell. Investigations failed to produce tangible evidence against either man.

Whether or not such suspicions had any foundation, what the report of the Fluency Committee, reinforced by a spate of information leaks by former and serving officers of the British security services, clearly indicates is that the services had been heavily penetrated by Russian Intelligence. Furthermore, that the penetration had not been confined to the known spies of the pre-war Cambridge Apostles. So great was the degree of penetration achieved, and at such a senior level, that it is inconceivable that the Russians would fail to introduce 'sleeper' agents into the security services under deep cover. This is the natural logic that fed the work of Chapman Pincher, Andrew Boyle and Nigel West in the late 1970s/80s.

What the controversy also identifies is the dichotomy within the security services about its current operational role. The surprising thing would be if no such dichotomy existed. In effect, what the public are beginning to sense is a power struggle within the service. Idealism is not a human phenomenon which was the sole prerogative of the youthful Marxist Apostles of Cambridge in the 1930s. More specifically, it is not one which is strictly confined either to youth, Marxism or the 1930s. The decadence, privilege and homosexuality of the Apostles tell us more about the nature of the Establishment, its contemptuous disregard for conventional social standards, and the arrogance of its exercise of unaccountable power. That the British security services have been, and are still, infiltrated by Soviet sympathizers is something a prudent public should accept without reservation. It is not for that reason alone, however, that the dirty washing of past years is being exposed to the public.

The successful conclusion of the Second World War did not signal an end to fascist tendencies in Britain's hard right. Neither did the Establishment origins of characters such as Blunt, Philby, Burgess and MacLean reflect the dominant political persuasions of the Establishment power brokers. The indefinable, amorphous entity of the British Establishment is elitist, paternalistic and authoritarian. It is apolitical only in the sense that it is beyond the conventional forum of party politics: the Establishment is about the politics of power. Whatever governments may come and go the Establishment intends to survive forever. It is in that context that the controversy over past scandals within the security services has to be viewed. What the public are seeing is a movement to realign the security services to a posture more in keeping with extreme right-wing perceptions of trends in British society. It would be foolish for the public to ignore evidence of the subversion and penetration of the security services by left-wing traitors; it would be no less foolish not to be aware of the possibility of the security services being used as an instrument of the far right.

Having concluded that the British security services are insufficiently accountable to the public for their errors of professional judgment, and that they have been penetrated to an extent whereby only the British public are kept in the dark about their activities, the next question is whether they are professionally efficient and competent. Evidence that the services are unaccountable and harbour disloyal personnel in their ranks is not in itself evidence that they are ineffective or incompetent. Much has been made of Geoffrey Prime's conviction in 1982, when it was revealed that he had acted as a Russian agent for years in the top security Government Communications Headquarters at Cheltenham. It is true that Prime eluded the security net and would not have been exposed had it not been for information provided by his wife. On the other hand, there is no security system which is impervious to internal treachery. Defectors from the Soviet Union and its satellites show that their security is no less fallible than that of the West. This fact is in itself highly significant for it shows the weakness of the idea that internal security in a democracy can be enhanced by emulating the security tactics of police states. How then can the public assess the professional competence and efficiency of the security services?

Formed in 1883, the *raison d'être* of Special Branch was to combat the activities of Irish Sinn Feiners in conjunction with a similar initiative in Ireland. For the next hundred years the IRA did not go away and neither did Special Branch, and over the years the role of SB expanded and diversified. Having been formed to combat one form of internal security risk, a logical step was to involve the Branch in additional areas of security, notably the other political extremists which posed a threat to Britain – British Nazis, communists, socialists. War between Britain and the Axis nations created new demands.

During the Second World War MI5 had some responsibility for the prosecution of enemy agents. After the war SB undertook this role almost exclusively. As administrators of the Official Secrets Acts, SB operated in a grey, indeterminate area somewhere between counter-intelligence on the one hand and conventional policing on the other. It might be said that their function was to make counter-intelligence more socially acceptable by assembling evidence and presenting it in criminal courts, often on behalf of the Intelligence agencies.

A more controversial aspect of SB work was, and is, surveillance on persons identified as political extremists, suspect fringe organizations and front organizations for foreign interests. Although some prosecutions have resulted from SB and MI5 activities in these areas, they were few and far between. Operating largely from the headquarters of the Metropolitan Police at Scotland Yard, SB prided itself on its anonymity and saw itself as a power behind the scenes operating in an Intelligence gathering role. Its ways were secret, the information it dealt with was classified and its professional competence and efficiency awe-inspiring. It was the proud boast of many officers that they had never arrested anyone throughout their entire service with SB. There were large numbers of Metropolitan Police officers who were not so sanguine about SB's standards. Of the many police critics, some of the most vociferous were themselves senior Special Branch officers.

Recruited into Special Branch at an early stage in their careers, officers had little or no experience in practical police work. Although they attended CID training courses their sphere of operation allowed them no scope for reinforcing their training with practical application. Secrecy surrounding the Branch prevented any objective appraisal of identifiable objectives, far less achievements. Other police officers regarded with deep suspicion a system apparently largely geared to the endless accumulation of information and 'intelligence' which did not appear to lead to positive action and tangible results. Generally speaking, there was a lack of knowledge about the Branch's functions, making it difficult to level constructive criticism against it.

The eruption of IRA violence in mainland Britain provided the perfect opportunity for Special Branch to silence the critics: a chance for the anti-IRA section to channel some eighty years of Intelligence collation to operational use and confound the sceptics. In the event, SB proved to be what operational officers had long suspected: a damp squib. Although the IRA offensive was precisely the contingency the Branch had been created to combat, it proved incapable of mounting any adequate or relevant response to the emergency. Through no fault of their own, officers completely lacked operational experience. It was not surprising that they lacked basic skills in assembling evidence for presentation at court, interrogation and the techniques of prosecution.

More damning was the revelation that the bulk of the Intelligence painstakingly acquired was, in the main, valueless. Most of it related to Sinn Fein front sympathizers who had been vociferously political over the years without being terrorist activists. Much of even that information was out of date, in addition to being irrelevant. In a number of cases, if the records were to be believed, SB officers had been carrying out surveillance on subjects who had been dead for some years. Hard intelligence about IRA covert operations, Active Service Units, logistical support, bases and safe houses proved virtually non-existent. In operational terms, the much vaunted secret files of Special Branch produced in a word: zilch. Such Intelligence as there was, not surprisingly, emanated from sources in Ulster and Eire and owed little to the efforts of SB in Britain however diligent these efforts may have been.

In order to offer effective opposition to the IRA, the Metropolitan Police formed the Bomb Squad (subsequently the Anti-Terrorist Squad), led and staffed by operational detectives from the CID who were able to apply wide-ranging practical experience to the peculiarities of IRA terrorism. A number of SB offices attached to the unit went on to make invaluable contributions to some of the successes achieved.

One inescapable conclusion emerged. The concept of accumulating masses of secret Intelligence unrelated to a specific aim, in this instance that of mounting prosecutions, was at best an academic exercise and at worst expensive and futile. In peacetime a democracy must depend ultimately on its courts for its protection against any criminal or terrorist attack. This in turn requires the detection, apprehension and prosecution of offenders. Intelligence and information gathering which are directly related to that process as part of a cohesive operational strategy have a vital role to play. Internal security which gathers intelligence for its own sake acquires a distorted perception of its functional objectives. More crucially, by continually viewing society and its relationship with society through a 'wilderness of mirrors', that relationship too may become distorted.

The IRA campaign of terror launched on mainland Britain in the 1970s parted the curtain of secrecy which had for so long cloaked the activities of Special Branch. What was revealed did not inspire confidence in the professional competence and efficiency of this branch of the security services. Special Branch failed primarily because of the secrecy in which it worked. Since much of the information accumulated had no direct operational application, the Branch collected garbage. With no real means of distinguishing between information and operational intelligence, garbage was piled on more garbage. Protected from independent scrutiny and assessment, the process of mindless accumulation continued for years. Despite external suspicion and internal rumblings of dissent, no means existed to challenge official perceptions of aims and objectives. At a time of security crisis, the suspicion and dissent proved well founded by the revelation of innate incompetence and inefficiency.

The Littlejohn, Marks and Terpil affairs all suggest that the British security services not only engage in activities and operations which may not always be in the best interests of British society but, having done so, get them wrong. The first is bad enough, the second is inexcusable. These services, nevertheless, remain unaccountable to the public for their operational activities or their errors of professional judgment. All the evidence publicly available points to these services having been extensively penetrated by elements which are either sympathetic to the aims of Russian Marxism or are unsympathetic to the anti-authoritarian principles of British democracy. This makes it unclear precisely who they are working for and what they are working against. The flaws exposed in Special Branch, when events forced secrecy to be removed from some of their activities, suggest the probability that, in addition to being unaccountable and severely compromised, British security may also be incompetent and inefficient. How can any of those issues be satisfactorily resolved unless their operational validity can be subjected to independent public scrutiny and appraisal? Clearly, they cannot be resolved in any other way. Yet Britain does not have any independent body capable of undertaking such scrutiny and appraisal, nor the constitutional format.

The problem of ensuring the accountability, loyalty and efficiency of a democracy's security and Intelligence services without unduly impeding their operational capability is not unique to Britain. The same problem was, and is, being faced in the United States. There, fears that the CIA and FBI, not to mention a series of other Federal security agencies, had acquired powers which placed them beyond the control of government and above the law proved well founded. Excessive autonomy, secrecy, and their involvement in covert operations free from any effective democratic scrutiny, allowed the security agencies to disregard the constitutional rights of American citizens and threatened to undermine the society they were ostensibly protecting. Despite fierce opposition from the Intelligence community, a Freedom of Information Act was passed and other measures taken to demolish the wall of silence surrounding government bureaucracy and to make agencies more publicly accountable.

A fine balance has to be maintained between allowing security services excessive unscrutinized freedom which can be abused, and creating so many restrictions on their operational activities that they may become impotent. The longest serving Federal judge in American history, and one of the most eminent, was Judge Learned Hand who was born in 1872 and died in 1961. In a speech on 24 October 1952 he addressed the following words to the Board of Regents of New York State University:

> I had rather take my chance that some traitors will escape detection than spread abroad a spirit of general suspicion and distrust which accepts rumour and gossip in place of undismayed and unintimidated inquiry.

This declaration was in accord with his belief that the preservation of democracy depended on the strength of will of the people to sustain it.

In the absence of that public will, no government or, least of all, security service can prevent the inevitable erosion of democratic and libertarian values. The object of 'undismayed and unintimidated inquiry' is to establish truth, and truth is not something a strong democracy should fear even though at times it may appear unpalatable. Truth often appears most unpalatable when it fails to conform to conventional wisdom. How would the activities and motivations of the security services stand the test of 'undismayed and unintimidated inquiry', and how well would the private reality match the projected image?

Deprived of the advantages of information which has been tested and supported by an open process of objective investigation, the British public are expected to be satisfied with doctored releases designed to manipulate public opinion and not to inform: unofficial and unattributable leaks of doubtful origin and even more doubtful authenticity; and speculation based on misinformation and innuendo. Security services and the police conform to the long-established trait of the ruling Establishment which resents and actively fights the intrusion of the public in the governing process. Among the security services this has produced an incestuous element of inbreeding: a self-perpetuating clone mentality which jealously guards itself from open minds.

The functional existence of any security service is based on a social recognition that knowledge is strength: British security services deny society the strength of their knowledge by failing to prosecute. A society which cannot identify its enemies as a result of criteria only vaguely comprehended cannot effectively defend itself from them. The greatest indictment of the security services is that they assemble, collate, interpret and process their information, seldom if ever submitting it to public examination. Too often, particularly in the late 1970s and early 1980s, information is released with an ulterior motive.

Foreign embassies and diplomatic missions in London all house Intelligence representatives of their respective nations who engage in a variety of information gathering activities. These activities range from the most sinister forms of espionage to simply co-operating with British services. Agents who enjoy diplomatic cover are immune from prosecution in British courts, however horrendous or criminal their actions. This applies equally to British agents posing as diplomats in other countries. In 1971, as a result of information supplied by a KGB officer who defected to the West, Oleg Lyalin, 105 diplomats and members of Soviet missions in the UK were expelled by Edward Heath's government. This represented only the tip of the iceberg of eastern bloc agents, including Polish, Czechoslovakian and Hungarian, active in the UK. An effective counter-intelligence service is clearly necessary, therefore, and, since those with diplomatic immunity cannot be tried in British courts, surveillance and, as a last resort, expulsion are the only options.

Acts of espionage, subversion or terrorism carried out without diplomatic status of course invite prosecution. It is important, therefore, to draw a clear distinction between foreign diplomats who are spies, and British and non-diplomatic foreign nationals who engage in the same activities.

In carefully orchestrated leaks to the media and 'defence experts', who are carefully cultivated by security services, it was revealed that Oleg Lyalin had confirmed the existence of detailed plans by the USSR to deal with Britain in the event of hostilities. As a preliminary to a surprise attack on the UK, a devastating campaign of internal sabotage was intended to be launched by teams of native British fifth columnists strategically located throughout the country. Using weapons and explosives already cached in convenient sites near nuclear, radar and other sensitive defence centres, acts of sabotage intended to disrupt and neutralize British defences would be carried out. These plans, in fact, are much in accord with similar western contingency plans for implementation in Soviet satellite countries should the occasion arise. In that context, the information made public is a matter of concern but not surprising.

What is more remarkable is information made public by Chapman Pincher, a confirmed friend and confidant of members of British security, and someone deeply concerned about the Soviet influences at work within the security apparatus. According to Pincher, this fifth column, numbering several hundreds, operates under deep cover, and the identities of some of them are known to the security services. That being the case it seems incredible that none of the known potential saboteurs has ever been prosecuted. The reason for this, if Chapman Pincher is to be believed, is that no action can be taken by the British authorities until these people have actually broken the law. Clearly some message is intended for the British public. A plea is being made for stronger laws and more power given to the security forces who find themselves impotent in the situation of having saboteurs poised at Britain's throat. For many, however, the message will be different. It is to scrap the security services and start again from scratch.

While conscious of weaknesses in the law as it stands, there are few experienced police investigators who would not hotly dispute the premise that known potential saboteurs cannot be prosecuted. British citizens who have agreed with a foreign power to engage in armed insurrection in the UK, at some unspecified time in the future, using weapons and explosives, actually or constructively, in their possession, or available to them for that purpose, are most unlikely to be impervious to criminal prosecution and conviction. Whatever the flaws in the British judicial system, lack of flexibility under unusual conditions is not too often one of them. With credible evidence of the facts, moreover, there is no professional investigator who would not be confident of achieving success in identifying and prosecuting others not now known, and finding some arms caches. This would put under pressure those who remained undetected; more importantly, it would alert the British people to the dangers they faced.

If the British security services have the knowledge claimed by Pincher, then they are playing Russian roulette with the lives of the British people. Far from advancing the argument that the law is weak and that the security services need more power, it merely increases suspicions that our security lies in the hands of flashy and unprofessional dilettantes.

Concern in the security forces and elsewhere about Russian Intelligence and the growing influence of left-wing Marxist sympathizers in

Britain is real and justified. What we are seeing is a movement to turn the security services towards the right: to realign them to conform with a divided society of the future. A drift by the services in either direction will have the most profound implications for our future.

During Sir Harold Wilson's terms in office as Prime Minister, he became convinced of a conspiracy by elements of MI5 to secure his downfall. He suspected he was the object of MI5 surveillance technology and expressed the belief that the service harboured a fascist clique. 'Fascist' may have been a more emotive than precise definition of factions within MI5. One thing was clear, however: the political affinities and affiliations of some in the service were inimical to those of Harold Wilson. The security services had more representatives in Parliament than the Labour MP Tom Driberg, and not all of them on the Labour benches. Several Tory MPs were directly linked to the secret service.

Harold Macmillan, who had a generally low opinion of 'spooks', as Prime Minister, instructed the secret services to stop running members of parliament as agents. The Whitehall corridors of influence, power and patronage are complex and tortuous, however, and in the security world relationships are not always publicly exhibited; when they are, they are not always what they appear to be. When is an agent not an agent? Was the junior Tory Minister who allegedly recruited the Littlejohn brothers an agent? When the security services seek out and cultivate MPs the purpose is to have the MPs' influence exercised on their behalf. It would be naive to suppose that politicians do not seek the same in return. Are parliamentary 'agents' who resist the government in parliamentary lobbies going to support political opponents in the security field? Can politics be left out of the security services? If not, what secret struggles are taking place in the subterranean 'wilderness of mirrors' they inhabit?

There is now no conceivable way of proving whether or not Sir Roger Hollis, deceased in 1973, was a Soviet agent. A number of inquiries have exonerated him. Despite these, and the futility of attempting to establish guilt at this late stage, strenuous efforts are still being made publicly to impugn his reputation. One credible interpretation of what is happening is that it is not Hollis who is being attacked. Those who are being attacked are senior security personnel who have remained loyal to Hollis and to his principles of operating secret security services in a democracy.

Hollis was reputedly associated with surprisingly liberal attitudes towards the role of security in a democracy. By some accounts he resisted efforts of more aggressively inclined officers to impose their own form of tyranny intended to protect society from some other form. It is said that he resisted the temptation to allow guilt to be established by assertion and suspicion instead of by tangible evidence. In the context of a British Security Chief, of course, this would be consistent with the policy of a Russian agent attempting to subvert the security services. Equally, it would be consistent with the responsible servant of a democracy. Hardliners are determined to raise the spectre of the former; those of more liberal persuasion cling to the latter.

The available evidence suggests that the British security services are not publicly accountable; that they have been penetrated by agents of a foreign power; and that they may be professionally ineffective and incompetent. When one adds to that the indications of an internecine struggle between left and right for control of the rotting carcase, the implications for the British nation are horrendous.

The microprocessing and computerized records and covert and overt audiovisual surveillance technology deployed by the security services will be vital elements in determining the future nature of British society. Control of these services by either political extreme would create a secret weapon poised over the jugular vein of British democracy. The existing secrecy surrounding the services is such that control could pass to one or other of the extremes without the public being aware until it is too late. The left makes no secret of its ambitions to control the instruments of power. The right is more subtle but no less dangerous. If it believes that the authority of the state is under siege from the left, it will act as if this is the case. Naked ambition for power is a stimulus for action. Fear of the ambitions of another is also a stimulus; the fear is no less real simply because it may be groundless.

# 5
# Soldiers of the Queen

Totalitarianism is not a form of government the British people would deliberately choose, and violent revolution is alien to the national character. On the other hand, totalitarian government rarely evolves as a direct expression of a people's will, and, in a modern state, successful revolutions are rarely achieved solely by means of an organized mass uprising.

The twin threats to British parliamentary democracy stem from the same basic source. This a shared belief by the political extremes that the uncertainties of government by popular consent make the parliamentary system inimical to the realization of the forms of society they wish to create. Democracy, like Christianity, is a highly subjective concept. Protestants and Catholics both profess to be Christians, yet at the extremes they are less tolerant of each other than they are of non-Christians. The word democracy falls from the lips of political extremists with equal conviction, yet their commitment to it is more than matched by their desire to destroy each other and impose a totalitarian government.

The Marxist left is openly dedicated to the overthrow of the British parliamentary system. With some justification, the left view the system as a divisive capitalist instrument designed to diffuse the collective will and to control the aspirations of the masses. There are few parliamentarians who are not conscious of institutional imperfections and the obstacles these can create for radical measures for political, social and economic reform. As an institution Parliament is an instrument of evolutionary, not revolutionary, change. That is both its strength and its weakness. In an egalitarian society evolutionary change is associated with continuity and stability. In a non-egalitarian society, however, the slow pace of evolution merely extends the time-scale for existing inequalities to become rooted. Given the Marxist view of British society as non-egalitarian their opposition to parliamentary democracy is understandable.

Much of the support by the extreme Right for elected parliamentary democracy is firmly rooted in cynical self-interest: Parliament has never seriously threatened the established social order in Britain and as a medium for change Parliament has consistently operated as a moderating influence. That support would evaporate if a democratically elected government appeared determined to pursue extreme radical policies: a massive redistribution of wealth with punitive taxation, wholesale state ownership of industry, banking and commerce. The commitment of the extreme Right to parliamentary democracy, therefore, is conditional. What is not so clear is the precise point at which the commitment would be terminated. This would be determined by the degree to which the Right felt threatened and the time available to mount a defence against the threat posed. If the threat was considered mortal and the danger imminent, the obvious defence would be to suspend parliamentary democracy.

The characteristic traits associated with the electorate's attitudes towards major change have been those of tolerance, moderation and innate conservatism. It is these traits which influenced an orderly transition from the days of autocratic monarchy, through the evolutionary stages, to the existing form of parliamentary democracy. The entire process has consisted of a series of compromises between the ruling Establishment and the forces of reform. The process allowed a degree of power sharing without the accompanying demand for the Establishment to relinquish entirely its social influence and power. In the past the orderly transition towards an egalitarian society has been a source of strength for the Right at the expense of the extreme Left. The political Right has retained the power to influence the nature and pace of social change. The extreme Left has never had that power and is consistently denied the means to acquire it. At the same time, however, the evolutionary political process has also contained the seeds of destruction for the far Right. However imperceptible, the effect of progressive liberalization over the decades has been the gradual erosion of power from the Right.

The logical and inevitable consequence of a process in which power is inexorably moving away from the Right is that the point of no return must eventually be reached. The devolution of power must reach the stage where it is no longer capable of being controlled or effectively influenced by the Establishment. When that point is reached, power which has devolved to the people cannot be democratically recalled. Power is indispensable to any form of authority, and it comes in two forms: the power of reason and the power of force. Democracy relies on the former; totalitarianism on the latter. The extreme Right in British politics has consistently lost ground in the realms of political, economic and social power. Whether they would lose if it came to the power of force has not yet been put to the test.

The predominant social trends in twentieth-century Britain have moved gradually, but remorselessly, away from the authoritarianism of the hard right in British politics. The right wing of the Conservative Party viewed with dismay what they regarded as a retreat from the ideals of capitalism into the insubstantial conservatism of Ted Heath, who appeared to advocate a pinkish social concern. This was the same Ted Heath who had identified an 'Unacceptable Face of Capitalism'. The economic benefits of unfettered capitalist free enterprise looked dubious. As a system it became discredited when the most fervent advocates of free enterprise, the major industrialists, appeared to be the first to demand government money. It seemed the 'freedom' they had enjoyed had been put to singularly unenterprising use.

The greatest threat to authority was posed by the wholesale rejection of traditional social and moral values in the 1960s, causing trauma for every established form of 'natural' authority and 'ordained' order.

It is tempting to trivialize the components of the anti-authoritarian trends which have characterized twentieth-century British society. That would be to underestimate the powerful reactions caused by permissiveness, liberalism and anti-authoritarian militancy in a society rooted in tradition. Even liberal opinion has found disquieting features, such as a sense of anarchy and over-indulgence, in the process. For the extreme Right unless the process can be reversed, every political, economic and social indicator suggests that their power will slide away. The opening years of the 1980s are a crisis point for the reactionaries. It is the point when they must either reconcile themselves to relinquishing power in the existing system of parliamentary democracy or make a concerted effort to change the rules of the game – yet no reactionary force willingly surrenders power and the commitment of many of them to democracy is slight.

The heavy cloud for extreme Right and moderates alike is the resurgence of the far Left. While the threat of a Right-wing dictatorship emerging in British society seems only a possibility, the threat to parliamentary democracy from the militant Left is both implicit and clearly expressed.

The traditional separation between moderate socialists of the British Labour movement and the revolutionary Left has rarely brought major disagreement about ultimate political and social ends. The fundamental disagreements which have proved irreconcilable have concerned the pace of social change and the means of achieving goals. The forces of moderation in the Labour party, which until the late 1970s had been the dominant influence in the party, have always believed that the pace of change and the methods should accord with parliamentary democracy. All Socialists want to see Britain as a one-party Democratic Socialist State. The difference between moderate and militant Socialists is that the moderates see the one-party state as the logical outcome of democratic Socialism, while militants see the one-party state as the means to create Socialism. The first is a democratic goal: the other a totalitarian route which has historically always proved to be an end in itself.

In what many regarded as a belated recognition of the extent to which the revolutionary Left had infiltrated and subverted the democratic process in the Labour Party, the Labour leader Michael Foot set out the fundamental distinctions. In the second of two major articles, published in *The Observer* on 17 January 1982, he vigorously attacked the militants and revolutionaries.

In denying the militant belief in undemocratic means to achieve Socialism, Michael Foot quoted R.H. Tawney who in 1953 wrote: 'The fact remains that the prizes, however glittering, won by way of totalitarianism, are rarely those which they sought. The means destroy the end ... The truth is that a conception of Socialism which views it as power, on which all else depends, is not, to speak with moderation, according to light. The question is not merely whether the State owns and controls the means of production. It is also who owns and controls the State. It is not certain, though it is probable, that Socialism can in England be achieved by methods proper to democracy. It is certain it cannot be achieved by any other.'

Foot also quoted a passage from the work of Ignazio Silone, Italian Socialist writer of the 1930s: 'Every means tends to become an end. To understand the tragedy of human history it is necessary to grasp that fact ...' and ... 'An inhuman means remains inhuman even if it is employed for the purpose of assuring human felicity. A lie is always a lie, murder is always murder. A lie always ends by enslaving those who use it, just as violence always enslaves those who use it as well as their victims.'

Foot likened the present-day extreme militants to the anti-democratic Russian nihilists of the nineteenth century who attacked Alexander Hertzen who, although a radical contemporary of Karl Marx, held fast to the principles of democracy. Hertzen had rejected the 'syphilis of revolutionary lusts' and lamented the ease with which his opponents despaired of everything, 'the ferocious joy of their denial and their terrible ruthlessness. Despite their excellent spirits and noble intentions our bilious ones can, by their tone, drive an angel to blows and a saint to curses.' According to Michael Foot, Hertzen 'saw the fallacy in the

Marxist method even while he recognized the glory of the Socialist ideal', believing that, 'remote ends were a dream, that faith in them was a fatal illusion; that to sacrifice the present, or the immediate and foreseeable future, to these distant ends must always lead to cruel and futile forms of human sacrifice'. According to Michael Foot, this was, 'a considerable prophecy for a democratic Socialist to make nearly 100 years before the Stalin show trials, the Stalin famines or the Polish Gethsemane of Christmas 1981'.

In the article Michael Foot defined the core of his own democratic Socialist beliefs when he attacked 'those who dismiss Parliament as at best a mere platform'. He said, 'Human beings and human communities cannot, by those who call themselves democratic Socialists, be viewed and used as guinea-pigs or ant-heaps or, to use a more accurately horrifying metaphor, vivisected dogs. They must be moulded, consulted, and made the true masters of their fate. For one thing this means the pace of industrial change must be suited to men and women and not vice versa. The whole process of industrial change must itself be made subject to persuasion, to industrial democracy, to the democratic will of the communities involved.'

He went on . . . 'To many (and to me), the Hertzen doctrine may still appear too adamantly stated; some faith in those remote ends is required if the future is to be defined at all. But the Hertzen doctrine certainly is required to rectify the balance between ends and means, to give a chance to breathe to those who must live from week to week, from day to day, to let them estimate for themselves what may be the nature and the scale of the sacrifice. Each generation, which can only live once, has the right to make its own choices. Socialists must insist on that principle no less resolutely than they seek to enlist enthusiasm for the creation of a new society.'

The attack by Michael Foot, himself once regarded as being on the extreme Left of the Labour Party, was launched in recognition of the contagious nature of a new strain of 'syphilis of revolutionary lusts' being spread by the 'bilious ones' among the militants. The sweep and passion of his attack portrayed the urgency he attached to their exposure and the extent of the threat they posed to parliamentary democracy. Bearing the imprimatur of Michael Foot, for many years a doyen of the far Left of British politics, the warning was both timely and one which cannot be ignored. It tacitly acknowledged the realignment which had taken place on the Left of the political spectrum. It had been a realignment of international, not merely national, scale. In Britain, as elsewhere, philosophical divisions between factions on the far Left had been temporarily bridged by a joint commitment to the politics and strategies of revolution.

The most notable paradox of Left-wing militancy in the United Kingdom in the latter half of the twentieth century has been the marked decline of the official British Communist Party at a time of ascending fortunes for Marxist politics. Although consistently denied political credibility by the traditional conservatism of the British electorate, it is significant that the major party of revolution in the United Kingdom derived no benefits from the growing revolutionary militancy of the Left. This reflected, too, the disillusionment of militants with the Communists' strict adherence to the Kremlin's policies. The world history of the extreme Left is littered with internecine battles between Marxist factions. As organs of Russian foreign policy, the official communist parties have often proved the most disruptive element in the entire international revolutionary movement.

Leon Trotsky had much earlier expressed the belief that excessive Russian national self-interest would eventually prove to be incompatible with the Marxist aims of international communism and those of individual, national revolutionary movements. This has often proved to be the case. National alliances between militant and revolutionary groups were frequently shattered because of changes and reversals of Soviet policy which were directly related to Russian interests and not those of revolution. Time and time again, local and national initiatives had to be aborted because of the refusal by the official Communist Party to deviate from the Moscow line, regardless of major inconsistencies. Adopting the Trotskyist line, Marxist theoreticians rejected Russia's automatic supremacy in the interpretation and application of Marxist ideology. More importantly, they rejected the authority of the Kremlin, preoccupied as it was with Russian national and imperialist self-interest, to determine local or national objectives.

The Soviet suppression of the Hungarian Uprising in 1956 emphasized the imperialism of Russian policies. At the same time, the fact that the uprising had taken place reinforced the importance of a national dimension in the revolutionary process. While revitalizing the revolutionary threat to western democracies, the realignment of the Marxist Left has considerably undermined Russian influence. This has profound implications for both the West and the USSR. Freed from the constraints of Communist Party discipline and Russian foreign policy objectives, the realigned militant movement is free to develop its own strategies and tactics and, where necessary, vary them according to national circumstances. This poses, if anything, a greater threat to democracy. It also poses a threat to Russia, however, since Russian strategic objectives may not always coincide with those determined by national movements preoccupied with local issues.

One important factor in the revolutionary realignment was the evidence that the Russian experience is not the only model for successful revolution. The success of internally managed revolutions, in China by Mao Tse Tung and in Cuba by Fidel Castro and Ché Guevara, highlighted the weakness of constantly bowing to Russia as the unique authority on revolution. Strained relations between China and Russia over the years, in turn, highlight the dangers to Russia in revolutionary movements which do not defer to the authority of the Russian experience. The first step in the realignment process, therefore, was for the revolutionary movement to liberate itself from the domination of Russian imperialist aspirations before turning to the nations controlled by their regime.

Once liberated from the doctrinal discipline of a Communist Party committed to the Moscow line, Communists were free to form their own alliances of convenience and establish broadly based coalitions within the national political framework. This did not mean that all Russian influence disappeared or that dialectic differences were resolved. It simply meant that the alliances were no longer compromised to the same extent by contradictions. Differences were subordinated to the one common goal of revolution: the destruction of parliamentary democracy. What evolved was a synthesis of two concurrent themes no longer regarded as incompatible: specifically nationalist strategies within the international Marxist framework.

The far Left gradually shed the stigma of Russian oppression and the post-revolutionary excesses which had traditionally tarnished the Communist image in the eyes of the British masses. Marxist theoreticians produced new revolutionary strategies which broke away from the vertical, hierarchical rigidity of Communist orthodoxy. Instead of the revolutionary Left forming the vanguard and the cause for the masses to follow, the roles were reversed. The new strategy was to follow the voice of public protest. The bourgeois nature of particular protests, and the lack of Marxist purity in their immediate aims were ignored. However misconceived the popular movement in Marxist terms, it is now the function of militants to provide the logistical, administrative and organizational structures to further the voice of protest. Regardless of the immediate cause, the protest will eventually be politicized and moulded along revolutionary lines. Examples of the diversity of the process in operation can be seen in militant connections with Anti-Nuclear, Anti-Nazi, Gay Liberation, Womens Rights and Civil Rights movements. In accord with contemporary revolutionary principles, revolution cannot take place in a modern state until the social conditions necessary for revolution are established. It is the primary function of the revolutionary, therefore, to foster the required conditions with the aid of whatever movements of protest exist in society.

The British masses have shown that they cannot be roused to organized militancy by Marxist rhetoric or by recondite political or social issues with which they cannot identify. Any degree of active public protest generated over artificially contrived issues is short-lived, soon evaporating with time or in response to minor concessions by government. The public are now encouraged to identify and develop their own political, economic and social grievances unencumbered by Marxist rhetoric, so that active public opposition to government and the institutions of state power is likely to be more deep-rooted and unlikely to evaporate so readily in the face of cosmetic reform measures. With real grievances identified by the public and opposition based on genuine convictions, there is no need for Marxists to lead the public. In the absence of major measures of reform, often unacceptable to government, protest over issues of public concern develops its own militancy. Marxists need only fan the existing flames, provide the wherewithal, and follow the public lead.

The adoption of this policy has provided the militants with the finest form of protection they can create in a modern society. Attacks by government or by the security services on movements of legitimate protest, far from hurting them, merely strengthen the position of the militant activists. For this reason Marxists deliberately create provocation and invite retaliation by the security forces. Retaliation merely alienates the genuine protesters from the state, widens the area of conflict, and makes increasing numbers receptive to Marxist agitation and propaganda. The more violent or punitive the measures adopted by the reactionary forces, the more favourable the social conditions for revolution. That does not mean that militant activists have evolved policies which are invulnerable in democracy. They remain as vulnerable as ever to the corrosive effects of progressive democratic reforms on their public support. It is for this reason that they fear the centre ground of politics more than their ideological enemies on the far Right.

Although a coup d'état by the Right of British politics is feasible for reasons which are discussed later, it is not a realistic option for the extreme Left given the strength and stability of the institutions of state power in Britain. Denied the option of seizing power, Marxist revolution must be seen in the context of a protracted war, not a single decisive battle. A series of campaigns have to be fought simultaneously on a variety of fronts, largely independently of each other. This means progress is not always chronologically consistent and it is difficult to determine the course of the mainly underground war at any given time. In essence, however, there are three phases in the successful revolutionary war.

Phase one is the process of making democracy unworkable even if this means the emergence of a totalitarian right-wing regime. An essential element of phase one is to ensure that the ideological hard core of the revolutionary movement cannot be isolated or neutralized at any time during the next two phases either by reactionary or counter-revolutionary forces. Phase two is the revolution itself: establishing a revolutionary regime out of the democratically ungovernable chaos created in phase one. Again, this is a battle not a war. Phase three is the consolidation of the revolution: the final destruction of all effective reactionary resistance. It does not end there, however: it is in phase three that the icy cynicism of revolutionary politics is revealed as the 'syphilis of revolutionary lusts' described by Hertzen. Phase three sees the ritual of revolutionary cannabalism, when temporary allies, necessary for the earlier phases, have to be eliminated in the interests of Marxist 'revolutionary purity'. Phase three is the proof of Ignazio Silone's words: 'A lie always ends by enslaving those who use it, just as violence always enslaves those who use it as well as their victims.'

Although the official British Communist Party has declined as a visible force in national politics since the realignment of the left began in the 1960s, it remains intact as a powerful weapon in the revolutionary armoury. Security service estimates placing overt membership of the Communist Party at 30,000 and covert membership at around 50,000 may be unreliable, but they are nevertheless important. The Party is nationally organized, disciplined, and has a defined administrative and logistic support structure. These factors are far more important in the revolutionary context than numbers: the idea is to create a revolution not to achieve it by popular vote.

The number of groups, alliances and affiliations of the extreme Left – Trotskyist, Social Workers Party, Workers Revolutionary Party, Workers Socialist League, International Marxist Group, Committee for a Workers International, the Militant Tendency – indicate that polemical factionalism and titular divisions have been bridged during phases one and two of the revolutionary process. Phase three comes later. The only way for the public to monitor the threat posed by the revolutionary process is to compare trends in society with the strategic and tactical objectives of each phase.

Phase one requires society to be destabilized by a combination of tactics. The democratic process has to be turned in such a way that it will tear itself apart. Efforts have to be made in every field to shift the voice of protest and dissent from the paths of democratic expression: protest is manipulated into civil disobedience, and, where possible, civil disorder. By linking itself to legitimate movements of social discontent, whether in local communities or national organizations, Marxist ideology assumes a direct relevance to real issues of concern for ordinary people without any need to express it in terms of political ideology. By becoming immersed in day to day issues which concern the public – work, health, education, welfare, local planning, public corruption, police misconduct and the like – Marxists become identified as fighters for the legitimate aspirations of society's underprivileged.

In revolutionary terminology this is a period of construction. There is no need for the reluctant public to be persuaded to elect for Marxism: it is enough that they support Marxists. It is this active public support which Marxists were formerly denied by the Communist insistence on politicizing protest movements along dogmatic ideological lines. This does not mean that ideological principles are being sacrificed: merely that they are submerged. They are still tightly held by the hard revolutionary core of Marxist activists.

Throughout Britain the Marxists run training courses for militant activists. The Communist Party, through its established connections overseas, provides selected cadres with opportunities to attend international courses. The Workers Revolutionary Party maintains a country mansion in Derbyshire through which it is estimated more than 2000 potential strike leaders have graduated since 1975. The International Marxist Group and the Socialist Workers Party both run intensive cadre courses. These are designed to provide a national framework of strategically located groups capable of reacting quickly to localized controversy. With the aid of professional expertise supplied in the form of advice, media exposure, printing facilities, organizational and administrative backup, relatively insignificant local issues can be fanned into civil disobedience and disorder of national dimensions. Recruitment takes place in universities, colleges of further education and schools where Marxism is indoctrinated in sociology students as objective truth; and in extra-curricular meetings where more open indoctrination is practised.

In the tradition of Anthony Blunt, efforts are made to identify and recruit suitable candidates for the revolutionary cause. Some of these are groomed for active protest operations at the grass roots of society. Others, as in the cases of Philby, Burgess and MacLean, though no longer necessarily for Russian masters, are assigned to penetrate the establishment power structures and conceal their Marxist affiliations. Industrial labour relations remain a fertile field for economic and social unrest fomented by Marxist agitators. The trades unions have traditionally provided the extreme Left with a platform from which to exert influence on trades disputes disproportionate to their active membership. The same power base has also enabled them to extend this disruptive influence into the Labour Party through its affiliation with unions.

The Socialist Workers Party adopted a resolution, at a conference in November 1981, to make intervention in industrial disputes the prime target of its future activities. With fifty or more fulltime, paid organizers, trained in the techniques of fomenting industrial unrest, providing professional backup facilities for militant shop stewards or other strike leaders – some Marxist trained – the potential for industrial subversion is unlimited. Roger Rosewell, a former Trotskyite and National Industrial Organizer for the Socialist Workers Party, defected from the SWP in 1974, since when he has been active in exposing the threat from the extreme Left. In a pamphlet entitled *Dealing with the Marxist Threat to Industry*, published by the right-wing Aims of Industry in 1982, Rosewell set out the training programmes, recruitment, organization and structure of the Marxist thrust in the industrial field. He also provided a vivid example of the 'success' which industrial subversion can achieve, and identified his source:

It is drawn from a recent issue of Socialist Press, the paper of the Workers Socialist League. In an article about British Leyland's Cowley plant in Oxford, Alan Thornett, the well-known Trotskyist shop steward otherwise known as 'The Mole', recalled that there had been more than 1000 stoppages in that factory between 1964 and 1967. This averages more than one a day. It is a staggering figure and occurred when Thornett and other Trotskyists dominated the shop stewards committee. It is simply inconceivable that all of these strikes were either spontaneous or necessary. They were the product of concerted agitation which urged workers to strike before procedures were exhausted. They are a grim reminder of why British Leyland declined.

The importance of the industrial relations field, however, has been overtaken in the second half of the twentieth century by the enormous expansion of the role of social services. This has provided a unique opportunity for revolutionaries to widen their infiltration horizons and broaden the front of social confrontation and protest. The complementary growth of the social sciences educationally and the social services in the areas of health and welfare at local government level enabled the Marxists to permeate the fabric of society on an unprecedented scale.

The Welfare State has given the militants the same sort of leverage in the social field that industrial disputes provided them with in industrial relations. They have been able to create and exploit social conflict and confrontation by manipulating issues of genuine social concern. Through industrial disputes they exploit the economic reality that while industry may pay some workers all they deserve and others all that is available, no industry can pay all workers everything they would like to have. In the same way, no government can implement all its progressive social policies at once. What is economically possible will never amount to all that is socially desirable. Exercising their influence in both the industrial and social fields, Marxists assume the classic revolutionary posture. They have the power to make constantly escalating demands, which cannot be met, without having to accept responsibility for meeting the expectations thus created. There is an important bonus for the Marxists in this infiltration into the social services: not only can they undermine the democratic fabric, but they are also being paid by a democratic government to do so.

In every aspect of phase one of the revolutionary process the objectives are to stimulate confrontation, social divisions and unrest in the community and a general revulsion with the democratic process. This policy, however, has to go hand in hand with measures designed to defend the revolutionary core: measures to ensure that the co-ordinating centre cannot be isolated or vulnerable to a pre-emptive strike by reactionary forces of state power. In the opportunist areas of industrial disputes and shifting social causes, the necessary protection comes from the cover provided by the legitimate public concern with the disputes or causes. The very nature of these forms of activity, however, means that they are essentially unstructured. They can inconvenience and weaken a strong democratic government, but they will not prove fatal. Public support can provide useful fodder for the revolution but not the stable framework or secure political and institutional bases necessary for ultimate success. Under the tutelage of revolutionary theoreticians, like Regis Debray, who have studied carefully revolutionary successes, and failures, in South America and elsewhere, it is now acknowledged that the popularity of a movement is not in itself enough.

In creating the conditions for revolution, the Left must establish a credible political framework at national level at the seat of government power. This must be supported by local bases where, through the activities of Marxists in support of popular movements of protest, local aspirations are made to appear to be inextricably linked to Left-wing activists. In this way genuine public support will rally to the extremists in response to any attack by the institutions of democratic government. The practical effect of this public support, although not the intention, will be to further the revolutionary aims of Marxism. The practical truth of the revolutionary strategies evolved by Debray and the others have become increasingly clear in Britain since the end of the 1970s.

Post-war Britain saw the Parliamentary Labour Party firmly established as one of the two parties of government in the United Kingdom. The Marxist Left, while rejecting the supremacy of a democratic parliament, recognized the reality of the Labour Party's power. The revolutionary Left also recognized that the legitimacy the Parliamentary Labour Party had acquired in the eyes of the British electorate was, at the same time, both a strength and a weakness. The more the PLP acted as a responsible party of democratic government, the more it found itself in conflict with its grass-roots supporters.

The British Labour Party comprises not one party but three. As a child of the trade union movement it owes a filial duty to organized labour interests. Although trades unions sponsor Labour members of parliament, they are elected by constituencies. While constituency parties have an historic affinity with Labour, their wider socialist aims do not always coincide. The elected representatives of the Parliamentary Labour Party, if it is to form a democratically elected government, have responsibilities which transcend both organized labour and constituency Labour parties. In accepting parliamentary election members of the PLP undertake a responsibility to the entire electorate, including the elements which do not subscribe to socialist aims. Faced with economic and social realities, successive Labour governments have found themselves unable to fulfil the aspirations of either organized labour or the Party constituency machinery to the extent, or with the speed, they would have liked. Recognizing the structural weaknesses of the Labour Party, the militants set about exploiting them.

The Marxist campaign to infiltrate the unions, traditionally a source of militant strength, was stepped up and, through the unions and sponsored candidates in the PLP, militant influence was nationally expanded. This was not always resisted, a fact which may not be unrelated to security service estimates of some sixty Labour MPs and about twenty Labour peers being secret members of the Communist Party.

The most dramatic impact was made when the militants organized a concerted campaign to gain control of vulnerable constituency parties. In some areas this amounted to little more than a handful of dedicated party workers, but, in a number of key constituencies, the weak local organization proved incapable of resisting the extremists' sustained and professionally organized subversion tactics. The process started in the 1960s and 1970s gathered momentum with the defeat of the Labour government in 1979. Much of the success of the campaign stemmed from the front organization for Marxism, the Militant Tendency. This carefully orchestrated organization projected policies of political ambiguity designed to attract those of the Left who, while inclined to militancy, would stop short of revolutionary Marxism. By blurring the fundamental divisions between the democratic evolution of Socialism and the anti-democratic revolutionary route to the one-party state, the Militant Tendency avoided the philosophical schisms which had traditionally caused the revolutionary impetus in society to falter. By the time moderate forces in the Labour Party became aware of the threat from the extreme Left, it was estimated that the Militant Tendency had in excess of fifty fulltime organizers operating within the Party ranks. The militants had achieved the remarkable revolutionary feat of creating a party within one of the two parties of government – a party which was independently funded and professionally staffed, with its own printing facilities and *Militant* newspaper.

Militant penetration of the Labour Party achieved the two revolutionary political objectives. One was the achievement of a national forum at the centre of British politics, the other was the creation of geographical power bases in the peripheral regions of the nation's political and social life. The extremists newly acquired influence was sensationally demonstrated in London in 1981. In the Greater London Council elections of that year the Labour group was successfuly led into the election by Labour moderates. As a preview of what will happen in phase three of a successful revolution in Britain, the moderate leadership of the Labour group was unceremoniously ousted immediately after the election by a Left-wing putsch and replaced by a group fronted by Kenneth Livingstone.

Control of local government authorities at a political level, even on a temporary basis, has enabled the extremists to introduce populist measures and policies which, however financially misconceived, expand their public support among the underprivileged. Unprecedented finance is now at their disposal for projects and propaganda which are designed to consolidate the already powerful influence of militants in the social services. They have the legitimate power to appoint sympathizers to positions of influence in the executive branches of local government. Not least they have a platform from which to obstruct and resist the social and economic policies of central government. Politically the revolutionary Left has the means nationally and locally to give tangible support to every disaffected section of British society, to encourage dissent, protest civil disobedience and civil disorder. They will soon be so deeply entrenched in the social and political fabric of society – if not so already – that they will be virtually impervious to any reactionary attempt to dislodge them, short of totalitarian measures or a major realignment of the moderate forces at the centre of British politics. The first would be welcomed by the Left: the second would be more dangerous since it would erode the popular support so recently and hard won.

Phase one of the revolutionary process in Britain has been achieved. The forces of revolution have been strategically deployed throughout society. Industrially, socially and politically they are poised to take advantage of public discontent, to create social divisions and to promote confrontation and conflict. They have created the basis of a recognizable framework on which to build the machinery of alternative government in the event of the collapse of democratic consensus within British society.

Phase one and phase two of the revolutionary process are in some senses akin to cold war and conventional war. Phase two is when the cold war of phase one is transformed into violent insurrection. Unlike conventional war, however, phase two is not signalled by any formal declaration. For this and a number of other reasons it is not always possible to discern the start of the revolution phase. There is a very fine line between civil disobedience and disorder on the one hand, and revolutionary insurrection on the other. It is a line which is not even always visible to the revolutionary protagonists themselves.

The transition between 'creating the conditions necessary to sustain the revolution' and the revolution itself is further complicated by the lack of agreement among revolutionary theoreticians about the relative importance of phase one. Some subscribe to the view of the revolutionary hero, Ché Guevara, that: 'It is not necessary to wait until conditions for making revolution exist; the insurrection can create them.' The more cautious heed the words of Mao Tse Tung, 'Engage in no battle you are not sure of winning'; and Lenin's 'Never play with insurrection'. In this context the words of Lenin are less persuasive, for if the Russian Revolution had awaited his arrival it might never have taken place.

Only the objectivity of an historical perspective can accurately define the events which signal the transition from phase one to the commencement of the revolution proper. If this is so, it is conceivable that the revolution, as in Russia in 1917, can be under way without the knowledge of the society in which it is taking place. It is conceivable that history books in the future will point to the fires burning in Bristol, Toxteth and Brixton in 1981 as the signal flames of revolution in British society. If they were not the flames of revolution, they were the clearest indication that the potential for violent insurrection is present. All the elements necessary for phase two of the revolutionary process exist.

In at least one part of Great Britain the revolution is in full operation. What is taking place in Ulster is revolution and one which threatens the stability of Eire as much as the UK. The reality is that the British Province of Ulster is at present ungovernable, and the revolution is being contained by the power of the military forces deployed in the Province. It is also being contained in Ireland by the Irish Sea. What the revolutionary forces in Ulster have, and the revolutionaries in mainland Britain do not have, is sanctuaries. The success of the Irish terrorist forces is directly related to the Republican ghettos in the Catholic city centres from which they can launch their offensives and to which they can return. Similarly, Brixton, and similar inner-city ethnic centres, pose a revolutionary challenge to the cohesive integrity of the British nation. They represent a mortal threat to the security of a tolerant democratic society. They raise the spectre of established bases within the national boundaries from which organized forces of intolerance can attack the weak and defenceless in society with impunity, returning to the sanctuary of ethnic fortresses where they can remain impervious to the power of reason and conciliation.

Social tolerance must always be seen as a reflection of a democracy's strength, not its weakness. West Indian Brixton illustrates the point. When compassion and social tolerance are so abused that they are discredited they cease to be virtues: instead they become vices of moral weakness. Mugging is not an exclusively Brixton phenomenon any more than it is West Indian in origin, but it has come to represent a public perception of a nation in turmoil, one in imminent danger of breaking down in the face of crime and general disorder. In the same way, Brixton (with other West Indian centres) has come to symbolize the impotence of democracy in the face of social intolerance. This is hardly remarkable since no other group in the United Kingdom has more emphatically and comprehensively embraced the phenomenon of mugging than the young blacks of Brixton.

Legally, mugging may be robbery, assault and/or theft. Morally and ethically, it is a violent expression of contempt for the right of the individual, and the weak, to exist in society free from tyranny by the strong. It rejects every form of public decency striven for over centuries of social evolution by the forces of tolerance and moderation in British democracy. Mugging, unchecked, signals to every intolerant element in society that democracy in Britain is weak and that any aspiration, however extreme and however violently sought, is capable of realization. It is an assault on human dignity which demeans the whole of society. When the mugger bludgeons our old, weak and infirm with impunity, it is a proclamation to every barbarian that our commitment to civilized life is but a veneer. Failure to respond effectively to violence and degradation inflicted on the old who gave us birth, and the weak and infirm entrusted to us, indicates there is no indignity we will not tolerate; no tyranny we could not view with equanimity; and no debasement we could not accept.

The fundamental problem is an issue of individual liberty and natural justice, and society has to affirm that these freedoms are not negotiable. The problem transcends race, colour or creed; it transcends questions of racial equality, social deprivation or political freedom. There is more to mugging than moral outrage or the social diagnosis of its causes: Brixton and similar inner-city centres have produced the precise territorial and social conditions defined in revolutionary literature as ideally suited to revolution on the one hand and totalitarian dictatorship on the other. In the terminology of revolutionary strategy Brixton is an embryo 'foco': a geographical sanctuary which, properly nurtured, can provide the potential urban guerrilla with the secure base and territorial support needed before effective insurrection can be mounted against the state institutions.

In 1981 an alienated black youth showed itself capable of expressing its desolation and anger in the form of mindless violence of the most ruthless kind. The violence erupted from ghetto fortresses, and when it was over the youths who had perpetrated the violence merged back into the ghettos to be enveloped in the ethnic solidarity which sustained and protected them from retribution – the same ethnic solidarity which for some ten years before had sustained and protected those in the ghettos who had made a lifestyle of illegal drugs, vice and mugging. Wedded to a revolutionary cause, made attractive under whatever guise by the extreme Left, ghetto violence can be manipulated for political ends. The revolutionary potential of these urban 'foco' in Britain poses a challenge society ignores at its peril. Phase two, the revolution, is the phase of armed struggle. Unrest and dissatisfaction with ghetto conditions have already produced mindless violence which is a small step from urban terrorism: terrorism which in turn would be a small step from revolutionary insurrection.

The threat also has to be seen in the context of a British society struggling to come to terms with the wider social issues of general economic decline, long-term mass unemployment, and the incursions of technology on the working and private lives of its people – all the conditions which have historically made people increasingly receptive to the poisonous racialism of the far Right, the conditions in which totalitarian solutions become attractive to a susceptible public disillusioned by democratic inertia. Unless the forces of social moderation face the problem of inner-city ethnic disaffection, the results will be certain: solutions will be provided by one extreme or the other, neither of which will have any qualms about using repugnant means to achieve equally barbarous ends.

Throughout the campaigns in phases one and two of the revolutionary process, there is at least one constant factor in the stratagems and tactics: the belief that the institutions and instruments of power will instinctively opt for social repression when faced with significant gains by the revolutionary Left. This reaction is not only anticipated, it is invited. There is nothing which will advance the interests of the Left faster and more certainly than the introduction of oppressive measures by the Right. That is why, if Chief Constable James Anderton did not exist the Left would have to invent him, or someone like him.

In advocating greater police powers, a return to 'measures previously rejected as too repressive', more police, less accountability and more autonomy for chief constables, harsher prison sentences, and more secrecy about Special Branch activities, police operations and internal investigation of police misconduct, Anderton is providing the Right's predicted response to the Left's social strategy. The theoreticians of the Marxist Left openly acknowledge that it would be impossible for revolutionary forces to emerge victorious from open confrontation with the united might of state power. Impossible, that is, unless in the process of confrontation the institutions and instruments of the state adopted repressive measures which more immediately threatened democracy than any threat from the Left. The first signs of such a posture are already visible. The threat to individual liberty and democratic freedom from the Right comes in two forms: the first is the danger of a sudden plunge into outright totalitarianism, the second comes from the uncontrolled deployment of computerized and security technology throughout society and the associated erosion of human values. (This latter threat is considered at some length in the remaining chapters of this book.)

The task of Right-wing extremists wishing to install a totalitarian form of government merely involves securing the co-operation of the services by convincing them that action is necessary to forestall the progress of the extreme Left. This may not prove as difficult as many might believe. The standard configuration of the security, military and police services to counter criminal and civil disorder, subversion and insurgency has been evolved to confront the challenge of the political Left. There are no military services in the world who have more experience than the British in the waging of revolutionary war in a counter-insurgency role. Garrisoning an empire in its twilight years,in the face of nationalist and communist movements seeking independence and power provided the British services overseas with unique experience in supporting civil authorities. This corporate experience has been honed in unconventional internal security campaigns in Malaya, Kenya, Aden, Cyprus and latterly – and perhaps more significantly – Ulster. No section of the British nation is more aware than the services of the effectiveness of the revolutionary process: the progression from legitimate protest, through the stages of civil disobedience, disorder, government instability, to the ultimate decline of society into open insurrection. Many of the general public are already dismayed by signs of growing criminality, moral permissiveness, Left-wing agitation and subversion of government institutions, industry and society generally. There are many who believe society is in imminent danger of collapse into criminal disorder, civil anarchy and/or Marxist totalitarianism. Under those circumstances it would be surprising if the armed and security services, who have had to confront similar phenomena so often throughout the world, did not share this perception.

The United Kingdom Land Forces (UKLF) provide the command structure for all army formations in the United Kingdom. They are deployed into ten (or eleven) command Districts: London District, South-East, South-West, Eastern, Western, Wales, North-East, North-West; Scotland, which is subdivided into the Highlands and the Lowlands; and Northern Ireland. In the event of war, the military structure is designed to mesh into the Civil Defence infrastructure, which is similarly regionalized in anticipation of war being a nuclear one. Each region is designed to operate largely autonomously under the direction of politically appointed regional commissioners. In the event of a nuclear holocaust, although many senior government ministers would survive, there could be no guarantee that national government could continue in the immediate aftermath of attack. For this reason, although having successfully led the vast majority of the British population to total destruction, the government in power might not have the means available to ensure the extermination of the remainder. Regional commissioners, therefore, would have the absolute authority, and power of life and death, over any of the population surviving in their respective regions. Theoretically, district military commanders would be there to support any action taken by the commissioners on behalf of or against civilian survivors. In the contingency plans for civil defence, regional commissioners will also be assisted by police liaison officers. Their role will be to co-ordinate the activities of police mobile 'Flying Columns' under the directions of the regional commissioner.

Although the police plans are fully integrated into the overall strategy for civil defence, there is one loose end. There are at present over forty police forces in the United Kingdom each with its own chief constable. Police force boundaries do not coincide, therefore, with those of the civil defence and military. This is irrelevant in the context of a nuclear war since no one can foretell what will be left, and clearly police structures need not conform to civil and military defence positions. If the proposals of Chief Constable James Anderton and the other supporters of a national police force are ever implemented, however, the police command structure would conform precisely to civil defence and military formations. If such a move has little or no relevance to the needs of a war, what purpose would it serve? The creation of 'about ten Regional Police Forces' advocated by Anderton would, he claims, produce a 'cabal of police' Commissioners who would be more likely to 'speak with one voice'. And, 'The opportunities in emergency for the immediate and urgent unification of police effort in the national interest would be readily apparent.' Whatever emergency James Anderton was alluding to, one thing is abundantly apparent: with the thinnest veneer of public respectability and political legitimacy, a Right-wing totalitarian regime could be created overnight in the United Kingdom.

The underlying strategic premise in the civil defence contingency plans, to be implemented in a time of nuclear war, is that democratic government will have ceased to exist and that, until conditions improve sufficiently to permit its return, it will be necessary to institute an arbitrary, authoritarian and totalitarian regime. It is openly accepted that this regime will be required to act ruthlessly and without compassion against a disorientated population desperate for food and the basic necessities of survival. Anyone attempting to oppose the triumvirate of regional commissioner and military and police commanders will be summarily executed. The machinery for this form of government already exists. To set it into motion does not require a nuclear war or even the threat. All it would take would be for a right-wing government to announce that, in order to prevent the country disintegrating in the face of anarchy and disorder, a state of national emergency was being declared and regional commissioners had been appointed to assume the executive powers of government. The assistance of the monarchy would be sought to give the action some semblance of legitimacy and, in the interests of preserving the stability of the kingdom, it is unlikely that it would be withheld.

It was revealed in the 1970s that Cecil King, a former Chairman of the Mirror group of newspapers, and one-time important influence in Fleet Street, had convened a secret meeting with a number of distinguished public figures in a London hotel room. At the meeting, to the reported astonishment of those present, King expressed concern about various trends in society and distaste for the Wilson government. He then floated the idea of organizing some form of political coup with the intention of establishing Lord Mountbatten as a national supremo presiding over a  coalition government of right (?) thinking public figures. When vague details eventually surfaced in the press, the affair was greeted with derision and regarded as evidence of King's derangement, who was thought to have been unable to adjust to the oblivion of retirement from public life. Reports identifying Lord Solly Zuckerman as one of those present claimed that he had stormed out in reaction to what he considered to be proposals verging on treason. It was never publicly confirmed that Mountbatten had any knowledge of the Cecil King proposals.

It may be that the affair was a direct product of King's state of mind. Madness and paranoia have proved not to be insurmountable handicaps, however, to the establishment of tyrannical dictatorships. There was nothing deranged in King's choice of Mountbatten as a figurehead for his proposed regime; Mountbatten's enviable war record as a military commander and hero, and his post-war stature as the man who had co-ordinated the emergence of India and Pakistan as independent nations, were unique qualifications for the role. As an Admiral of the Fleet, he retained strong links with the military services; the Mountbatten Report on Prisons had given him some influence in the civil police and prison services; and his blood connection with the Royal family left him untainted with the stains of party political opportunism. There would unquestionably have been some support from the extreme, and not so extreme, right; with careful preparation, there would have been support from elements of the various services bound by oath of allegiance to the Crown; and there would have been sympathy among the general public. How much support, how tangibly it would have been expressed, and for how long are questions which cannot be answered. At most, the Cecil King affair demonstrates that the idea of a Right-wing coup is not alien in the corridors of power, and in a mechanical sense it is feasible.

Since the 1960s there has been an increasing cross-fertilization of police and military contingency planning at command and lower levels. This has been in response to a joint appreciation of the need to prepare for the possibility of military intervention in a peacekeeping role in the event of a breakdown in law and order. Increasing emphasis has been placed on training for this eventuality in military colleges. The growing threat of terrorist activity and events in Ulster have influenced the police to view the prospect of military intervention in civil affairs more routinely than hitherto.

In April 1980 James Anderton delivered his speech claiming that 'quiet but hardly bloodless revolution' was in progress. Coincidentally, or otherwise, that same year Lieutenant-General Sir Frank Kitson was appointed Deputy Commander-in-Chief of United Kingdom Land Forces. In 1971, then a Brigadier, Kitson had published *Low Intensity Operations*, which subsequently became regarded as a definitive military manual on counter-insurgency, subversion, and the peacekeeping role of the military in support of civil authorities in the event of crisis. Promoted Major-General, he was then appointed Commandant of the prestigious Military Staff College at Camberley. In this capacity he expanded considerably and controversially the training curriculum of officers being groomed for staff appointments by giving a high priority to military intervention in support of civil authorities. Sir Frank Kitson's counter-insurgency credentials are impeccable and his international reputation as an expert solidly based. His operational experience includes active service in Malaya, Kenya, Cyprus and Northern Ireland. Opera-tional experience was reinforced with intense and wide-ranging academic study of revolutionary theory, from the writings of the Chinese general Sun Tzu in the fourth century BC to the work of contemporary writers such as Regis Debray.

In *Low Intensity Operations* Sir Frank predicted that the British military would have a major role to play in dealing with the revolutionary process of civil disorder accompanied by sabotage and urban terrorism by the late 1970s. He argued that the appropriate military response would have less to do with the destruction of large, heavily armed guerrilla groups and more to do with isolating subversive elements from support bases within the community. To combat this he advocated the allocation of greater resources to the training of military forces in counter-insurgency techniques and the creation of more psychological warfare officers, and urged that more psy-war teams of officers trained in the techniques of propaganda, mass communication and public persuasion be formed. Largely as a result of General Kitson's research and the influence of his acknowledged military expertise in the field, rapid progress was made to redress what he had identified as British military deficiency in the field of psychological warfare operations. Psy-war courses were started in the early 1970s at the Joint Warfare Establishment at Old Sarum. By October 1976, according to Peter Wilson in his book *War on the Mind*, 262 civil servants and 1858 army officers had graduated from these courses. Assuming the numbers have remained reasonably constant, this means that something approaching 10,000 civil servants (including security service operatives) and military personnel will have been trained for psy-war operations by 1984. A high proportion of those will have gained direct operational experience in Northern Ireland.

The need for the services to develop psy-war capabilities to counter insurgency and civil insurrection is undeniable. As an instrument to counter revolutionary forces such capabilities are invaluable. It must be remembered, however, that they have a dual function: they are intended on the one hand to isolate and alienate the revolutionary forces in the community; on the other hand, such personnel are trained in the techniques of rallying community support for the regime it is working for at the time. The basic techniques of black propaganda and misinformation of psy-warfare would operate just as effectively in support of totalitarianism against the forces of democracy were the confrontational postures reversed.

By tradition and training the military, police and security services have been conditioned to confront the revolutionary forces of the Left. Many are convinced that such a confrontation in Britain is inevitable. The more polarized political, economic, social and geographical divisions become, the weaker democracy becomes. The longer the extreme Left are allowed to establish revolutionary conditions in society without

121

being effectively challenged, the more difficult the task of the services. To leave the forces of revolution to take the initiative indefinitely is to defy every principle of political and military logic. If the democratic process is seen to be too weak to launch a counter-offensive against the Left, then it will have failed. The test of a democracy's strength is largely subjective in any event: it is enough that the security forces see it as being too weak. The structural and organizational fabric for the institution of an alternative form of government is in existence: it is operationally and administratively feasible; and the trained resources are available. All it takes is for the ball to be set rolling.

Parliamentary democracy in the United Kingdom is unquestionably under threat. It faces simultaneously challenges from both the political Left and Right. It is at risk no less from those who declare their allegiance to democracy than from those who openly proclaim their enmity. The Right offer the dubious attractions of authoritarian paternalism: an automaton society 'forced to conform and obey', conforming to those who instinctively know what is best for all and obeying those who recognize their own 'natural' qualities of leadership. The conflicting social, economic and political pressures, the raw violence, and the harsh intolerance are all evident. All the ingredients associated with the emergence of totalitarianism are furiously fermenting. Only a fool could deny that some modified form of totalitarian control holds some attraction. It is tempting to see a temporary suspension of democratic rights and compromise on questions of freedom as worthwhile sacrifices in the short term to achieve social stability.

History teaches that rights once suspended or ceded, however, are difficult to recover and individual liberty can be enslaved. Marxist revolutions and Right-wing coups are not the only ways in which a people can lose their liberty in a modern society. In some instances unwittingly, and in others through apathy, the British people in the 1980s have been allowing their precious freedoms to be systematically eroded in the specious interests of 'security'. This disregard for the lessons of history is bad enough: but it is tragic and farcical that the erosion of freedoms is tolerated to further security policies which are untenable and socially divisive.

# 6
# Computers – to Serve Them All Our Days

In the opening years of the 1980s the world witnessed the death-rattle of industrialized society. Precisely where the post-industrial era will lead society is no more clear than the ultimate course of the Industrial Revolution was to those who took part. Nations have already plunged into bankruptcy in a world which faces the imminent prospect of a collapse of international finance. The industrial society produced a human race conditioned to expectations of material growth: a growth limited only by man's ability to produce the goods. Technology enabled man to produce what he could not do unaided. As new technology replaced the old, however, the numbers of people involved in the production process gradually diminished.

The productive capacity of technology is now virtually limitless. It is producing for markets conditioned to expectations of material growth in which demands are insatiable. To meet the demands, increasingly sophisticated technology is being deployed. Even fewer people are required to be involved in the production process. The market appetite for consumption remains as strong: the demand is there and the technology exists to meet the demand. For increasing numbers of the world's population it is the means to pay that are non-existent. Nationally and internationally, for producers and consumers alike, the future stability and security of the human race will be determined by the answers to two questions. How are those who are surplus to the needs of technological production going to be provided with the means to pay for what is being produced? And what means are going to be employed to pacify them when their demands are not met?

Advances in modern technology have knocked national and international societies out of synchronization. Technical innovations have moved faster than mankind's ability to comprehend the nature of the changes being wrought. To paraphrase Michael Foot, 'human beings and human communities' ... [are not] ... 'true masters of their fate'; his stricture that 'the pace of industrial change must be suited to men and women and not vice versa' is not being applied nationally or internationally. The 'chance to breathe' is not being given to 'those who must live from week to week, from day to day'.

British society must come to terms with new realities. The end of the industrial era has arrived with a lurch which threatens to disorientate the whole fabric of society. Social principles which applied in an industrial economy apply no longer. National and individual wealth are no longer – if they ever were – related directly to the human capacity to produce wealth, and human endeavour no longer plays a major role in deciding how it will be distributed. In the post-industrial society, the transition between what society was and what it is to become will depend entirely on the value placed on human dignity. How the value will be determined depends on society's resolve to control its technology, not forgetting those who create and use it. Quite simply, society must decide if it is to rule the machine, or allow the machine, and those who control it, to rule society.

Every advance in computer and microchip technology has come to be hailed as a technological breakthrough which will revolutionize the human condition. The omniscience attributed to the new technology and the pace of its expansion cause us to ignore, or overlook, the more disturbing features of the growth process. No one really knows what it is doing or where it is leading. Until a high level of understanding, and adaptation, is achieved, technology's capacity for serious social disruption will at least equal its potential benefits. For too long computerized technology has been regarded with amused or irritated tolerance by an uncomprehending public. It has been regarded alternately as little more than a glorified abacus, and as a sophisticated servant of society, capable of working faster, more reliably and more accurately than its human master.

Shrouded in technocratic mystique from all but the initiated, microchip computerized technology is creating its own religion with its own computer shrines for its worshippers. Technology is the modern equivalent of some ancient pagan god. Like so many before, it is a demanding god. Its insistence on homage from its adherents is matched by its demand of obeisance by non-believers. Its High Priesthood of programmers and operators perform the required rituals, couched in an attendant and suitably arcane language which only the initiated can understand. Technology is applying its own truths and standards to society and its own definitions of heresy and blasphemy to those who might oppose its progress. It is this religiosity which is bludgeoning society into a mute acceptance of all that is bad in technological expansion: the belief that its progress is preordained and therefore inevitable.

Technology will become uncontrollable unless a conscious effort is made to control it. Even now there are doubts as to whether it is capable of being humanly controlled. Society is already being shaped and moulded by mechanically inspired moral values which are insidiously being imposed. The uninterrupted progression of these values can only have the most horrendous consequences for human relations and social interaction. Society is being progressively dehumanized and is acquiescing in the process: the human master is rapidly being enslaved by the mechanical servant and its acolytes. The term 'technological progress' camouflages the imposition of tyranny. Mechanistic procedures and values are increasingly replacing human experience in a growing range of human affairs. There is no place in the belly of the mechanical beast for the subtle intangibles which influence human behaviour and the relations between one person and another. Where in the computer printout are we to look for compassion, love, sympathy, sadness, despair, tolerance, ambition, elation, fear, suffering or joy? Where, in our dealings with the one-dimensional images it projects, are we to find some reflection of the inner being? Above all, where on the implacable bottom line are we to look for human understanding?

The gathering momentum of computer and microtechnology already poses for society a problem of terrifying dimensions. As the century reaches its closing years the need to confront the problem will become increasingly critical. Unless it is confronted in the not too distant future the time will come when it may be insoluble. The first essential step must be the recognition that what is already identifiably wrong and dehumanizing in the technological process is not peripheral, it is central. Computers are not being designed to complement the existing industrial, commercial, social and ethical mores in British society. Values in all areas of British society are changing to comply with the demands of computerized technology. Each new technological development and each successive generation of computer accelerate the pace and broaden the nature of these demands.

Advancing technology offers society the prospect of universal good and at the same time universal evil. It offers humanity on an unprecedented scale opportunities to attain what is socially desirable. Increasingly, however, that is being overshadowed by the apparently irresistible compulsion to attempt to make what is possible to attain socially desirable. In deciding between these two prospects, the determination of the individual's intrinsic worth in society is at stake. If society is aware of what is at stake it may elect the former alternative. In that event, the individual will be valued above the seductions of mechanical expansion for its own sake. Failing this the individual will become no more than an adjunct of technology, always to be subordinated to its apparently infinite potential and expendable in the face of its progress.

The conflict is between two elements in society engaged in a struggle which has taken place in one guise or another from time immemorial – a struggle to control society. What is different is that the participants can no longer be clearly defined by class divisions and, even less, by degrees of wealth. The division is between those who are not of Orwell's 'New Aristocracy' and those who are.

On the one hand there are those who are deeply suspicious of large vested interests, favour socially orientated economics and regard a bureaucracy as an enslavement; identify the authoritarian vision of an ordered society as tyranny, hold that individual rights are sacrosanct in any society which values freedom, and contend that mechanical efficiency, whatever superficial attractions it may offer, must always be weighed against the need for human beings to control their own destinies. Against those are ranged the organized forces of industrial and commercial self-interest, economists and bureaucrats; the forces of authoritarianism who view an unordered society as a disorderly one per se; those who view individualism as anarchy; and those who accept without reservation that technological progress is a goal so worthwhile that human participation can readily be sacrificed in order that it may be attained.

Clearly, this is and will continue to be an uneven struggle. All the traditional might associated with the structural organizations of the big battalions are ranged against unco-ordinated pockets of resistance which emerge only occasionally; the certainty of material wellbeing for a few is balanced against a possibility of economic uncertainty for all. The security offered by compliant conformity is weighed against the unpredictability of individual freedoms being exercised with a minimum of external restraints. It will often appear as a conflict between what is seen to be immediately practicable and something which may be capable of existence only as an ideal. If the ideal were to prove an abstract concept, efforts to attain it are not invalidated merely because it proves unattainable.

Opposition to the unrestrained, uncontrolled growth of computer and microtechnology is often derided by the 'aristechnocrats' of the post-industrial society. The aristechnocrats accuse the opponents of technology of intangible fears and of combatting an inevitable progress. These accusations are misconceived in both their assumptions. Tangibility is not the only reality: intangible fears are just as real as a computer even if the fear subsequently proves unfounded. No process which is capable of interruption or change can properly be described as inevitable, and the human condition will not necessarily be advanced by technological progress. Every step which erodes mankind's self-sufficiency provides another hostage to fortune. More and more responsibility for human affairs is being ceded to computers with little guarantee that man retains the right to recall that responsibility and power.

The most terrifying aspect of the new aristocracy is the fallibility of the aristechnocrats in relation to their technology and the increasing use of flawed technology in security. Not all those involved in technology are blind to the dangers of the machines they are creating. In an article in *The Observer* (15 August 1982) journalist John Davy reported an interview with Professor Joseph Weizenbaum of the Department of Computer Studies at the Massachusetts Institute of Technology. In the context of computerized weapons systems, Professor Weizenbaum quoted from a paper circulated by the director of a university computer laboratory which receives funds from the US Defense Department:

... these systems are responsible in large part for the maintenance of what peace and stability there is in the world. But they are also capable of unleashing destruction of a scale that is almost impossible for man to comprehend ... There is no stemming this trend in computer development ... The computer has been incorporating itself, and will surely continue to incorporate itself into most of the functions that are fundamental to the support, protection and development of our society. Even now there is no turning back ...

On the subject of how much trust we can place in the computer systems and their programmes, it was pointed out:

Many large systems now in use have been built up cumulatively so that NO ONE knows all the rules by which they are operating. 'Decisions' may be made by computers whose programmes nobody can any longer survey or take responsibility for. Such systems cannot be challenged or changed without falling apart; they can only be 'fixed' usually by adding further programmes. Thus their very conservative obscurity reinforces our own tendency to treat them as oracles of unchallengable authority. This opens the door not only to delusion but to corruption. When President Nixon ordered the bombing of Cambodia, the Pentagon computers were fixed to produce false 'secret reports' for senior politicians. George Orwell's Ministry of Truth, busy rewriting history, was mechanised.

Weizenbaum denies that computers are equipped to make judgments, dismissing the idea as a sinister delusion. 'During the Vietnam war', says

Weizenbaum, 'computers operated by officers who had not the slightest idea of what went on inside their machines effectively chose which hamlets were to be bombed.' He is even more scathing about the 'computer bums' who inhabit the world of computer technology. These are the 'compulsive programmers' . . . 'haggard and obsessed young men who work at their computer keyboards for twenty hours at a time' . . . 'whose only reality has become the vast and ramifying system of programmes and sub-programmes which they construct, reconstruct and try to control'. While attacking the oversimplification of 'real life' when 'model' worlds are produced for computer programmes, and their lack of relevance to life, Weizenbaum says: 'The computer programmer is the creator of universes for which he alone is the law-giver.' However: 'Paradoxically, within the rigid and ordered world he has created, the programmer is not so much omnipotent as helpless.'

It is Weizenbaum's belief that unless people wake up to the dangers of computer technology, the ultimate effect will be more malign than benign. He queries, 'Are there any exceptions to the rule that we take some of the finest fruits of genius and pervert them?' and asks, 'Is there perhaps a law?'

Computer technology more than any other modern development has advanced the likelihood and the feasibility of an Orwellian 1984 society emerging in Britain within the span of the twentieth century or shortly after. The evolution of this pervasive technology has successfully overcome many of the most obstinate technical barriers to the establishment of any form of totalitarian regime. A totalitarian regime depends heavily on centralized planning and power. Computer technology makes this possible as never before.

Even when they have been established, totalitarian regimes have traditionally been vulnerable to unrest among the labour force necessary to sustain the regime's industrial and economic base. Repressive measures could at best achieve only a token compliance from a sullen and uncooperative work force. The economic crisis culminating in Poland's virtual collapse in the 1980s exemplifies the dangers to a totalitarian state of a disaffected work force. The more repressive a regime is, the more it must rely for support on a massive state bureaucracy and security apparatus which itself produces no wealth but makes heavy demands on the wealth of the state. These demands will be disproportionately high, leaving less available for the work force. A disaffected work force produces less, making it more difficult for the regime to satisfy the demands of its bureaucracy. Additional repression further alienates the wealth creation sector without significantly improving the economy. However repressive, therefore, past totalitarian regimes have had to face the added difficulty of providing enough wealth to sufficient supporters to ensure a continued loyalty.

In the short term these factors were less important. In the longer term they imposed real constraints on the forces of totalitarianism. A regime could exist without the active support of the working masses, but it could not have any great life expectancy without some degree of co-operation. It could forcibly repress opposition within the working masses, but it could not afford for long to oppress all of them without jeopardizing the co-operation needed to sustain the apparatus of power.

Advances in computer and microtechnology have significantly reduced the ability of working masses to influence the repressive instincts of totalitarianism. There is no longer the same dependence on a massive work force within the production and wealth creation sector of the economy. More and more computer technology is being applied to the industrial, agricultural, commercial, administrative, telecommunications, transport, government and internal security machinery of the developed and developing nations. The more it can be applied the less dependent a potentially totalitarian tyranny is on the working masses. With the support of a relatively narrow band of technologists, in a country highly developed technically, a regime can become virtually self-sufficient. Controlling the production and distribution of its own wealth, it can create and sustain well-paid and well-equipped military, internal police and security services. As technology advances, the constraints on repression are progressively relaxed. The masses come to be regarded as an unnecessary evil sucking the nutrients from the economic blood of the aristechnocratic élite: parasites with an insatiable appetite, forever taking and contributing nothing.

Technologically, the UK is already highly developed, and technology is making it increasingly efficient in its industry, commerce, agriculture, transport and communications, and less reliant on a large work force. Britain is not short of wealth: it merely has too many people who want to share in it. Computerized technology can increase the already centralized arms of government, and is being deployed more and more by the security agencies, government and private elements in society. There has never been a time when so much information has been stored about so many citizens, and there has never been a time when it could be so quickly accessible. This inordinate mass of information is being indiscriminately collected and stored, often with no immediate justification. What it all means is that the nation is uniquely vulnerable to totalitarian repression in a way previously unimaginable.

Stripped of the emotive connotations, the differences between concentration camps, gulags or forced labour camps and British prisons are more imaginary than real: as institutions there is little to choose between them. It is true that millions have died in concentration camps and gulags through policies of exterminating state enemies. The difference lies not in the individual institutions or the forces which run them, however. Police, security and prison authorities have far more things in common with each other than they have things which keep them apart. The essential difference is in the democratic system under which British institutions operate. It is only democracy that restrains them from the worst excesses which all such institutions are prone to indulge in, with or without state authority.

It is the British democratic process, weak though it may be, and not the institutions which operate within it, that protects the British people from authoritarian tyranny. Once that is grasped it becomes easier to see how, far from sustaining the freedoms associated with democracy, these institutions, unrestrained, can threaten the very democracy they believe they are protecting. Authority and tyranny are not the same things, yet the excessive use of authority is invariably tyrannical. No one who exercises authority on behalf of the state, particularly in the law enforcement or the security services, will ever willingly concede that that power is excessive. It is unlikely to be conceded, whatever the extent of the power, that it is enough, or that it is available to the degree necessary to maintain the state's authority.

Democracy is founded on the power of reason, but this does not preclude a democracy's right to react with necessary force to defend itself against aggression from any source. Reason alone can never prevail against mindless violence or terrorism. It is sometimes necessary for state institutions to react forcefully, or to undertake covert actions which may impinge on individual democratic freedoms or those of society generally. When this happens, however, it is essential that the state define the precise nature of the threat being combated. The public should be given the opportunity to assess whether the danger merits waiving individual freedoms. This is particularly true of the police and security services. The developments in computer and surveillance technology have made this more imperative than ever.

Masses of information is being accumulated about millions of British citizens and no one knows why, often least of all the people who are accumulating the information. The police and the security services are allowed to collect, store and retrieve limitless information about the public. Since it has become possible to do this, they consider it unnecessary to ask if it is desirable to do it. Much of the information is never used, which is just as well since a significant amount of the information is misleading.

There is a lack of discrimination about the whole process of gathering, storing and disseminating information: in the main it is acquired at random, often from unreliable sources. The mere act of recording the information gives it a degree of authority which does not accord with the reality. To conform to the mechanics of the record system it is ruthlessly and indiscriminately summarized with sometimes disastrous effects on its accuracy and context. Such information is stored unprocessed until activated, if ever, at some future time. Each snippet of information is an unspecified accusation intended at some future time to support a specified allegation against the person it relates to. Almost without exception random information stored is designed to allow a sinister interpretation to be placed on the subject's future activities. However far removed by time, place or the nature of the event, however ill-founded the original information and however misconceived the new information, each will give spurious credibility to the other. When subsequently applied out of context to unrelated events it can become a denunciation quite without foundation.

The American judge, Learned Hand said:

> The community is already in the process of dissolution where each man begins to eye his neighbour as a possible enemy, where non-conformity with the accepted creed, political as well as religious, is a mark of disaffection; where denunciation, without specification or backing, takes the place of evidence; where orthodoxy chokes freedom of dissent; where faith in the eventual supremacy of reason has become so timid that we dare not enter our convictions in the open lists, to win or lose.

1982 was heralded as Information Technology Year. In March of that year two journalists, Duncan Campbell of the *New Statesman* and Steven Connor of *Computer*, wrote in the *New Statesman* of the breathtaking scope of involvement by the police and security services in the latest information technology. In common with so many other revelations about security, the disclosures were as interesting for what they did not tell as for what they revealed. The article told of a government computer centre, designated MoD-X Computer Centre, operated by MI5 in the heart of London's Mayfair. According to the story, the centre had started operations 'in the early 1970s, equipped with the then largest British made computer, an ICL 1907'. The article described how in 1977/8 the computer complex, described by the Ministry of Defence as a 'classified database', placed orders for more advanced computers:

> The computers ordered by the Ministry of Defence were a double or 'dual' ICL 2980, largest of the company's powerful 'new range', plus a 2960 (for back up). The most formidable part of the MI5 specification

was for a huge 'disc store'. There were to be over 100 disc store units of ICL's type EDS 200 – the largest then made. This electronic memory, even by the standards of an industry accustomed to superlatives, could only be called gigantic. Together, these discs can store 20,000 million characters, letters or numbers; 20 'gigabytes' of information. This is the equivalent to the information in a library of about 50,000 paperback books. Or, it could store personal dossiers on some 20 million people, if these consisted of identifying particulars and about 150 descriptive words.

The Campbell/Connor article made four basic points:

● The data storage capacity of the computers, estimated to have cost between £15 and £20 million, is two and a half times that of the already controversial Police National Computer. The PNC itself has forty million personal records, and is checked tens of thousands of times daily. Information has often leaked from it.

● MI5's access to other departments' files is unlimited, according to details in their Charter which have been published in Australia, but never before in Britain. The Charter also says that their information system should be 'comprehensive'. The Ministry of Defence has stressed, in unpublished evidence to the Lindop committee, that the new data protection laws should allow exemption so that the security services have access to personal files held elsewhere in government.

● MI5's files are in addition to more than 1.3 million Special Branch files already on computer at New Scotland Yard. This system, which was known to the Lindop committee, provoked for them 'new dimensions of unease'.

● Development work on MI5 computers and associated networks to tap into other government computers has been under way since 1972. A succession of plans to create a network of central government computers has been tested – and, a computer executive from ICL says privately, is under active development within the company . . . unofficial sources say that the network gives or will give MI5's computers direct access to the records of the DHSS, Inland Revenue and other departments.

The writers make this point: 'The critical question about "MoD-X Computer Centre" is of course the use to which they put the computer. What exactly does it store, about whom, and for what purpose is the information kept and used?' Not surprisingly, the writers could not say. Some things are certain beyond reasonable doubt, however. A great deal of the information will be absolute rubbish: much of it will relate to perfectly ordinary and innocent citizens by any legal standards; and, whatever the intended purpose of the information, some of it will be abused, misused and given a credence it does not warrant. As with all computers, the first principle of computer technology applies: GIGO – garbage in, garbage out.

GIGO is a convenient acronym for this basic principle except for its tendency to understate the problem. Garbage is not always instantly recognizable as such, and this is particularly true of unprocessed information. The situation is akin to a financially stretched mother who finds a tin of salmon in the street, not realizing it has been condemned as a health hazard. Having examined the tin and found it apparently undamaged she serves it to her children as a treat. To the children, mother is an unimpeachable source and they eat the salmon, which is contaminated with botulism. Coming from mother, the salmon carries the highest possible seal of approval although it is poisonous. Official records and computers have the same capacity for endowing their sometimes poisonous information with spurious authority.

The leader page of the *New Statesman* provided a backdrop to the article quoted. The leader argued for public debate before security systems were implemented and attacked the 'combination of technology and [public] ignorance' as being deadly. The leader-writer quoted Kipling who 'tried to put the warning in the mouths of the machines themselves':

Remember, please, the law by which we live
We are not built to comprehend a lie.
We can neither love, nor pity, nor forgive
– if you make a slip in handling us, you die.

The writer continued:

One thing we know, or should know, about MI5, the 'Security Service', the spooks under all their aliases, is that their whole business is built on lies, evasions and fantasies – most notably, on the fantasy of its own non-existence. Any hardware and software they are allowed to procure unsupervised will amount, in practice, to an attempt to comprehend a lie. If we allow it to happen we will have no one to blame but ourselves.

The *New Statesman* is a self-proclaimed radical, left-wing magazine, which has carried attacks on the institutions of authority for years. Any undisguised bias should not, however, be taken to mean the magazine is always wrong. Moderate opinion in Britain has too long been reluctant to look objectively at the police and security organizations and identify their shortcomings. The mistaken belief that constructive criticism would somehow undermine the stability of these organizations has led to society being dangerously exposed by the institutional inefficiency and incompetence which is endemic in their internal affairs. Responsible opinion has too often discarded evidence of major flaws in the philosophical, social and operational strategies of all organizations connected with security, government and private. Criticism has too often been rejected as propaganda from the lunatic fringe of political extremism. Few, if any, truly understand all the implications for society of modern developments in information technology. The police and security forces probably understand less because they apply different values and do not identify the same dangers: they do not identify the same dangers because the dangers do not apply to them to the extent they may do to others.

It is hard for those who have no direct experience of 'intelligence' records, criminal or security, to appreciate the inherent dangers in much of the unprocessed 'official' material. It is even difficult for those who make the records to comprehend how trivia once recorded can take on an authority and substance which does not accord with reality. Take as an example the case of an imaginary airport loader, John Smith. To police the job description in itself is considered indicative of criminality. John Smith earns high wages and has a wife who runs an active mail order agency from their home, which is in a middle management suburb near an international airport. Their joint incomes service a mortgage and allow each of them to have a car. Concessionary air fares allow them to have frequent foreign holidays. A working class background, little formal education and few social pretensions separate them from their aspiring executive neighbours. The Smiths appear to enjoy a lifestyle above that which could reasonably be expected. Stimulated by news of recurrent airport thefts, a public-spirited neighbour tells his local bobby about the airport employee with the enviable lifestyle who, with his wife, is constantly to be seen carrying packages in and out of the house. 'I don't suppose there's anything to it, but I just thought I'd mention it.'

Having no personal knowledge of the Smiths, the bobby decides there is no direct action he should take to investigate what is no more than gossip. At this point the instinctive caution of organizational man takes over. If it were to transpire subsequently that the airport loader was, in fact, a suburban equivalent of Al Capone, and it came to light – as it most certainly would, given the public-spiritedness of the 'good neighbour' – that the bobby had received information and done nothing about it, things would rapidly become uncomfortable for the officer.

Being an experienced officer, well versed in the art of administrative self-defence, he takes steps to divest himself of responsibility for action. He first passes on his information to a disinterested CID officer; he then approaches the Station Crime Collator where he receives a rapturous welcome. The Collator, whose existence depends on someone somewhere taking his role seriously, seizes on the information and commits it to record. The information is placed in a Street Index and a Nominal Index. The record reads like this:

**SMITH, John**
**1.10.84**
B. 1.1.45 in London. No Trace CRO. Airport Loader of 'Mon Repos', Snobs Row. Information received from P.C. 49 'T' Cautious. Neighbour reports packages seen taken in and out of house – possibly stolen property. Subject drives Blue Ford Mustang, Reg. No PPP 111. Wife Thelma drives red Mini Metro TTT 222. No Trace Vehicle Index. Both take frequent holidays in West Indies. May be involved thefts at Heathrow Airport.

Sometime later a major theft takes place at Heathrow. Smith and 200 others are questioned. The investigating officers contact the Collator to ask if anything is known about Smith. The Collator gives the information recorded on 1.10.84. At the same time he makes another note on the record card.

**2.7.85**
Information received from Heathrow Serious Crime Squad – Det. Sgt. Rickett. John Smith questioned re £100,000 diamond theft at Heathrow. Not charged.

Acting on the information supplied by the Collator, D.S. Rickett obtains a search warrant and searches Smith's house. Smith expresses resentment at the search. Rickett resents Smith's resentment. Rickett reports search to Station Collator who makes a fresh entry.

**3.7.85**
D.S. Rickett executed search warrant at 'Mon Repos' re £100,000 diamond theft. No trace stolen property. Smith reacted aggressively – may be violent. Not charged.

The same day D.S. Rickett, in accordance with force instructions, forwards a brief report of the executed warrant to the force headquarters at New Scotland Yard, in order to have a central record of the unsuccessful search in case any complaint should be made by Smith. The report is allotted a General Registry correspondence number and filed. The name John Smith is indexed with the relevant correspondence number. Any future search on the name will produce the report.

A few days later two young officers temporarily posted to plainclothes duty with the local Crime Squad browse through the station records to familiarize themselves with possible suspects involved in criminal activities in the area. They read the three entries about Smith. Patrolling in the vicinity of 'Mon Repos' they see Smith and his wife in one of their cars with a number of packages. Smith starts to move off in the car and is stopped by the police. Questions are asked about the packages, and Smith and his wife are asked to leave the car in order that it may be searched. An irate Smith refuses and demands to see a search warrant. He is told that a search warrant is not needed and this time is more forcefully requested to get out of the car. A now aggressive Smith does so and punches an officer on the nose. Two more entries appear on Smith's record at the station:

**6.7.85**
Smith arrested by P.C.s Proboscis and Tender for assault on police. Fingerprints taken. Bailed to appear at Astfelt Mags. Court 20.7.85. Car and home searched. No trace stolen property.

**20.7.85**
**SMITH, John – CRO No. 99999/85**
Appeared Astfelt Mags. Court. Pleaded 'not guilty'. Found 'guilty' Assault on Police. Fined £100. THIS MAN IS VIOLENT AND OFFICERS SHOULD APPROACH WITH CAUTION.

There was no factual error in any one of the entries as they related to John Smith's circumstances. The flaw is not in what the records say: the flaw is in what they do not say. When 'Mon Repos' was searched the police were looking for stolen property; they did not find any and the record said so. If no lies are recorded why should the public worry? The police need information to operate effectively. Smith did act aggressively – he was violent and the court conviction proved it.

Although factually correct the notes made about Smith were one-dimensional, and in the end the records created their own reality of the character. It is an example of what Learned Hand referred to when speaking of the dangers of a situation where 'denunciation without specification or backing takes the place of evidence'. Police and security records should be looked at in terms of 'accentuating the positive and eliminating the negative'. Information which relates to guilt is positive and should, therefore, be accentuated: information relating to innocence is negative and irrelevant and is, therefore, eliminated. The concept of an individual's innocence is one which is not recognized by the professional police or security officer. They may occasionally apply the word 'innocent' to a child or to a victim of crime, but it will never be applied to describe an individual in any police record or report.

The public en masse may be emotively referred to as innocent to justify police or security measures. As individuals, however, members of the public are in one of two groups: those who have been found guilty and those who have not yet been found guilty. An individual acquitted on trial is found 'not guilty': but that is not to say innocent. In police internal records and reports opinions are constantly expressed about an individual's guilt without supporting evidence. In officially protected documentation unwarranted guilt can be freely attributed. In direct contrast to the legal principle that an individual is innocent until proved to be guilty, officers are actively discouraged from expressing a belief in an individual's innocence. An assumption of innocence is incompatible with security standards of judgment. The result is a constant thread running through surveillance records: a conscious and deliberate effort to place some sinister significance on the most innocuous human behaviour.

In an article in *Police Review*, Lord Ritchie Calder describes at first hand a classic example of the one-dimensional nature of surveillance records. Before the outbreak of the Second World War, he had been active in fund-raising to provide medical aid for Republicans in the Spanish Civil War. He knew that he was at the time under Special Branch surveillance. He had even had drinks with one of the officers who was reporting on him and they had enjoyed a friendly relationship. After the World War had started Calder found himself in a position of influence within the security services. He used this influence to get hold of his own dossier compiled by Special Branch before the war.

His reaction to the contents varied from indignant outrage to bewildered amusement. One entry described how at 10.30 pm one evening he had left the HQ of the Spanish Medical Aid Committee accompanied by a beautiful actress, also a fund-raiser for the cause. He had been seen to enter the actress's flat and stay there until 2 am when he was seen to leave. Some might say, lucky Ritchie Calder. Certainly no officer reading the entry would have any doubt about the 'hanky-panky' going on there. The entry was factually accurate and was remarkable only for what it omitted to say. Not only had Ritchie Calder gone to the actress's flat and left at the recorded times: so too had the entire Medical Aid Committee. They had all gone to the flat to have coffee and to continue the meeting. Having read his own dossier, Lord Calder concluded that the irresponsible and misleading trivia had been compiled to produce a purpose-built scenario. Both in what had been included and what had been omitted, the information was intended to place the worst possible interpretation on the most innocent of actions. The dossier had ultimately done him no harm as his subsequent elevation to the peerage testified. Special Branch deserved no thanks for that. The amount of valuable public resources expended on accumulating the rubbish, and the extent to which surveillance had been prolonged by the heaping of distortion upon misrepresentation of fact can only be guessed.

It is true that very little of the garbage pumped into the system is ever put to any use, but this is little consolation. Such records, whether computerized or manually recorded, are like inter-Continental ballistic missiles sitting in concrete silos: relatively harmless until someone presses the buttons. Information, however, is more invidious than missiles and less detectable when activated. It is from the type of records and information described that decisions are made in the police and security world: they are the stuff of positive vetting. Officially and unofficially, judgments are made from which there are no appeals. As Free Text Retrieval Systems for computer databanks become more advanced, individuals will increasingly assume artificial paper identities. The relationships between citizens and the authorities will become one-dimensional as a result of contrived, purpose-built scenarios designed to place the most sinister interpretation on individual character traits.

Much of the public controversy over the Data Protection (Lindop) Committee report centred on the need to protect the confidentiality of information stored in databanks with questions about unauthorized access and distribution of the information. The only people who have difficulty in gaining access to information are those to whom it applies. Over the years, Criminal Records have been a prime example of the social dilemma which can arise from record banks. Despite the alleged confidentiality of Criminal Records relating to criminal convictions there is no one in Britain with the right contacts who cannot discover the details of an individual's convictions. Whether by bribery or influence, close contacts among serving and former police officers, personnel who are or have been in government security agencies, and senior personnel in the private security industry can produce any details required. The controversy over confidentiality is artificial and misconceived, tending to obscure wider issues.

Writing about Chinese society in 1934, Generalissimo Chiang Kai Shek wrote:

> The general psychology of our people today can be described as spiritless. What manifests itself in behaviour is this: lack of discrimination between good and evil, between what is public and what is private, and between what is primary and what is secondary.

The General is not a source which immediately springs to mind when one seeks an authority on democratic principles. As leader of the Kuomintang party in succession to the founder, Sun Yat Sen, on whose death in 1925, Chiang had moved the party away from principles of social concern, parliamentary democracy and public welfare into a corrupt, reactionary military oligarchy. Fifteen years after writing the words the General found himself ejected from the Chinese mainland to end his days as an exiled warlord on Formosa (now Taiwan). (His successor in China was Mao Tse Tung.)

Chiang Kai Shek was ejected for lack of support by those he regarded as spiritless. Whether or not this was because they had recovered their spirit or their capacity to discriminate between good and evil is a matter for historical conjecture. It may be that what he identified as spiritless was despair which concealed fundamental feelings of frustration, resentment and anger inevitably destined to culminate in an explosion of violence. In any event, both the words he used to describe the Chinese condition in 1934 and the General's ultimate fate may have more relevance for Britain fifty years later than is immediately apparent.

Technology confronts modern society with precisely the same choices of discrimination as those posed by Chiang Kai Shek for China. Technology's potential for good has to be balanced against its potential for social evil. With technology man can achieve goals which were formerly beyond reach. The question is how worthwhile are the goals now attainable. It may be good that more and more people are being released from the 'tyranny' of physical labour by technology. Is it also good that for hundreds of thousands of young people the former tyranny of work is being replaced by the prospect of a lifetime of playing with computerized toys and Space Invader machines? Is the condition of society improved by having peoples' endeavours channelled away from useful to useless activities? While the major effort of the computer industry is applied to feeding the insatiable demands for toys and games from its largest consumer market, people are dying for the lack of blood dialysis machines.

The principal feature of modern technology is the irrationality of its social acceptance. Society is being moulded to conform to what technology can do, instead of technology being designed to do what society needs to be done. First the machine is created. Society then asks what it can do and does it. Before the machine is created no one asks why. Once the machine has been created, the question is regarded as superfluous. This applies to information technology as much as any other. Before getting heated about the confidentiality of records other questions should be answered: why are the records necessary? What form will they take? What is there which makes them, and for whom should they be, confidential? The answers demand adequate discrimination between good and evil, public and private, and what is primary and secondary in society's commitment to democracy. The matter of Criminal

Records and the distinction between those and the indiscriminate storing of randomly collected and unprocessed information highlights the issues.

The case for keeping Criminal Records of those who have chosen to break the law is self-evident. Democratic laws are intended to protect the tolerant in society from the intolerant: the weak from the strong who would otherwise misuse strength; and the law-abiding from the criminal. The law should reflect forms of conduct which society collectively considers unacceptable. Open trials are intended to protect both the accused and society from any malpractice. When the accused is properly convicted, it is by the standards set by society, and punishment is determined in the same way. It is society which determines the process, but it is the individual who elects to set the process in motion. When members of society choose to break the rules they, in effect, elect to sacrifice their precious rights of anonymity and privacy.

Society is entitled to know the identify of those who have criminally rejected its values and, by the same token, it is entitled to know how serious was the act of rejection. It has to be recognized that transgressors cannot be socially assessed purely on the basis of criminal actions which may be unrepresentative. It also has to be recognized that behaviour patterns change and that people can rise above previous indiscretions if they are given an opportunity to do so. It would be an intolerable burden for individuals genuinely attempting to reconstruct a respectable place in society constantly to be branded with labels such as embezzler or child-molester because, in the past, they had either embezzled or molested a child. The fact is, however, what has been done cannot be undone: the act cannot be de-enacted but it can be re-enacted. In a free society a convicted person has the right to apply for any employment regardless of their past. Equally, in a free society, an employer has the right to employ anyone considered suitable regardless of the person's past. At the same time both parties should have the right to know what judgments have been passed by society about each other and about themselves.

When a person voluntarily commits a criminal act and is properly convicted, private actions become public property. Genuine privacy for the individual is a crucial element of freedom, but privacy is not about publicizing what is good and concealing what is bad. Concealment of a criminal conviction is not an act of privacy, but secrecy; and unnecessary secrecy is not compatible with democracy. The challenge to democracy is not that of keeping criminal records secret: the challenge is for society to foster responsible public attitudes to the information the records contain. Armed with knowledge, an employer is still free to employ the convicted rapist as night porter in a nurses' home, the arsonist in the explosives factory, the drug addict in the pharmacy, and the mass poisoner in the laboratory. To do so, however, is to accept responsibility for the action.

The factual content of Criminal Records is intended to protect the public, and the right to make open enquiry is a well-established safeguard of freedom. Yet the public are denied free legitimate access to Criminal Records and are legally prevented from making open enquiry. The result is that information contained in these records has become a form of black market currency. Those who have legitimate access to the information supply without authorization thousands of times each year those who do not have legitimate access. The system leaks like a sieve; any real measure of confidentiality is non-existent and it is regarded with contempt by those who are charged with operating it and those who wish to take advantage of what it contains.

Examples of abuse are legion, but the principle involved and the inherent dangers were exemplified in the Ladbroke Casino affair. In May 1981 a former police inspector and a Director of Ladbroke's pleaded guilty at Nottingham Crown Court to corruptly paying a police sergeant to supply them with details of car owners from the police computer. Private investigators had been employed by Ladbrokes to record the car numbers of punters patronizing competitors' casinos. The car index numbers were supplied to the police officer and in return for a reported fifty pence per car, the computer was used to provide the ownership details. The owners would then be contacted by Ladbrokes and persuaded to frequent the Ladbroke Casino. The records in this case were not Criminal Records, but the principle is the same and the Ladbroke affair provides a good example of the illicit information industry in action. There is unlikely to be a private investigator or senior private security operator in the country who has not had occasion to use it.

The basic information in Criminal Records Office files is factual and relates to criminal convictions and court proceedings. These are matters of public record, and it is in the public interest that both the public and the subject of the files should have free access to them. To the extent that they are factual, they can reveal nothing to the subject nor anyone else not already known. Because they are not made available to the subject or the public, however, these files often contain opinionated and inaccurate information which will invariably be slanted to the subject's detriment. Suspicion will be voiced which is incapable of proof and unsupported by tangible evidence. In this way, persons convicted of criminal offences, in addition to suffering the consequences of past crime, may also unwittingly suffer for what someone has thoughtlessly recorded.

It is impossible to comprehend the full implications for society of its failure to discriminate between what is public and what is private in relation to criminal records files. It is only possible to note some features of the system. The lack of public access to the files denies the public protection from criminals in society who may intend them harm: the convicted embezzler who applies for a position as an accountant or cashier without disclosing the previous conviction; or the child-molester applying to work with children. The subject of a file has no protection from having unfounded accusations recorded. Perhaps the most ominous feature of all, the system has created a covert industry based on the circulation of illicitly obtained information which involves numerous police officers in professional malpractice. In most cases the technical breaches of confidentiality are well intended and often work in the public interest. The Ladbroke affair shows this to be not always the case.

A clear distinction has to be drawn between the information on criminal records files and the most sinister form of records: the records which are compiled at random or as a result of covert surveillance; and which are rarely subjected to any objective test to confirm their substance – the type of records which create the one-dimensional John Smith of society, or Ritchie Calder's. Calder probably never knew the purpose of the paper scenario being prepared for him. It is equally probable that the person making the record did not know either. The distorted information had only one logical interpretation: as a form of paper character assassination. Even though the lies did not prevent Calder serving in a sensitive post during the war, the information still lay there like a malignant cancer waiting to attach itself despite his newfound eminence. If history had taken a different course and fascist elements of the British Right wing had achieved power, who can say where the scenario would have led him?

There is a need for the state to keep information relating to internal and external enemies, and clearly this information has to be protected if it is to retain its value. At the same time, information which is false at the time remains false however much time elapses. It is also true that the longer it remains in existence the more difficult it becomes to identify the basic falsity. In the incident recorded about Calder and the actress, the passage of time could only enhance its credibility. As a professional security document the record was monumentally incompetent and fatuous. If Calder and the actress had been engaged in subversive activities, the record was framed in such a way as to provide them with the perfect cover: by implication their association was no more than a love tryst. By any objective professional standards it was a record which should never have been brought into existence. It was nevertheless created and stored in the same way that thousands of records still are.

The John Smith syndrome arises because of the basic lack of respect officialdom has for the individual in society: a lack of commitment to democratic principles. On a technical level, a paper John Smith is created as a result of the bureaucratic mentality which cannot discriminate between action and records, thus confusing the latter with the former. Too often in the police and security world, clandestine manoeuvering is preferred to open investigation, while in reality the latter almost invariably proves more productive. John Smiths are a result of official attitudes to innocence, the refusal to accept that innocence is in itself positive and that to accept an explanation of innocence is preferable to recording an accusation or suspicion unsupported by evidence. As things stand, no one can say they are not a John Smith, and no one knows how many there are.

Before his retirement in 1982, John Alderson, then Chief Constable of Devon and Cornwall Constabulary, instituted a movement to destroy the vast bulk of all Special Branch records held in his force. He judged it to be what many had long contended: a heap of bumpf which served no useful operational function, but posed a potentially deadly health hazard for democracy. This largely unprocessed garbage is compiled and preserved in perpetuity by officers who, under the protection of the Official Secrets Act, are relieved of any necessity to demonstrate any purpose, relevance or result for the information they so assiduously accumulate.

There has never been a time when the various institutions of government have had so much personal information about so many people. Computer technology has swept away the constraints previously placed on governments who might wish to impose unwelcome controls on society. The mass of the public are no longer protected by individual anonymity from the attentions of government. Never before have governments and their institutions had the same administrative capability to segregate and divide society into selected groupings: the means to divide and conquer. Computerization, microtechnology and continually advancing surveillance equipment are rapidly reaching the point where the power of the electorate to control government will be grossly outweighed by government's power to control the electorate. In the same way, the power of government over its own technology will be less than the power of the institutions operating the technology over government. The new technology has its own dynamism and develops its own logic: a logic which complements perfectly the rationale of authoritarianism and bureaucracy. It provides the means, the justification and the impetus to create the regimented orthodoxy of a programmed society – a society in which traits of individuality, dissent and protest are registered as non-conformism. Once these are readily identified they can more easily be eliminated, and it will then be possible for the whole of society, not just the 'undisciplined and crime-ridden community' identified by Greater Manchester's John Anderton, to be forced to 'conform and obey'.

Government has over 200 computers and databanks in operation, and these are certain to be increased in number and capacity. The scope of the information contained in these records is already formidable and continues to grow. The activities of the Departments of Employment, Health and Social Security, Education and Science, the Ministry of Defence, Home Office and the Inland Revenue and a myriad of other offices of government are rapidly being turned over to high technology. There are many sound reasons why this should be so, providing always the anticipated benefits are not allowed to conceal the potential hazards. What is technically possible is not always socially desirable.

Nowhere is this more evident than in the activities of security (government and private) and the police. To combat what they see described as growing lawlessness in society they are turning more and more to modern technology for answers. At the same time they ignore the evidence and the apparent paradox that the lawlessness they identify is growing apace with the technology they are increasingly deploying. If advanced information and surveillance technology is seen by police and security forces as a solution to growing lawlessness, then they clearly must know the nature of the solution. It must, therefore, be possible to impart this vision to the public, yet they seem reluctant to do so. Technology certainly makes it possible to accumulate, store and retrieve information to the nth degree. It does not mean it is desirable to do any of those things; far less does the new capability make the information so treated accurate or valuable.

Bureaucracy has a tendency to make information an end in itself, and information technology increases the tendency. A complex modern society needs to record a massive amount of factual information as a means of reference: a factual history of the social interaction between government and the individual, and that of individuals with each other. The extent to which this is done must be kept within clearly defined limits as far as government is concerned, and that applies to police and security agencies alike. The foremost principle must be to protect society from records designed to produce a preconceived, misleading scenario. There is no room in records for a process of selectivity which seizes anything which can be made to appear to support a preconceived notion, and discards anything which does not support the preconception.

When society is asked to choose between 'good and evil', then it must opt for human dignity, liberty and the freedom of the individual. When discriminating between 'what is public and what is private', it will not go too far wrong if it identifies the governing process as being public, and the personal affairs of the individual as private – in the national context, 'what is primary' is to aim in society to make what is worthwhile and desirable, possible; and what is very much 'secondary' is making what is possible desirable. Whether those choices are to remain in the hands of the public will depend on how effective the safeguards created to protect society are against the potential tyranny of advanced technology being indiscriminately deployed. If the safeguards are inadequate or ineffective, the dynamics of technology will impose their own controls on society and these will become irreversible.

Unless consciously controlled, successive generations of computers will increasingly be utilized by the police and security services in the role of public surveillance. This expansion of computerized security technology is already changing the whole complexion of internal security in the United Kingdom. The next logical step in the escalation process is to activate the technology from a passive surveillance role to a more active one. At present many of the most sophisticated information computers are under-utilized in the sense that they are being fed only by human hands, even although they are capable of being linked to other compatible information systems. The pressure to provide these links will in time increase.

Private security agencies are becoming heavily involved in the extension of electronic fund transfers at points of sale to counter fraud. When transactions involved cash, proof of identity was not a critical factor. Cheques, cash cards and credit cards and electronic cash transfers make the matter of identity crucial. As electronic systems, already being used by banks, supermarkets, shops and garages, spread through society the importance of identification will increase. Security people will advocate, as some already do, the issuing of identification cards which can be electronically scanned and verified. To be effective this would require computer access to central databanks. This would represent a quantum leap in the intrusion of surveillance and security controls on society, with all that implies for personal privacy. Given the extent of the information and personal details already contained in government and commercial computer databanks, mutual access computer systems offer undreamed possibilities for citizen surveillance.

A computer profile of an individual would show financial status details from banks, employment, tax, credit and hire purchase sources. Information on computer at Swansea's Driving Vehicle Licence Centre about vehicle ownership is readily available but cannot be too heavily relied upon. This could be supplemented by information from garages where petrol is bought by credit or cash card. Information from this source would provide details of vehicles used even if not owned. From purchases made in this way, a computer profile would provide a picture of an individual's lifestyle. It would also detail a record of physical movement from payments made at garages, restaurants, shops, hotels and any other venue where non-cash transactions were made. When all this is added to the infinite diversity of other information on record in police, security and other government department systems, the true potential for computer surveillance can be appreciated. When computerized information systems are deployed in conjunction with other related surveillance technologies (discussed in the following chapter) and when considered in the context of uncontrolled developments in the ever-growing private security industry, there are no grounds for complacency about the future of democratic social freedoms in Britain.

The unholy combination of computer technology and security surveillance devices has placed awesome power in the hands of government and all those who are involved in deploying the apparatus. The degree to which the public can be confident that it will be used responsibly is governed by the amount of faith they have in those who have power. In this respect, every democracy has been provided with a salutary lesson by the American experience of Watergate, when the nation's constitutional freedoms were seriously threatened by the activities of Richard Nixon's conspiratorial henchmen. The President's Office, the Attorney General, the CIA, the FBI, Inland Revenue and many of the most senior officials of the executive arms of American government deployed the full range of surveillance technology in an orgy of illegality. Under President Nixon, democracy in the United States teetered for a time on the brink of a totalitarian abyss. The Watergate revelations, by exposing the criminality in the US government, prevented Richard Nixon completing his second term in office. Democracy survived, but only just. Whether it would have survived had Watergate not surfaced and Richard Nixon and his associates been given another term in office with all the technical apparatus of government at their disposal is a matter for conjecture. In 1983, the exposure of 'Liffygate', in the Republic of Ireland, demonstrated to the public in that country and the United Kingdom that the misuse of computer and surveillance technology by government is not a uniquely American phenomenon.

In the Fianna Fail government of Charles Haughey, which took office in 1979, the state's surveillance and security resources were deployed against politicians and journalists who had the temerity to oppose the views and policies of the Taoiseach. With the collusion of the then Minister of Justice, Sean Doherty, the Police Commissioner, Patrick McLaughlin and his Deputy Commissioner in charge of security matters, Joe Ainsworth, telephones were tapped; it was not only opposition politicians who were bugged, members of Haughey's own party suspected of disloyalty were also subjected to surveillance. On 29 January 1983, in *The Spectator*, Irish journalist Bruce Arnold described the circumstances

which led to him being subjected to surveil
that a Charles Haughey supporter Arnold was
questioned in print Haughey's integrity as a polit
civility, and attacked him both for his policie
policies. He also queried the nature of Haug
Although Haughey threatened Bruce Arnold and hi·
*dent*, with legal action, no legal proceedings were ins
Doherty, McLaughlin and Ainsworth handling justi
courts seem to have become as superfluous as in the l          ⸗ under
Richard Nixon, Spiro Agnew and Attorney General ⸗uin Mitchell. In
Eire, democracy again saw the dangers of corrupted power and surveillance technology. Again democracy survived. Would it have survived
another term of the Haughey government's eccentric style of security
and justice? Can democracy rely on Liffy-Watergates always breaking
before it is too late?

Computer and surveillance technology does not pose a single danger
to democracy, but a series of dangers on different levels. It would be
inappropriate to describe technology as a dagger pointed at the heart
of mankind, a bomb capable of indiscriminate destruction, or even a
sophisticated guided missile. It should be viewed instead as a multi-
purpose weapons system as yet not totally integrated. At present its
power is limited to the destructive capacity of the individual weapons
of the system. Once it becomes fully integrated, its destructive power
will exceed the sum of the parts to a degree at present unimaginable.
Control of the power may not even always rest with government. For
governments to have the power is bad enough, as the examples have
shown; the hands of government are not the only ones, however, to
have access to the levers.

*In conclusion*

# 7
# The Technology of Tyranny

The arms industry has always benefited from mankind's inability to reject what is technically possible because it is socially and morally undesirable. The international nuclear arms race provides the classic example of the difficulties involved in attempting to reverse technological momentum once it has been set in motion. Security technology is closely linked with the arms industry and its success is founded on much the same perverse logic: having developed the technology to threaten society with the one hand, it offers to counter the threat with the other, at a price.

One extract from the advertising literature of a major multinational company (a highly ethical one as far as ethics in the industry go) in the field of esoteric surveillance and security technology defines the problem with unconscious explicitness when it boasts:

> The officers of our firm are *the inventors* of much of *today's eavesdropping equipment* which was *developed for government agencies.* Now *we hold the patents* on the *anti-bugging equipment being introduced to the public* and, of course, available exclusively from our own R & D facilities.

The statement illustrates by 'chicken and egg' the inexorable progression of Big Brother technology. First a disease is cultivated and disseminated, then an antidote is produced; the disease is then made resistant to the antidote, calling for a new antidote; and so on ad infinitum. Once the technology has received the seal of approval from government agencies the way is then clear to manipulate public morality. The justification which leads to the self-perpetuation of the technology rests on the acceptance of a mind-bending falsehood: the premise that parallel lines will converge somewhere this side of infinity.

The commercial logic of the situation is unassailable: if you want the benefit of surveillance or security technology go for the best available; if you wish to overcome the most sophisticated security or surveillance system, go to the salesman who provided it in the first place. Along the corridor from the government agency which wants devices to counter eavesdropping will be another agency which wants a device which cannot be detected; the immovable object countering the irresistible force. Ultimately, of course, the former proves no more immovable than the latter proves irresistible and this merely fuels the race.

The belief that the parallel lines of measure and countermeasure will eventually coalesce into some form of technological social harmony is based on the principle of the ultimate supremacy of machine over man: a supremacy which has as its corollary man's subservience to the technology he created; and a subservience he has historically refused to concede to his fellow man, claiming that such subservience amounted to tyranny. There is no reason to suppose that controls which amount to tyranny in the hands of man will prove to be any less tyrannical when exercised by machines.

The progress of surveillance and information technology in the latter half of the twentieth century clearly demonstrates the erosion of individual liberties which have run parallel with the advance of the technology. Increasing inroads have been made into social freedoms, sometimes visibly but often imperceptibly. More controls are being imposed without any general appreciation that it is happening or of what is being sacrificed.

Before looking at the devices currently available, and in use in varying degrees, in the nebulous world of law enforcement, security – government and private – and increasingly in industry and commerce, it is important to understand the nature of the market forces. The impact made by any particular device will not wholly be governed by the extent to which it is used. The mere existence of a device will be sufficient to generate a reaction in excess of any real impact by its application.

The success and future prosperity of many sections of the security industry, both in government and in the free enterprise sectors are largely determined by the generation of fear in society. Whether the fear is soundly based or spurious is irrelevant. Bugging and debugging is a case in point. No one can possibly know how many eavesdropping devices are in existence, let alone how many are in use at a given time. An educated guess, which is the best that professional sources can provide, is that the use of bugs is more extensive than the public generally realize and considerably less than the security world would generally have us believe.

The mere existence of bugs has generated a whole new area of expertise: debugging. This is, more often than not, an exercise which proves that no bug has been planted, thus ensuring the same degree of confidentiality which would have operated whether the search had taken place or not. At the same time it has to be borne in mind that an unsuccessful search may simply prove that the device which is being sought is more sophisticated than the technology used to find it; and, even if the covert devices are discovered, confidentiality can still not be guaranteed if someone reveals what has transpired. So long as such devices exist technology is nevertheless needed to counter them.

Until society takes steps to curtail and control the process, the security technology industry will remain in the business of self-fulfilment. The futility of so much of the process was highlighted by the revelation in 1982 that a journalist had somehow managed to breach the confidentiality of the communications system in the White House in Washington; a system regarded as near immune to covert penetration as contemporary technology can make it. If the President of the United States cannot be sure of making an untapped phone call what chance have lesser mortals? Although enormous strides have been taken in the technology of covert surveillance, there is much that has changed very little. The technology may have made significant inroads into the art of snooping, but the results obtained will almost invariably depend more on the quality of the agent employed than on the sophistication of any technical apparatus.

The enormous upsurge in the extension of credit in the form of loans, credit cards, mortgages and the like has opened up endless opportunities in the field of status enquiries and debt collection. The growth of government benefits in social security and the general permeation of the state into all aspects of society through tax, grants, immigration, vetting procedures, national security, crime, drugs, pornography laws and countless other ways have made privacy for the individual a thing of the past. Relatively few ordinary citizens have any conception of the extent to which their private lives are the subject of intense interest for one organization or another. Few realize, for instance, how many investigative arms of government, local and central, there are. These range from local government enforcement officers dealing with rent arrears, school attendance, rent rebates, food, health and hygiene, licensing authorities, and other aspects of local community life. The Police, Customs and Excise, Inland Revenue, Ministry of Agriculture, Fisheries and Food, to name but a few, maintain specialist investigators in addition to their normal work complement, as do the Gas and Electricity Boards, the Post Office and British Telecommunications, right up to the security and intelligence services. When those, and many more, are added to the untold numbers in private security firms, industry and commerce, all of them constantly seeking, acquiring, exchanging, recording, and in some way processing information about individuals for one reason or another, it gives some idea of the extent to which information and the product of surveillance activity are in constant circulation.

As one of the major growth industries of the twentieth century, security in all its guises – private investigators, government agents, police, company security – has created a network of information sources which range across the face of society, linked together by ties of mutual aid, current and past associations and a common interest in overcoming the barriers of confidentiality and privacy when these interfere with the immediate objective. In day to day work in the information trawling industry, an agent need rely less on technology than on access to the information network.

The time-honoured professional skills of bribery and deception remain as effective as ever as a means of acquiring confidential information. Doormen, waiters, hotel staff, milkmen, neighbours, caretakers and porters, cleaners, office staff and all the traditional sources are as fertile as they ever were, given suitable motivation financial or otherwise. Despite the proliferation of information stored in official and unofficial locations, and the increased opportunities for gaining access to them, there comes a point where records themselves lack sufficient immediacy and physical surveillance becomes essential. The quality of this form of surveillance will be determined by one primary factor: how much the individual or organization instituting the surveillance is prepared to pay; or in the case of government or police agencies, how many resources are to be allocated to the particular project.

There are a few basic factors which anyone contemplating financing physical surveillance should consider at the outset. Premises are stationary objects and lend themselves more readily to surveillance than people, who are not. Ethical operatives who offer surveillance services will stipulate that results cannot be guaranteed and as a first step will try to establish whether personal surveillance is the most appropriate means to obtain the required information. In the main, responsible operatives will not break the law to secure positive results unless offered a lot of money and some not even then. Less ethical or irresponsible operatives, on the other hand, will often be more willing to break the law to secure the desired result for less money – an attractive proposition for the client. This course has at least three dangers attached to it: if the operative is stupid enough to tell you he is prepared to break the law he is stupid enough to get caught; an operative who will undertake illegal actions on your behalf for money may sell you out for money; and, in either event, you may both end up in prison.

The first thing anyone contemplating the use of private investigation facilities should be aware of is that the whole field is a veritable jungle of evasion and subterfuge. With relatively few exceptions, the majority of private investigation agencies in the United Kingdom are self-employed individuals with no staff. There are no recognized professional standards, although attempts have been made by those in the field to form professional associations with varying degrees of success. In the main, however, they have proved relatively ineffective because no one is quite certain what qualities a professional investigator should have. To that extent at least they are no different from the police who tend to view the concept of professionalism in criminal investigation as an aberration.

Private investigation not unnaturally attracts a high number of former police officers and members of other government security agencies. This background does not necessarily indicate competence, but it is a useful starting point. One reason for scepticism about the professional capabilities of 'international detective agencies' which have no employees other than the proprietor is the likelihood that no single individual has the all-round ability to perform all the services offered equally well. The operative who is highly experienced in the investigation of complex frauds is unlikely to be similarly experienced in the techniques of shadowing or tailing a subject; a former traffic patrolman, on the other hand, may be admirably suited to the latter task, while he may have considerable difficulty in writing any complex report for a client. Those agencies who do have employees tend to suffer from the difficulty of paying permanent employees who have special talents high enough wages to keep them on in the periods when those talents are not required. The obvious advantages of the former police or government agents are that they will have had some experience which is relevant to certain situations they will confront; their former colleagues will give them some access to the records; and, if they meet a situation with which they are unfamiliar, they will know who to contact with the particular expertise required.

The most basic of all forms of surveillance is to place an operative in a convenient, suitable location with instructions to take a note of anyone seen entering or leaving the premises. Providing there is a clear view of the doorway and the operative can be sited unobtrusively that, more or less, will be that. There are a few considerations, however, which influence the procedure. An operative is subject to the calls of nature which must be answered and it is an invariable law of surveillance that, if anything is going to happen, it will happen at that time. An operative who has to stand in the open in a blizzard is unlikely to be unobtrusive; it is usually better to abort a surveillance temporarily than risk its existence being revealed or suspected. Lastly, two pairs of eyes are always better than one.

Two operatives should be used when possible: they should be sheltered from the elements and from observers; and enthusiasm should always take second place to caution. There are a number of useful professional tips for the would-be client and watcher/s. Surveillance always carries the risk of failure whatever resources are utilized. Accepting that a risk factor may be involved, a process of rational deduction may often produce key times when surveillance is most likely to pay dividends. By reducing the number of hours the cost can be cut, and this saving may allow the use of an additional operative.

Static surveillance on any premises is usually best carried out from some other building to which the watcher/s has ready access and which provides internal freedom of movement and an uninterrupted view of the subject premises. Alternatively, official watchers commonly use a nondescript van. This is just what the name suggests: a commonplace van with some special but outwardly unremarkable features. One essential feature is that it should permit whoever is in the van to see out without those outside being able to see in. An added touch of authenticity can be added by opting for a van carrying the identification marks of a public utility. A workvan, an open manhole, a tent, these are all ever-present features of British life and are regularly used as a cover by police and security surveillance teams, and by criminals disconnecting alarm systems to premises. From a surveillance viewpoint a British Telecom cover has the added attraction of good camouflage for electronic equipment. (This is unnecessary for official telephone tapping since this is done at exchanges.) Other forms of electronic or wireless eavesdropping are limited in their effective transmitting ranges and therefore need to have receivers or taping facilities not too far distant.

The next step in the surveillance art has to come to terms with the irritating fact that people tend to move from one place to another. It is worth bearing in mind, however, that many of a subject's movements are relatively insignificant and unrelated to the objective in hand. The more rationality can be applied to the surveillance, the cheaper and more effective it is likely to be. A static observer well located will invariably have an advantage over a watcher who is moving and so be more likely to be wrongfooted. Add to this the increased likelihood of detection by the subject, and some of the advantages of attempting to analyse and anticipate a subject's movements in advance become more apparent.

Most people have a basic pattern to their day's activities: the office worker leaves home at much the same time every day; travels to work by the same means, and probably by the same route; and his destination will be the office. If he is known to leave home at 8 am to catch the

8.30 am commuter train to London, is it vital to follow him from his home to the station? Or can that part be left to chance and the subject picked up at the station by an agent waiting there? Since the 8.30 does not stop until Victoria Station terminus could the subject equally well be picked up there at 9 am? This is more important than it may seem when a client is paying for surveillance.

An agent who has to be at the subject's home in suburbia at 8 am may have to travel for an hour to get there and he will arrive at least half an hour before the appointed time if he is a conscientious agent. This means the client's money meter will start ticking over at the rate of £15-20 per hour from 6 am. By 9 am, when the subject has arrived at Victoria three hours later, the client has already incurred a bill of £45-60 plus travelling expenses – or £225-300 for a five-day week. If it is at all feasible it is more cost effective to employ more operatives for shorter periods than to engage one operative over more hours in any day. It may be possible to identify peak hours during each day when the subject is most likely to engage in whatever it is that interests the client. An errant spouse, for example, is less likely to indulge in extramarital dalliance before work than during or after.

If cost is not a critical factor in determining the resources to be deployed and intensive surveillance is necessary on a 24-hour basis, the minimum effective number of operatives will be unlikely to be less than eight operating in pairs with two pairs functioning at any given time. While it is true that the majority of unofficial surveillance operations are carried out with far less than those numbers, it is also true that many surveillance operations are expensive failures. Most of those which fail do so because too few operatives have been used for them to cope with the unexpected. Clients who value a successful operation above cost should be chary of engaging operators who underestimate the resources required.

A prospective client seeking an effective surveillance team, or alternatively, anyone who suspects that he or she is the subject of such a surveillance operation may profit from some knowledge of tactics involved. One sound piece of advice which can be used as a standard of judgment is that surveillance, while it may not be an art, requires skills which relatively few operators have in equal measure. This means that some of the worst are so bad that their ineptitude may be too unbelievable and thus risk being overlooked on that basis. Some of the best, on the other hand, may be better than one might think possible. Any prospective client should, therefore, demand to know in some considerable detail the structure of the surveillance team to be used and the techniques to be employed. The four principal matters will be the numbers and quality of operatives, the vehicles, communications and technology. A subject on foot in an urban environment should have at least two operatives assigned on foot. Since there is no certainty that the subject will remain on foot each operative should have a backup vehicle conveniently located. It is usually difficult, if not impossible, for a vehicle to follow someone on foot in a town or city and the solution to that problem depends on effective communication between those on foot and those in vehicles. Where intensive surveillance is justified, it will almost invariably be as important to hear what the subject is talking about as it will be to see what he is doing and since it will only rarely be possible for an operative to eavesdrop without risking disclosure, only technical equipment can assist.

There is one overriding principle which governs all surveillance activities: regardless of whether what is being done is legal or illegal, the important thing is not how you do it, but that you do not get caught doing it (unless, of course, some purpose is served in making the subject aware of being under surveillance – extremely useful, for example, as a means of exerting pressure and creating nervousness). It is always important to have a degree of flexibility and to be unobtrusive; it is rarely possible to be either if watchers maintain too close a proximity to the subject. Crowded streets offer more camouflage for watchers than deserted ones, but they also afford more risks of losing sight of the subject. The more crowded the streets the easier it should be to close in and the less crowded the location the more important it will be not to do so. It will often be more advantageous to keep a subject under observation from the opposite side of the street, but it will almost certainly be a disadvantage when the subject turns into another street. The classic position is, therefore, to have one watcher behind the subject and one on the other side of the street. With more than two watchers it becomes easier to ring the changes by having watchers alternate their positions.

Dress will often determine the effectiveness of a watcher. Again flexibility and unobtrusiveness are key factors, with the watcher dressed in the same type of clothing as the subject. A casual shirt, blue jeans and hush-puppies might be appropriate dress for a pub snack at the local 'Fox and Goose', but will probably attract unwelcome attention in the cocktail bar of an exclusive city restaurant where cashmere coats, pinstripes and regimental, club or school ties are the norm.

One vital aid every surveillance operative needs is an adequate supply of cash, a cheque book and credit cards. With these there is at least a fighting chance of keeping up with the subject. Without these indispensable aids an operative may discover the frustration that comes with being stranded on the concourse of King's Cross station while the subject is travelling Inter-City to a distant, unknown destination. It is preferable, of course, to carry sufficient cash to meet any contingency, but this is often impracticable. Chequebooks, bank and credit cards will cope with most emergencies, such as unexpected hotel bills in Glasgow or a candlelit champagne supper in a Soho nightspot. It is worth bearing in mind however, that cheques and credit cards bear names and it can be embarrassing when settling hotel bills if the name differs from the one used to register. It is also worth remembering that a subject under surveillance who becomes suspicious may be able to trace an operative from cheques or credit cards used in places where he has stronger connections than the operative.

There are many tips available for those who wish to be successful in surveillance techniques: some are effective and some are quite useless if not counter-productive. There is one well-known truism: there is no substitute for practice. What one person may carry off successfully in surveillance will not always work for another. The most successful will be those who make the best use of natural cover. Sudden movements and changes of direction are usually dangerous since they tend to attract attention; this applies to the eyes as much as to the body. Some textbooks, for example, urge the watcher never to look directly at the subject when faced by him or her. There are times, however, when to avert the eyes quickly may arouse more suspicion than looking directly at the subject with an expression of vacancy.

Vehicle surveillance depends largely on the driving expertise of those engaged. It demands a high degree of mental and physical co-ordination. Taxis are quite popular with police and security services for surveillance in built-up areas. They have the advantage of being unremarkable, highly manoeuvrable, and accustomed to executing unexpected movements in heavy traffic. Increasingly, however, motorcycles are gaining recognition as the most effective means of tailing. They are less visible and more capable of coping with adverse traffic conditions than other vehicles, with more ability to switch traffic lanes and avoid the most common problem of being held up by traffic lights, buses and slow-moving vehicles.

The greatest single handicap faced by a surveillance driver is the fact that the subject knows the ultimate destination while the following driver usually does not. This inescapable handicap can often be mitigated by the initial steps taken to establish the subject's daily pattern: his clubs, pubs, restaurants and the like. It also helps, of course, if the surveillance driver is familiar with the terrain. An experienced police driver who has driven for years in a particular area will have obvious advantages; in the same way a taxi-driver will often be able to guess the options open or closed to a driver travelling in a certain direction. Good road maps are, of course an invaluable aid to a moving surveillance crew.

Whether the proposed surveillance is based upon static observation at a particular premises or foot and/or vehicle surveillance, a prospective private client usually has little choice other than to accept that the investigating agency will supply a reasonable standard of operative to undertake the task. It is unlikely that the client will be qualified to make a professional appraisal of the quality of operatives. What a client can do, however, is to establish at the outset the standard of communications, if any, which are to be utilized in surveillance. Operatives conducting a surveillance who have no means of direct contact with each other and who cannot be contacted by anyone else are only half operational. More surveillance projects – official and unofficial – have failed through a lack of, or faulty, communications than by any other means.

Given adequate communications links, minor hiccups during surveillance can often be redressed by quick remedial action: a relocation of foot operatives or redirecting backup vehicles, for example. Without communications operatives almost invariably end up hamstrung. Clearly, the more sophisticated the communications system used the better, but something is better than nothing. The prospective client is at least entitled to know.

The most basic requirement for any surveillance project is a centrally manned telephone number which operatives can use to give messages or seek fresh instructions. This may pose some problems for the one-man investigator, should he be part of the surveillance operation. One refinement is to supply operatives with bleepers, which means they can be made aware of attempts to contact them. The advent of Citizen Band radio has considerably increased the scope for two-way communications, providing a degree of confidentiality can be maintained by the use of a prearranged code. Radio-telephones and two-way personal radios are even better.

Once we leave the basics of personnel, vehicles and communications we enter the eerie Orwellian world of surveillance technology which has introduced new dimensions to the shadowy world of 'getting to know you, getting to know all about you'. Before looking at some of the more esoteric devices, the one which has considerably advanced the art of tailing is the electronic directional transmitter. This device can operate either from its own power pack or be attached in a discreet position to the electrical system of the subject's car. For obvious reasons the latter system has significant disadvantages, not least being the danger of discovery while making the attachment. To obviate this problem the transmitter, which can vary marginally in size from one type to another but is generally contained in a metal case about 4 inches X 2 inches X

½ inch, has magnets attached to the top with an antenna protruding from one side. It takes only seconds to fix the transmitter with the magnets in a concealed position on the underside of the subject vehicle. Once activated the transmitter emits a series of multidirectional pulses which are made audible to the receiver as a bleeping tone.

The pulses of the transmitter are audible to the receiver over a range of some three miles and the volume of the receiver will increase as the following vehicle closes on the subject vehicle, reaching a screeching crescendo as the cars draw level. Different sounds are emitted when the subject vehicle turns left or right; the distance between vehicles can be determined with reasonable accuracy by three receiver positions, long or 3-mile range, medium or 1½-mile range, and short-range of about ½-mile; and it is possible to establish whether the vehicle is moving or stationary.

This device clearly refines the art of tailing, making it possible to follow or track a vehicle without even seeing it. It also enables a vehicle to be traced in a built-up area even if it has been garaged or otherwise concealed, providing that the pulse has not been screened by some impenetrable barrier. On the other hand it does have certain problems if the transmitter is discovered and relocated, not the least being the possibility of the receiver vehicle finding itself trying to follow a transcontinental juggernaut across the Channel en route to Zagreb.

In common with most things in surveillance, the most sensational advances are siblings of military and space technology. In optic science they are the offshoots of the satellite 'spy in the sky' industry, and obviate the need to see in the dark. Binoculars by day are still practical aids to surveillance at long range, particularly when the subject is in motion, and it is possible to mount gyroscopic stabilisers on a moving vehicle to compensate for movement. Gyroscopically stabilized binoculars can be attached to cameras if necessary. For observation on a static or localized object or area, the higher magnification powers of telescopes may be preferable if a tripod or other support can be used without revealing the surveillance. The problem, of course, with both conventional binoculars and telescopes is that they only function under normal lighting. Three developments in optic science have overcome this problem.

The first was the discovery of the infra-red beam. It was found that, with an apparatus sensitive to infra-red waves, a person or object can be detected in the dark. With technological man's instinctive grasp of life's priorities, one of the principal advantages found for this was to enable snipers to identify and shoot people in the dark. It is now possible to buy lightweight, hand-held adaptations which enable one to see an object at a range of 500 feet in the dark. The device comes complete with a mounted infra-red light source powered by its own batteries. It has one possible drawback, however: although the infra-red beam is invisible to the naked eye it is visible to anyone else who happens to be scanning with infra-red detection glasses. Since there are only two ends to a single beam it does not take a genius to work out the location of the person operating the beam.

This rather unsatisfactory state of affairs was to some extent alleviated by the next development. This came from the discovery that all darkness is relative. The secret was, therefore, not to introduce fresh artificial light into the darkness but to amplify the existing light – street lighting, human habitation, fires, and the natural light afforded by traffic, for example. There are now goggle masks which fit over the head and allow the watcher to see considerable distances in darkness. The obvious advantage of the light amplification apparatus is that it is completely passive with no beams to lead back to the viewer.

As one might expect, infra-red aficionados did not simply fold up their tents and steal off into the night in the face of this development. They discovered that it is possible to detect and capture the image of an object by the heat it radiates. As a result the surveillance industry now has devices which not only see in the dark but through fog or smoke as well and convert objects into red images on to a black viewing screen. It is also possible to take 'passive' photographs without a conventional light source with the aid of specially treated films. Since every living body, or heat source, gives off its own identifiable print, it is technically possible to take an infra-red picture of an object by residual traces of thermal radiation even when the object has moved away: the outline of a man who has been lying on the ground for some time is one example. Military research has already made progress in producing devices which can distinguish people hiding in undergrowth, and work is going on to refine devices which can effectively penetrate walls. Theoretically at least, if not in practice, there is no technical reason why such devices, or one based on similar principles, should not be available to the surveillance industry in the foreseeable future.

In the meantime surveillance must rely on the technology presently available and, in the field of eavesdropping, the problems of walls and distance have long been overcome. The principle is simple: if you want to hear what someone is saying, place a microphone as close to his mouth as possible, or, otherwise, conceal the microphone. Microphones, or bugs, used for covert surveillance are often described as sub-miniature and their ultimate success, or failure, depends largely on their sensitivity, size and range, which dictate their suitability for a given task. (A major supply company for bugs in the United Kingdom warn prospective clients in their catalogue that 'it is an offence to transmit any radio signal without Home Office licence in the UK. The Home Office *never* grant licences for use with surveillance transmitters.' They describe the range of 'micro-transmitters' they sell as 'the classic "bug" '; at the same time they warn, 'surveillance transmitters should not be used in the UK'. Quite so!)

Bugs come in two basic forms: there are those which need wires attached and those which do not. Dynamic and crystal microphones require no current since they generate an electrical current when hit by soundwaves, and this self-generated current can be amplified or transmitted to a nearby radio. Condenser microphones do require a current and they operate by causing variations in the current which equate to the sounds that approach the mike. Since condensers do not have to produce a current but merely change the form of an existing one they tend to be more sensitive than the dynamic variety. On the other hand they tend to be less selective in screening unwanted sounds from other directions whereas a feature of dynamic microphones is that they can be either omnidirectional or so designed as to pick up single-direction sound.

The scope of bugs is limitless. As most people are probably aware, these sub-miniature bugs can be hidden in, or made to resemble, tie clasps, tie pins, pens, sugar cubes, buttons, cuff-links, wristwatches, flowers, light sockets, and anything else that one cares to think of – providing you accept that these small bugs have a limited range. One widely publicized design in the 1960s in America was the 'martini olive' which had a cocktail stick as an antenna. Whatever method of bugging is eventually chosen, two basic factors remain constant: who it is that is to be bugged; and the best place to do it, depending on what is wished to be heard.

A place which is controlled by the watcher is obviously the easiest to prepare for eavesdropping or covertly recording conversation. The scope for planting bugs in one's own premises is limitless given that microphones can be secreted almost anywhere. Tape recorders can be hidden in desk drawers, cocktail cupboards or filing cabinets; microphones in telephones, chairs, lamps, air vents, desk tops; and there are few problems with hiding any wiring used in conjunction with the transmitters, amplifiers or recording devices. It has to be remembered that it is also possible for anyone else to introduce similar microphones or tape-recorders by way of a pen, tie-pin, wristwatch. Equally, both parties can introduce warning devices which will indicate if any active bugs are present. Devices are now sold in packages which incorporate both device and anti-device: for example, one company markets a desk top cigar humidor, for the host, where cigars lie on a removable tray under which is a voice-activated recording device, a telephone monitor, and a detector which warns of concealed body transmitters; for the visitor they provide a wristwatch which serves as a bug detector together with a small pocket tape-recorder – a combination which they describe as the 'ultimate miniature privacy system'.

Although such forms of audio-surveillance probably account for most incidents of bugging in the United Kingdom, they are generally regarded as being at the amateur end of the spectrum. The professional sector accommodates the person wishing to eavesdrop without being present. Given that some access to the location is possible any number of sub-miniature microphones can be concealed in the range of places already described. It may sometimes be possible to secrete a mini tape-recorder on location, perhaps in a briefcase for example. Special briefcases are readily available (at prices ranging from around £250-500 and upwards depending on the level of electronic sophistication required). These specialized briefcases can be obtained to include such features as: built-in voice-activated (VOX) microphones; 'touch' on/off controls; LED display; high performance surveillance amplifiers which are also suitable for use in conjunction with external microphones; and slimline cassette recorders capable of recording as much as six hours' conversation. A cassette recorder operating under the 'control' of a voice-activated microphone can record whole days of conversation. Voice-activated relays will sometimes have problems which can undermine the whole purpose of the bugging operation: if they are not sensitive enough, they may fail to activate the recorder if the voice is too low to register; and if they are over-sensitive they may be activated by background voices which will waste the tape. To overcome this there are available remote control, or 'command', transmitters which will activate bugs or tape recorders from a distance of about a mile.

The range of readily available bugs in the UK is as ingenious as it is varied in the field of self-contained battery-powered transmitters. They include such devices as: a 4 inches X 2 inches X 1 inch voice-activated, battery- powered transmitter, with a battery life of up to 1200 hours and fully adjustable VOX sensitivity setting, transmitting between 109 and 120 megahertz, with a 1-mile range, costing about £150; a 3½ inches X 2¼ inches X 1 inch, remote-controlled transmitter with 2000 hours of battery life while dormant, with a range of 1 mile, at a cost including the command transmitter of about £500; and a 3.5cm X 1.3cm X 1.2cm (including battery) sub-miniature transmitter with up to 60 hours continuous battery life, transmitting for a range of 600 metres maximum between 109 and 120 megahertz. Similar transmitters come in the form of Sheaffer pens complete with ink at about £150 and fully operational pocket calculators at about the same price. For something more permanent there are the two-way and three-way standard 13 amp adaptor wall plugs with built-in transmitters, operating off the mains electricity and using the earth wire as an aerial. These fully functional adaptor plugs transmit on a pre-set frequency and have a range of between 800 and 1200 metres; they cost between £80-140. No house or office should be without one!

The time-honoured practice of putting one's ear to the wall to hear what was going on in an adjacent room, or holding a wine glass between the ear and the wall for better reception, has now been refined by the Electronic Stethoscope. A sensitive microphone inside a stethoscope leading to a strong amplifier is considerably more effective for listening through thin walls than the ear or even the wine glass. Keyhole eavesdropping has become much more accessible with the advent of tube microphones. The tube microphone operates equally effectively under the door, through cracks in the wall, ceiling, window, or indeed any convenient hole; if there is no available aperture then one can be made. An aperture the size of a pinhole will suffice. Given that drilling through the dividing wall is necessary, there are a number of important considerations: the appearance of a clearly visible hole in the wall; any drilling from the other side of the dividing wall will almost certainly deposit debris inside the target area which may equally invite discovery. The drilling must therefore be stopped short of penetration into the target area and the penetration completed with needles.

Tube microphones can be made either from flexible or inflexible tubing. According to one published source a tube microphone can be constructed as follows: take a metal film container of about the size used for 35mm film with a lid; drill two holes, one in the lid and one in the side of the can; place a layer of cork on the bottom of the can; set a dynamic miniature microphone element firmly on the cork and extrude the wires from the microphone through the hole in the side of the can; procure a piece of thin, flexible plastic tubing with an inside diameter of ⅛ inch, or less; having located the hole in the microphone element place one end of the plastic centrally over it and glue the end of the plastic tube in place; feed the loose end of the plastic tube through the hole previously drilled in the lid of the can, but do not replace the lid at this stage; pack the inside of the can full of fibreglass resin to the top of the can; with the fibreglass hardened and the lid securely fixed, sound can now only enter the can through the tube. It only remains to attach the wires from the side of the can to an amplifier; push the end of the tubing through a hole; what you have, so we are told, is a tube microphone.

The professional can use the Spike Mike which is a form of contact microphone. A more orthodox form of contact microphone, costing about £100, is usually described as a Contact Window Transmitter and it is also suitable for doors. Measuring approximately 2¼ inches × 1½ inches × ⅞ inch including its battery, it can be stuck on to a window or door and monitors through vibrations the activity within. It transmits for a distance of about 800 metres on 109-120 megahertz. The principle of contact microphones is based on the fact that walls, windows, doors and the like vibrate to sound. The contact microphone takes those vibrations and reproduces the sound which created the vibrations in the first place.

The Spike Mike is another microphone which is useful for circumventing the sound-deadening effects of thick walls. Drilling is required but, unlike the tube microphone which must have a hole penetrating the target side of the wall, the Spike Mike need not break the surface on the target side. A hole is drilled into the surface of the dividing wall on the surveillance side, stopping before going all the way through. A spike is then driven some distance into the undrilled section of the wall without the spike breaking through into the target side of the wall. The microphone then slides on to the spike which acts as a sounding board for the vibrations in the same way as the wall. The essential things are to ensure that the microphone is in full contact with the spike, and to ensure the spike is not in contact with the sides of the hole which has been drilled since this will dissipate and weaken the vibrations.

It may not be possible to get close enough to the target area, in which case the directional or rifle microphone is a useful alternative. With this device, long popular in use in film and television studios and for outside broadcasts, conversation can be picked up at a distance of some hundreds of feet. By pointing it at a window, for example, it is possible to distinguish what is being said in a room from about 90 feet away. There are difficulties, not the least being unwanted noise. This has been overcome, to some extent, by frequency equalizers which, when hooked up to microphones, amplifiers or tape recorders, can boost or exclude sound – boost speech and exclude machine noise. One make, the Sennheiser rifle microphone, is sold by security device suppliers at £125-470. On the other hand, the DIY eavesdropper can make one.

The first stage is to get 36 pieces of ⅜ inch diameter aluminium tubing in descending lengths, each one 1 inch shorter than its predecessor, ranging from 36 inches to 1 inch long. Starting with the 36 inch piece, a symmetrical bundle is made using the lengths in descending order of size and keeping one end of the bundle flush, and gluing the pieces together to keep the bundle intact. The next step is to find a funnel which will fit as near as possible the dimensions of the flush end of the aluminium tubing. A sub-miniature microphone element is then placed in the neck of the funnel with the wires running out through the neck. Glue the microphone element and the wires in place, and using a good quality rubberized compound, cover the air space around the microphone element and the wires, sealing the entire assembly. Fit the flush ends of the aluminium tubing into the funnel and seal all the spaces with the compound. If the funnel does not take the flush end of the tubes immediately, the funnel can be hammered into shape; obviously, however, any hammering should be done before fitting the microphone element into the neck of the funnel.

Once the entire assembly has been airsealed, all that remains to be done is to run the output wires into an amplifier and mount the unit on a camera tripod. It is then merely a question of pointing the device in the required direction, although a few minor adjustments may have to be made. Wind may vary the direction of sound waves or, indeed, overpower the sound. To catch the soundwaves it will be necessary to 'pan' the microphone: unwanted sound can be excluded by plugging a cork into the particular tubes carrying the unwelcome noise by a process of elimination, and a piece of cheesecloth draped over the end of the tubes will reduce wind noise. There is one vitally important technical matter which must be borne in mind when an amplifier and a microphone are used together: all microphones have an output impedance and all amplifiers and transmitters an input impedance, and the two should be matched. Should the microphone have a higher or lower impedance than the amplifier, a transformer can be used to bring them into balance.

Developments in laser technology are now threatening to outdate conventional directional microphones. Infra-red laser beams, invisible to the naked eye, can be directed through a window at a range of up to a mile, or on to a sounding board such as a wall mirror, and used to record conversations in the room. The biggest boon to the audio-surveillance industry came with the telephone. With the aid of telephone taps, it is no longer necessary to get anywhere near the target area, providing that there is a telephone and that the subject uses it indiscreetly.

The most elementary form of telephone tapping involves finding a convenient location somewhere along the telephone wiring circuit. The first step is to strip off the main insulation cable and, having identified the two active wires, strip off the secondary insulation thus baring the wires without breaking them. A set of high impedance headphones are then attached to the exposed wires using a capacitor for one of the two attachment links. It is then just a matter of waiting for the telephone to be used. The obvious disadvantage of this form of tapping is the requirement to listen constantly with the headphones. This problem has been overcome by using transformers which feed the conversations into tape recorders and relays which activate remote control start switches on the recorder, ensuring that the tape runs only when the telephone is in use.

The two most common telephone bugs are the parallel and the series bugs. The parallel bug is attached in the way described and comes in two forms: one draws its power directly from the telephone line, and the other is independently powered by battery. The line-powered parallel bug will run indefinitely from the current on the telephone line, but because it feeds constantly from the current it is easily detectable. The battery powered parallel bug uses none of the telephone power but requires batteries to be changed or recharged at intervals. Series bugs on the other hand call for the telephone wire to be cut and routed through the bug. In this way any power loss is minimal and only then when the telephone is in use.

With access to the target telephone, a room and telephone monitor transmitter can be installed. This serves a dual function: when the telephone is in use it transmits both incoming and outgoing conversations; and when the telephone is not in use it transmits the sounds in the vicinity of the transmitter. It can be placed in the telephone or anywhere along the wire (the wall junction box for example), and can draw power either from the telephone wire or from batteries which will automatically charge themselves from the wire. They will transmit to a range of up to 800 metres.

Perhaps the most notorious of all telephone bugs are the infinity transmitters. Known variously as tele-infinity monitors or infinity transmitters, these are units which combine a microphone amplifier, switching device and transmitter. They are capable of picking up conversation within a 30-foot radius of their location and transmitting it directly over telephone lines, in theory at least, anywhere in the world providing there is a direct dialling facility to the doctored telephone. The entire unit can be attached to the telephone wire anywhere along the circuit inside the premises, or anywhere outside if an extension microphone can be secreted in the telephone or on the line. The bug remains inert until activated by a signal which is transmitted by dialling the appropriate telephone number and sending the electronic signal. The bug reacts to the signal by stopping the telephone from ringing and, in turn, transmitting along the line any conversation then in progress in the vicinity of the microphone. The device does not interfere with the normal use of the telephone. Obviously, the infinity bug will not transmit conversations on the subject telephone.

Surveillance gadgetry includes miniature cameras – a pocketsize Minox miniature camera with pull-push operation can be bought with an adaptor for linking with high-powered binoculars and a carrying chain which corresponds to distance settings on the focus dial for close-up photographs of documents and printed pages. The Rollei, Minolta, Yashica Atoron, all with their individual characteristics and price variations, can each facilitate surreptitious photography. Clearly there is nothing necessarily sinister about miniature cameras; miniaturization has many innocuous advantages not least in the sense of convenience. Anyone who wishes to know how the security industry defines a miniature camera need only look at the advertising literature: a microminiature professional spy system for undetected photography. It shoots extra-long distance or 8 inch close-ups and takes photographs around corners while the operator remains hidden!

With all the bugging apparatus available it may be unwise to use your own voice on the telephone. The Electronic Handkerchief – 'This incredible telephone turns a woman's voice into a man (sic) and a man's voice into something else entirely. Anyone's natural speaking voice is completely unrecognisable. Used for business (?) and to avoid harass-ment' – offers you instant disguise.

Those who operate in the security world when they are not practising deceit are trying to combat it in one form or another. The Polygraph lie-detector was technology's answer to the search for truth. The trouble with Polygraph machines is that they involve attaching the human subject to the instrument, demanding either compliance or compulsion of the subject. Technology has been able to overcome the problem by replacing the Polygraph with the Voice Stress Analyser or Psychological Stress Evaluator which does not require attachments to the human body.

The human voice, it seems, is modulated by physiological reaction induced by stress such as that caused by lying. Whereas the Polygraph operated on the principle of detecting the stress level by measuring the reaction of the body to stress, the PSE records the voice. The device then filters out the audible speech and displays the stress levels. Having first established a stress norm by analysing the response to a series of innocuous questions such as 'Is today Friday?' (making sure that today is Friday), the machine can in theory identify untruthful answers by displaying an increase in stress activity. The problem is that even their protagonists concede that these machines have a substantial failure rate, simply because some subjects can lie without experiencing any stress while others suffer stress even if they are not lying.

Of all the security technology available closed circuit television has enjoyed the most spectacular growth of all and, in the unrestrained hands of the police and commercial security industry, poses a major threat to every traditional concept of privacy and individual liberty. It also provides the clearest possible evidence of the risk society is running by failing to understand, or attempting to control, the growth of security and the virtually unchallenged control over the development and application of its technology. Regardless of social consequences, driven by the commercial attraction of making what is technically possible socially desirable, the security industry is foisting on the public a technological tyranny.

# 8
# Thin Trees with
# High Foliage

Most reasonable critics would concede that the police are not sufficiently accountable. The heat generated by public controversy over police accountability makes it all the more incredible that so little concern is expressed over the lack of almost any public accountability by the private security industry. As an industry, security has shown itself to have an insatiable appetite for growth and to feed on the exercise of power and authority. What is clear is that the private security industry is exercising more influence on the future direction of British society and making more impact on social attitudes than either it acknowledges or the public realize.

The difficulty of defining precisely what the security industry comprises means that estimates of its extent vary wildly. The British Security Industry Association, BSIA, is the major trade organization in the security field, with 73 affiliated security companies in 1982. These were engaged in activities such as cash-in-transit, guard and patrol, locks and safes, and manufacturing and installing alarm systems. BSIA claimed the 39,500 personnel employed by its membership represents 95 per cent of the industry in those fields. BSIA admits, however, there are hundreds of smaller companies and firms engaged in those and similar activities who are not affiliated. It is obviously in BSIA's commercial interest to give the impression of speaking for 95 per cent of the industry whether it does or not.

Thousands of security personnel are directly employed by firms, companies, and major corporations throughout the United Kingdom. Factories, offices, shops, hotels, hospitals, airports and seaports all employ security staff. There is hardly a shopping precinct in any major city or town where a security uniform is not to be seen. Even that is too narrow a view of the security industry. On top of this a vast range of technology is manufactured and marketed in the name of security, an alphabet that includes: access control systems for premises with identification procedures based on photographs, identification cards and fingerprints; alarm systems: audible and silent, internal and external, contact breaks, beams and rays, electronic and ultrasonic, triggered by contact noise or heat; ballistic protection: bullet-resistant jackets, shirts and vests, arms and ammunition; bars and grilles for doors, windows and kiosks; body search equipment and scanners for explosives and metal detection; cases, booby-trapped with dye-sprays, extending arms and alarms activated by releasing the handle release catch, for conveying cash, documents or valuables; special security doors, reinforced windows and fences, anti-vandal fences and microwave sensor barriers; field telephone systems; fingerprint equipment; floodlights and high-intensity lamps; bullet-proof and shock-resistant glass; homing devices; personal identity discs and cards; handcuffs; keys and locks; multi-purpose security control and monitoring systems; one-way glass mirrors for covert surveillance; night vision, infra-red surveillance equipment; personal protection devices – blinding lights and alarms; portable X-ray equipment, public address systems, radar equipment and radio communications systems; revenue control systems – security cash tills, cash dispensers, photographic recording apparatus; riot equipment – roller shutters, grilles and bars; safes, vaults and strongrooms; security boxes; security vehicles – armoured vans and multi-defence cars; anti-shoplifting devices; surveillance apparatus – listening devices and anti-bugging systems; video and closed circuit television systems; voice and data scramblers to prevent unauthorized interception during transmission – counter-devices to make unauthorized interception possible.

Alongside all this is an array of related services: security consultancies and private investigation agencies; test purchasing agencies; bodyguards and even one or two agencies which specialize in the esoteric field of ransom negotiations. There are services which, directly or indirectly, fuel the industry – insurance companies, loss assessors and loss adjustors; credit finance companies, rental companies, cash and credit card companies, a whole range of ostensibly unrelated interests which exert enormous influence on security practices and, therefore, on our daily lives.

It is widely accepted that the private security industry comprises some 250,000 people. In his paper to the 1980 International Fire, Security and Safety Exhibition and Conference (IFSSEC) James Anderton used the number 250,000, excluding 'many other security agencies and private police forces'. That number alone represents almost double the strength of the conventional police forces in the United Kingdom.

The largest security company in the United Kingdom is Securicor, which in 1982 disclosed an annual turnover of £194 million. Employing about 24,000 personnel in the UK and some 12,000 overseas, Securicor roughly equates with the largest police force in the country, London's Metropolitan Police. Some indication of its logistical capability is demonstrated by its operation and ownership of the largest non-governmental radio network in the United Kingdom. The second largest security company, Group 4, employing 5500 personnel, exceeds in numbers the Merseyside Constabulary with its 1981 complement of 4646 officers. The annual reports for 1981 by the Chief Constables of Merseyside, Cumbria, Warwickshire, Tayside, North Yorkshire, Gwent, Norfolk, Dumfries and Galloway were published in the *Police Review* on 20 August 1982. They showed a combined total for these forces of 11,537 officers: less than half the personnel employed by Securicor.

What the figures represent is a major switch in social emphasis and resources from public to private policing; from policing over which the general public may have some control to policing over which the public has no control. It is an indictment of the failure of the police, but much more of successive governments who over the years have failed to provide a police service directly relevant to the problems of society: more specifically, problems as they have been identified by powerful, and not so powerful, private organizations which have the means and the freedom to apply their own solutions regardless of the wider social implications.

As this alternative system of policing has grown, so increasingly has its collective power to impose its own security rationale and perceptions on an acquiescent society. Despite considerable unease about the growth of private security within the industry itself, the police and in Parliament and despite periodic reviews by the Home Office and other interested parties, the official attitude remains one of irresponsible complacency. In February 1982 the Home Office announced that a review had revealed no reason to introduce any regulatory or licensing controls. It was content to rely on self-regulation within the industry in the form of an internal BSIA inspectorate intended to establish and enforce standards within affiliated companies. However successful this may prove with the BSIA companies, what it cannot do is challenge the fundamental issues of private security in society.

Like 'police', the word 'security' has overtones of rectitude and substance which are often without foundation. It is often overlooked that private security operates just as effectively, and often more so, to protect what is evil in society as what is good. In the same way it provides an illusion of security where none exists. An authoritarian police state may appear to provide security, but the security enjoyed by the people is more illusory than real. As ever more of the conventional policing role has been ceded to private security, the public have increasingly been losing their right to decide their quality of life. Ethical and moral values are gradually being eroded and submerged in commercial security interests. Individual rights and liberties are being abrogated by an industry which has no higher duty than to operate profitably for its clients.

To attempt to justify this, one can point to the statistical failure of police and conventional law enforcement agencies to keep pace with crime in society. Statistically at least, at a time when the police are being paid more than ever before, and have more personnel than ever before, they are consistently presenting the bemused public with a diminishing clear-up rate at a time of rising crime. The police are withdrawing rapidly from property protection to be replaced by privately funded security personnel. There is a body of opinion in the police service which does not believe the police are capable of affording the public protection from burglaries, and for a period in the Metropolitan Police this became a reality. After Sir Robert Mark's dismemberment of the CID the importance formerly attached to the prevention and investigation of burglaries evaporated. The police investigation system virtually disappeared to be replaced by little more than an administrative recording system for identifying stolen property if it ever came to light. Since the 1960s, shoplifting has become virtually the exclusive province of private security. The police have no real role to play other than that of processing shoplifters apprehended by private security or shop staff. Industrial estates, shopping precincts, housing estates, schools, among others, are tended by private security organizations.

Although little public concern is expressed at such trends, the security industry is conscious of the danger if the public should ever wake up to what is happening. To try to placate the suspicious, the industry's highly sophisticated propaganda machinery reiterates the platitude that the service complements the police role. What is happening, in fact, is that private security in many areas of society is replacing the police. Britain has traditionally enjoyed a reputation for having fewer police per head of population than many other countries. If private security personnel are added to conventional police forces, the ratio changes rather dramatically from somewhere in the region of 1-400 to 1-150 or less. What is significant is not merely the statistical drama portrayed by the new ratio, it is the time-scale in which the change took place. In a matter of twenty years or so British society has seen a change in its internal security which has taken it from one of the least policed societies in the world to one which has a security apparatus numerically almost on a par with Soviet Russia – with barely a ripple of public disquiet. As the ratio of police/security personnel to public has increased, so crime has also risen. The more police and security, the more crime has increased and the less crime has been detected. In addition to personnel, there has from the 1960s been a quantum leap in the quantity and nature of security technology. In defiance of natural logic and social prudence, the interpretation of crime prevention produced by vested commercial interests, encouraged by police chiefs anxious to avoid charges of incompetence, continues unchallenged.

Since the 1960s, the private security industry has succeeded in establishing a complicated and extensive network of operatives, communications, transport and administrative backup facilities; and it has deployed a plethora of sophisticated electronic and computerized control and surveillance technology at every level of society free from any state or legislative restraints. It is evolving and imposing virtually unchallenged its own security mores regardless of the inevitable social consequences.

Although subject to the same laws as private citizens, private security cannot expect sympathetic consideration from a client-paymaster if moral niceties or legal technicalities are allowed to interfere with results. Despite the sanctimonious rhetoric from the industry's PR machine, private security is a powerful and influential force of reaction against individual liberty and social reform.

Existing resources as they are currently being deployed are incapable of stabilizing, far less of turning back, a rising lawlessness in British society. If it is accepted that the present level of crime is intolerable, society is faced with the choice of two solutions: on the one hand it can opt to increase the human resources and the technology deployed against crime; or it can make a concerted attempt to rationalize and restructure the existing resources.

Conventional wisdom in some police circles, as articulated by hardline officers such as James Anderton, argues for increasing police resources, centralizing and consolidating police autonomy, and granting stronger police powers. Not unnaturally this finds favour in the security industry since expansion in the police service augurs well for security too. In fact, free from the constraints on unlimited growth of conventional police forces, the private security industry, geared to growth through commercial profits, is already institutionalizing what hardline authoritarians in the public services can only hope to achieve by public persuasion.

Unquestionably, many police and security elements are genuinely convinced of the need for additional resources. At the same time, even the most intelligent, articulate and persuasive of advocates for increased resources, when pressed, concede that they cannot quantify in numbers, or cost, the resources which would have to be deployed to make any significant impact on crime in society. More significantly, neither can they define the extent of repression. Given an open-ended commitment by the public and government, if human and technical resources are

ploughed into law enforcement regardless of cost, and repressive measures applied regardless of social consequences, crime trends could be
altered. By the same criterion, however, there is also a level at which
the consequences of such commitment would become unacceptable to
a free people both on the grounds of cost and at the degree of repression.
Fortunately, those who advocate such commitment have so far been
unable to convince enough people that the potential benefits could be
reaped before reaching the level of unacceptability.

In essence, this is at the heart of the debate which is being conducted
within and outside the police service: a debate which is polarized between
those who favour strong law enforcement and those who see a more
tolerant, broadly based 'community policing' policy as the best long
term hope for an evolving society. It is a debate which in many ways
the private security industry is making increasingly irrelevant by pre-
emption. The industry is usurping the right of a free society to exercise
democratic choice in the way it will be policed, by providing an
alternative to those who can afford to opt out of the chosen system and
by offering, to those who can pay, the means of supplementing the
community system. It caters for sectional interests whether or not these
interests coincide with those of the community at large.

Funded by private money and with police collusion, the security
industry is foisting on society an interpretation of crime prevention
which flies in the face of practically every lesson learned by law
enforcement agencies and criminologists in the latter half of the twentieth
century. The industry perpetuates the myth that some form of effective
security in the long term can be attained by the creation of technological
or defensive barriers within society, which are largely incompatible with
democratic freedoms. They create divisions between those who can
afford to apply them and those who cannot.

The only form of security that has any relevance in a social context
is one which regards society as a homogenous entity entitled to an
equality of protection. The divisions created by the security industry are
not designed to advance this equality but to encourage dual standards
which have the effect of further dissipating social resources. The most
incredible aspect of the phenomenal rise of private security in Britain is
its unquestioned acceptance. There have been a number of direct
consequences, such as the withdrawal of police from traditional areas
of activity – property protection, for example. Police released from
property protection can now be employed in public relations roles. The
effectiveness of a police officer patrolling a factory estate could be
measured by the amount, or lack, of crime on the estate: the effectiveness
of the same officer engaged in public relations cannot be assessed. Given
a choice, who is surprised if the latter is preferred to the former?

There has been a concerted campaign over the years by the police and government to shift the emphasis of responsibility for the protection of the public away from the state and transfer it to the individual. The main thrust of crime prevention campaigns has been to instill in the public a sense of personal responsibility for self-protection. There is some merit in this policy as an element of a coherent strategy against crime, but there are limits. The emphasis on personal responsibility becomes an abdication of the state's responsibility for the protection of the weak in society. Commercial security, individual responsibility and security technology can never be properly regarded as an adequate substitute for conventional policing, yet officialdom and vested interests increasingly present them as socially compatible alternatives.

The 250,000-strong private security industry and a multi-million pound investment has done nothing to reverse or stabilize crime trends in society. It has not done so to date and it will not do so in the future in a free society because, quite simply, it is not designed to do these things. The whole philosophy of the security industry is predicated on the assumption of a growth in crime and a corresponding growth in private security and its associated technology. Unless crime, and the response to crime, conforms to that scenario the industry is dead. In allowing the industry to evolve and impose its own concepts and truths, society has allowed a ravenous beast to grow with no guarantee that it can be controlled when the need arises.

Not all security personnel and not every function performed are useless and unnecessary, nor is its technology all junk gadgetry. But much is. Advanced technology is short-circuiting the process of consultation and consensus, and society is in danger of having the tenuous social balance of compromise and consent destroyed. Technology is creating new social tensions faster than they can be assimilated. In the battle to decide whether man or machine will hold dominion in society, private security, allied to the technology of surveillance, is the most powerful and persuasive influence in society today for ensuring that man will be subordinate to the machine. Under the spurious guise of offering society technical apparatus for protecting it from the incursions of crime, private security is, in effect, perpetrating the ultimate crime on society: enslavement.

So long as man is allowed to retain individual freedom and independence of thought and action, technology can make no significant impact on crime, unless it is allowed to control the individual to an extent which is incompatible with a democratic society. By the time technology has effectively curbed crime it will have imposed a tyranny which will be far more unacceptable than any crimes from which it will protect society. Not surprisingly, such reasoning is anathema to the private security industry, but fortunately for them and its growth potential, the public seem unaware of the threat.

Based on the estimated 250,000 personnel engaged in security related functions, the annual investment in the private sector must be considerably in excess of £2000 million as compared to about £2500 million spent on conventional policing in 1982. Police costs are already causing budgetary concern as police numbers increase and salaries begin to outstrip those of previously comparable workers. Regardless of operational considerations, any government committed to maintaining police salaries at their present level and to making significantly greater human and technical resources available to the police service will find itself faced with a major problem of finance. Economic recession creates social tensions; the more social tensions there are the greater is the incentive to strengthen the police. The more resources allocated to policing the less there will be available for other public services, and the more politically sensitive will be the decision to allocate such additional resources to police. The same considerations do not apply to the private security industry.

According to some estimates the industry multiplied by a factor of six between 1970 and 1980 to a cost of £2-2.5 billion. Assuming a growth rate of only a third of that between 1980 and 1990 private security could comprise 500,000 personnel and cost £4-5 billion in present-day terms. This seems perfectly feasible when crime, violence and public disorder are constantly being shown to increase as fast or faster than the resources to combat them. Nothing like those figures would be acceptable if similar projections were proposed for the police. They would be rejected out of hand by the public on the grounds of cost and their implications for liberty. There are no such constraints on private security.

Far too little is known about the social consequences of the massive, selective public investment in security. What is clear, however, is that the disparity in resources between the public and private systems of 'policing' militates against the public's capacity to mount an effectively organized and co-ordinated campaign against socially disruptive elements. Now that all the resources currently subscribed by society are deployed by private individuals or organizations who decide the priorities. The priorities are based on the immediate interests of those concerned, not necessarily those of the community. What makes the situation even more disturbing is that these private interests have themselves created the problems. When innovations, such as open displays in shops, do not conform to the human reality, the logical and responsible response is to adjust the innovation and not to try to force mankind to change. Yet we now have the lunatic situation where excessive security resources are deployed to combat shoplifting – more than are deployed to deal with inner city muggings.

Effective crime prevention demands a close appraisal of the conditions and circumstances governing particular forms of crime: if there is food available, the only crime prevention measure which will stop a starving man from stealing food is to feed him. In this context, it is not theft which is the crime and the thief the criminal: it is the denial of food which is the crime and society the criminal. Crime prevention and security must have regard for the human condition. Free from public constraints, private security exaggerates the social importance of its own perceptions of crime and applies its own remedies. This has obscured rational social appraisal of cause and effect. It has distorted some of the fundamental realities about crime and the relative social significance of one form of crime against another.

Retail security has been one of the major growth areas of private security. In 1973 Home Office statistics and estimates for shop thefts by customers or staff placed the value in the region of £190 million per annum. By 1982 estimates produced by retail trade and security organizations place the annual total in excess of £1000 million – this despite roughly a six-fold increase in private security during the same time-scale. One major London store alone budgets £500,000 a year for security. It is the public of course who pay, indirectly, for this security in increased prices.

£500 million represents one-fifth of the total allocation of public funds to the police service in 1981. At the same time, a proportion of the police allocation is also applied to retail thefts: investigating offences and processing offenders. The public gives the retail industry £500 million a year to decide on its own security priorities, while it gives the entire police service only three times that to deal with murder, mayhem, riots, robberies and all other forms of social order or disorder. The £500,000 budget of the one London store would pay for about 35 police officers, the equivalent of what society employs to police a town of some 10,000 inhabitants. Looked at in that context it is hard to believe that the social consequences of shop thefts are really so overwhelmingly serious as the retail and security industries paint them. Even if they are, there is no evidence that any of the measures being employed are having any preventative effect on the rate of shop crime.

Corporate, public and other forms of fraud may account for anything between £5-9000 million annually. In one major scandal during the 1970s, it was revealed that the Crown Agents had dissipated some £250-300 million of public funds by a combination of fraud, corruption, and criminal or near criminal incompetence. This one matter, therefore, accounted for the equivalent of 25 per cent of all losses from shop thefts in 1981. Nevertheless, it is unlikely that the entire allocation of national police resources invested in specialist fraud investigators in any single year amounts to £15 million. Private security and surveillance technology are not the only means available to prevent shop thefts, but investigation is the only means to deal with complex fraud. There is something innately wrong with social priorities where £500 million can be spent to prevent the theft of cans of beans from shops, yet not enough can be found to investigate or prosecute the perpetrators of multi-million pound frauds for lack of funds.

Not all shop thefts can be prevented by acceptable measures, and, for those that can, there is no single panacea. A decline in honesty is not the only influential factor in shoplifting. It is significant that the private security industry and shoplifting have grown side by side in society: it is not clear which is cause and which effect. There were other changes which are ignored by current retail and security philosophies: changes which have also coincided with increased awareness of shop thefts as a major social problem.

Since the end of the Second World War, in place of individually owned shops entrepreneurial innovation has successively provided multiple stores, chain stores, supermarkets and hypermarkets. Self-service replaced personalized service and open display cabinets took the place of counters. Shop managers replaced shopkeepers, sales assistants were replaced by stackers, merchandizers, check-out attendants and cashiers. Time and motion studies were applied by efficiency experts and the concept of personal service was declared redundant. Shops were given over to the fast product, fast turnover and the fast buck. Customer relations was replaced by programmed managerial techniques based on statistical percentages, mathematical probabilities and market research surveys. Shops were made impersonal, catering for dehumanised customers, who were conditioned to want what was on offer under the conditions they were offered.

Modern advertising, marketing and merchandizing skills produced a consumer society with the emphasis on the disposable product. Market research deduced that the packaging and wrapping were more important that the contents. Pervasive and sophisticated advertising through television, newspapers and magazines created an acquisitive society: a general public conditioned to impulsive or compulsive buying. In addition to being encouraged to buy what they needed, they were brainwashed into believing that they needed what they had been conditioned to want. Indiscriminate advertising made no distinction between those who could afford to buy and those who had no means. Temptation was the name of the game, and instant credit facilities were designed to make the temptation irresistible. The public were encouraged to take what they wanted when they wanted it whether they could afford it or not. Under such circumstances theft was merely an extension of the process. The cumulative effect of the system was to produce a whole new class of people in Britain: the shoplifting class.

Membership of this new social class was not confined to those who had always seen crime as a way of life. It now encompassed the oldest and the youngest in society, the poor and the rich, the uneducated and the intellectual from all classes. The growth of shoplifting was a direct result of commercial decisions to revolutionize the social patterns of retail trading in the interests of expansion and efficiency. Having created the boom in shoplifting, the retail industry then turned to security to combat the evil retailers had themselves created.

There is nothing ethically or morally wrong in business interests introducing innovative techniques of selling to the public. In a competitive market, efforts to achieve efficiency are necessary and commendable. Traditional concepts of trading, however, provided a service for the customer, and did not attempt to sell when the customer could not pay. Commercial interests in the latter half of the century decided, for commercial reasons, to change the rules. The depersonalized service aligned itself to efficiency, however, with the objective of giving the customers whatever they could be persuaded to take regardless of cost. Society was manipulated to conform to new sales concepts.

Small privately owned shops died off in their hundreds of thousands unable to compete with huge chain stores with their loss leaders and massive bulk purchasing power. These shops closed because they had become uncompetitive. They were not forced to close because of staff thefts or shoplifting, which they suffered both then and now. A number of measures were taken which are as valid today as they were then. Management made increased efforts to employ honest staff and to ensure their loyalty. By their presence and involvement with staff and customers, management vigilance and supervision reduced the opportunities for theft. In the same way, the more closely staff assistants involved themselves with service to the customer the less opportunity there was for the customer to steal. Retail security was based on two pragmatic principles: the recognition that the public should not be presented with unnecessary temptation to steal; and the instinctive knowledge that good personal service provided the best form of security. Of course this form of security and service is labour intensive and, therefore, relatively expensive. The larger the premises, the greater the numbers of staff employed and the more customers there are, the more difficult and expensive it becomes to apply simple security. Prices would rise no doubt. Large stores might become uneconomical and be forced to close in the same way that the hundreds of thousands of small shopkeepers had been forced to close by the advent of large stores.

In retail trading, as in so many other areas where private security has become entrenched, management have done what they have always done when faced with a problem: they have plumped for short-term financial expediency instead of confronting the problem. They have elected to abdicate their managerial responsibilities in favour of a dangerous myth. In a futile effort to treat an epidemic of shop thefts of their own making, they are unleashing on the public a Frankenstein private security which justifies its virtual inadequacy by constantly drawing attention to society's rising crime and falling standards of honesty. The security industry has a vested interest in encouraging the public to believe that this is true, to justify ever increasing constraints on personal freedoms.

The word 'security' has become vested with unreal connotations of professionalism, experience and expertise. This is misleading industry and commerce into believing they are being given a protective service which too often has no substance. The private security industry has largely become a dustbin for gimmick manufacturers, fly-by-nights, criminals and cynical entrepreneurs masquerading as professionally knowledgable and responsible 'security experts'. So established have these become, so powerful and persuasive their influence that instead of opposing the process of exploitation, society is continually ceding more and more authority to the industry. Rarely has the client paid so much for so little. There are, of course, many responsible elements in the security industry, many who are disturbed by the headlong rush into arcane devices and surveillance technology, yet find their professional instincts in conflict with their financial self-interest.

A 1982 Department of Employment survey found that the average basic wage for staff and contract security guards and patrols, excluding overtime, was less than the national average for manual workers. The contract security element is generally less well paid than permanent staff. Recruitment, accordingly, is generally from the lower end of the unskilled labour market. The hourly minimum rate quoted for a Securicor static night guard in January 1982 was £1.61 per hour, and rates in summer 1982 could be as low as £1.23 per hour in some companies. These hourly rates bear little relation to the costs to the clients and the public who pay for contract security. Clients will pay anything up to £6-8 per hour for contract security staff and few pay less than £5 an hour. Many guards are conscientious and willing with no criminal convictions; but some are not.

A history of crime is no barrier to being employed in positions of trust in the contract security field. According to *The Guardian* (26 March 1982), a director of 20th Century Security resigned his directorship when

179

he discovered that the company's new security co-ordinator had been engaged less than a year after release from prison. Burglar alarm companies have employed burglars on their staff and one company in North-West London still does. Casual security personnel have been recruited in flophouses. Security companies have been formed and run by criminals of long standing. It would be wrong, of course, to give the impression that all security companies and personnel are unethical, inefficient and sub-standard. Some companies and staff are not any of these things. A prospective client, however, engages in a lottery with every chance of winning a lemon. Too often commerce and industry are paying executive level salaries for the privilege of employing human dross. Professional skills are attributed to people who lack the training, background and intellect that the security façade implies.

Reliance on private security has resulted in commercial and industrial management opting out of involvement in the conventional policing of the community. Instead of exercising their financial muscle, in terms of rates paid for policing to the local authority, and insisting on adequate police protection for their rateable property, management have elected to buy their own protection. In many areas this has become established as the social norm to the extent that the police have virtually absolved themselves of responsibility for the protection of property to the detriment of the entire community. Although there is now a return to it, in many places high profile policing presence all but disappeared, to be replaced with something considerably less efficient and socially less cost-effective.

The use of private security has dissipated enormous amounts of valuable community resources. Static guards presently employed to watch over a factory on an estate, for example, could equally well provide protection for others in the vicinity. Instead of having a number of patrolling mobile guards from a number of different security companies paying periodic visits to different premises on the same estate, a more rational system would be to have a permanent presence on the estate for the same money. Traditionally, the onus was on the local authorities to provide adequate resources to safeguard the external security of premises. By supporting private security, commercial and industrial management has curtailed the ability of local and central government to provide police for this purpose. At the same time it has reduced the influence of management on local authority policing priorities. If professional management had paid generally more attention to the police in the past, there would perhaps be less grounds for concern about today's lack of police accountability.

The most invidious influence of private security in society has been in the deployment of surveillance technology. According to such trade organizations as the Association for the Prevention of Thefts in Shops, something like 2 per cent is added to the nation's shopping bill as a result of shop thefts by both staff and customers. What this 2 per cent actually means is that 98 per cent of the value of all shopping transactions is honestly conducted.

It is rarely, if ever, possible for stock analyses to identify accurately the precise nature of stock shrinkage. Of the £1000 million annual losses attributed to staff and customer thefts, no one can say how much is due to human error in stocktaking, accountancy, pricing, deliveries and breakages. Certainly shoplifting is widespread and the evidence is that it is growing, but not all goods taken without payment are stolen.

Most authorities and intelligent people now accept that theft is not the intent in many cases when goods are taken. There are factors like senility and mental illness, and in young children an unawareness of criminal intent. The law recognizes that these incidents are not criminal acts. There are not many of the British public who can honestly say that they have never, at one time or another, inadvertently walked out of a shop without paying for an article. That is not necessarily theft. Customer crime is indeed more than society would wish to see, but considerably less than the retail and security industries would have society believe.

A company which suffers heavy losses from staff pilferage employs a number of dishonest and disloyal staff who are being presented with the opportunity to steal. If the problem is major, long-term and cannot be identified, the management is incompetent and the only solution is to sack the management and start again. If the problem is minor, short-term and has been quickly highlighted by internal procedures, corrective action can be taken. These are basic security truths; but it is palpably wrong and probably counter-productive to apply security measures which seriously infringe the rights of the innocent in society, while making little impact on the freedom of the guilty to continue their criminal activities.

The British public should have no illusions about the ultimate logic underlying the unrestrained deployment of security and surveillance technology. Its unimpeded progress must result in an escalation from the present level of surveillance and manipulation of people to the stage where it exercises control. No sooner is a new device or system applied than it is overtaken and circumvented by human ingenuity. Every new technical measure is met with a technical counter-measure. The inevitable response to each counter-measure involves placing additional restraints on the general public. In some cases, when an effective criminal counter-measure cannot be produced there is an escalation of violence.

In recent years millions of pounds have been spent by retail outlets on the installation of radio or electro-magnetic beam detectors at the exits to stores. In theory these are activiated when shoplifters try to leave with stolen goods. On 13 February 1983 *The Sunday Times* published a short article which revealed that an inventor in America was marketing a specially treated shopping bag which shields the contents from the radio or electromagnetic detector beams used at the exits of department stores. The article went on to quote James R. Finnelly, security director of a large Chicago chain store: 'The guy's selling a shoplifting device pure and simple – and what's more, it works, unfortunately.' The inventor is said to be presently, 'working on a new invention which he describes as "stealth clothes". These, apparently, are garments that will not trigger burglar alarms.'

In 1982 claims were made by private security sources that violence was becoming an increasing feature of shoplifting. The claims may or may not be solidly based. If the claims are true, it is even more questionable that they support the view that security in shops should be increased. Before the growth of private security, and the practice of conveying enormous sums of money in one vehicle through the streets became commonplace, heavily armed and violent criminal gangs of robbers were virtually unknown in British society. Security vehicles did not make armed robbers; they did, however, provide regular, visible targets. Huge sums of money promised rewards commensurate with the risks involved in violent criminal action. For a robbery team to run the risk of a heavy custodial sentence 100 times to net £100,000 is an unacceptable degree of risk for most professional criminals. To risk the same sentence once for hitting a security vehicle is vastly more attractive. This would not be so important for society if it could be shown that all the risks to the public were now being taken by professional security personnel. The effect has been quite the opposite, however: violent robberies are now a daily feature of British life. Even at the most elementary levels the benefits to the public of private security, and particularly of the deployment of surveillance technology, may not always be what they appear.

Responding to an article critical of the escalating use of technology in retail security published in the *Security Gazette* in February 1982, the Chairman of a major closed circuit television company wrote: 'The incidence of complaints by honest shoppers about the use of CCTV is negligible. It is normally welcomed, as a means of reducing losses and keeping prices down. *Shoppers do not expect privacy* except in fitting rooms, where it is obviously respected.' The assertion that the complaints about the use of CCTV are negligible is probably true. It would also be true, however, to say that the complaints from honest shoppers about shoplifting are negligible, but this does not mean shoplifting is unimportant. To claim that shoppers normally welcome CCTV is fatuous.

'*Shoppers do not expect privacy* except in fitting rooms where it is obviously respected' perhaps best sums up the value placed on individual rights by the security industry. What shoppers and the public expect is generally determined by what they get, and what they get rarely accords with what they are entitled to expect in the context of individual liberty.

Covert surveillance by CCTV cameras has spread to shops, public buildings, hotels, banks, factories and offices – in fact anywhere a camera can be introduced. This technology is the electronic eye of Big Brother, an eye ensuring that there will not be a person in Britain free from scrutiny.

The assurance that privacy extends to shop 'fitting rooms where it is obviously respected' is specious. On at least two occasions in major London stores this is known not to have been the case. Even if the assurance were true, it could not, by security logic, remain true. Every security and police officer knows that fitting-rooms are used by thieves to secrete stolen clothing under their own. Covert cameras are used in staff changing-rooms and locker-rooms to prevent staff pilfering. With security logic why should any place remain free from cameras which are, after all, being used to catch thieves. Why should an innocent shopper object to covert security surveillance in fitting-rooms, or even lavatories, if they are doing nothing wrong. The security mind in its enthusiasm is quite incapable of adequately discriminating between 'what is good and what is evil, what is public and what is private, and what is primary and what is secondary'.

In 1967 in the London suburb of Norwood Green, local police responded to complaints about male opportuning in a public lavatory which was attracting clientele from far and wide. Two experienced officers were given the task of dealing with the problem. With remarkable enterprise they found a concealed observation post above two cubicles in the male lavatories. Small holes in the ceiling gave them an uninterrupted view of all activity taking place in the respective cubicles. The vast majority of those kept under surveillance used the cubicles for conventional reasons, and the incidence of complaints from conventional users about this police scrutiny was negligible. Nevertheless, the individual's right to privacy is too important to be left to the private security industry to define its extent.

The pleas of self-interested security personnel for the public to take on trust what is being thrust upon them are based on the lie that the industry is capable of self-imposed restraints; the lie that integrity of the industry exists; and the lie that the security industry understands the technology and its social implications. The biggest lie of all is that the industry cares about any of these things.

The emphasis is already moving away from CCTV visibly deployed to covert surveillance. Pinhole optical surveillance is to visual surveillance what the Keyhole, Spike or Rifle microphones are to audio surveillance. Developments in the miniaturization of CCTV cameras, coupled with rigid and flexible fibre optic pinhole lenses, have meant that tiny CCTV cameras can be hidden in walls with only the requirement of a hole of less than $\frac{1}{16}$ inch exposed in the target area. Pinhole lenses, which can either be straight or right-angled, are available with adjustable focusing, although most are designed for fixed focus. The lenses are designed for use with $\frac{2}{3}$ inch vidicom cameras, which incorporate light level adjustments. Used in operations like the Iranian Embassy seige in London, this and similar equipment proves invaluable. In the context of private security, however, their use must be questioned. According to one security handbook, 'all these lenses, and many more, are being used by security companies to fight crime in retailing, industry and commerce.'

A technocratic utopia is being prepared for British society: a utopia in which the individual will have no relevant characteristics other than those capable of being fed into a machine. This will be supervised by a security apparatus filming the human form, checking memory banks for relevant information and storing new information in data information banks for instant retrieval. These systems will be useless, it is claimed, unless inter-organizational facilities are linked to enable reciprocal information transfers. By the end of the century it is anticipated that much of the country will have been rewired with fibre optic cable for television and telecommunications. Experimentation is already in progress to enable work and shopping to be conducted from home by two-way audiovisual communications. Problems will be created, it is said, by people who attempt to switch off at inconvenient times. To overcome this problem, it can be argued that it will be necessary to programme the input facilities into the home to override the internal controls. This would facilitate external audio-visual surveillance to be exercised on the household.

When the private security industry and other authoritarian forces project an image of society disintegrating under a sustained attack by criminal, subversive and anti-democratic forces of social disorder, they are not offering a warning as much as making a sales pitch. It is conditioning society to an apocalyptic vision of a future given over to rampant crime, rioting, street violence, looting, arson and anarchy, a society in which any form of security would be welcomed. If society accepts the vision, it will be succumbing to counsels of despair and hastening the conditions anticipated. By accepting the vision, society accepts the supremacy of security in all its forms and its right to be dominant in the public's affairs. By rejecting the analysis of a disintegrating society and pursuing alternatives, however, the influence of security can be brought under control. The evidence of the essential emptiness of the remedies being offered by security is all round us: a society of imposed authoritarian values enforced by conflict and confrontation. The futility of what is now being provided in the name of security, the crass stupidity of those who offer it as a solution, and the underlying self-interest which prompts the offer are all there to be seen by any who care to look. *Pissing tree + CCTV is not security*

In 1982 it was reported that police in East Anglia were deploying CCTV surveillance cameras to detect dogs fouling the pavements. This must rank with the importance of protecting cans of beans in supermarkets as a matter of pressing social concern. In June 1982 under the auspices of the British Standards Institute – a private concern not a public institution – a committee of representatives from bodies which included the police, private security, insurance, architects, fire officers, locksmiths, local authorities, the Home Office and the Department of the Environment met to consider how the future society could be protected from muggers, burglars and vandals. The blueprint for the future included all the mechanical solutions the public could have expected from the assembled bureaucratic, technocratic and vested commercial interests. Steel roller window blinds, CCTV entryphones at entrances, solid doors, spyholes, chain deadlocks, high visibility lighting, remote control TV cameras, tarmac and concrete paths rather than paving stones which could be thrown by rioting masses; social measures to co-ordinate public transport with closure times of clubs and pubs; in fact, anything to sustain a society under siege except arms.

One of the most significant advances in crime prevention made by the committee was a long overdue public warning about the dangers posed to society by trees. Many people may have been unaware of the malign and subversive influence trees have had on British society. Not any old tree, only the fat ones with low foliage. The Sherriff of Nottingham would have led a peaceful and contented life had Sherwood Forest not provided refuge for Robin Hood. The point was not lost to vigilant police crime prevention specialists who fearlessly exposed this implacable enemy of humanity. Counter-measures have been advanced. Only 'widely spaced thin trees with high foliage' will be permitted anywhere near human habitation in the future. By this means muggers will be prevented from hiding behind trees while waiting for potential victims. Sympathetic consideration would, no doubt, have been given to hardline proposals to eliminate entirely pestilential trees from all areas of human habitation, were it not for the 'bleeding hearts' in society who claim some unaccountable aesthetic pleasure from trees – 'wets' who regard trees as objects of beauty rather than dangerous instruments in crime.

Thin trees and high foliage security can be resisted if society has the will. There are whole communities and vast areas of rural, suburban and provincial Britain where the incidence of serious crime is uncommon, posing little danger to social stability. The thin trees security mentality is a national threat. Paradoxically, this is particularly true in the inner-city urban areas where crime is and has been for generations endemic. These areas have been turned into dehumanized wastelands by thin trees, concrete and steel security mentalities. Financial and technical resources have been wantonly dissipated and misdirected in the same way that security measures are being now wasted operationally, strategically and philosophically. Just as lunatics cannot be allowed to run the asylum, self-appointed watchdogs have to be regarded with caution and even those who are publicly appointed have to be subject to scrutiny lest they become so affected by their working environment that they cannot see the wood for the trees.

# 9
# Re-addressing a 'Post' Society

As a post-imperial power, Britain no longer polices the world: as a post-industrial society, it no longer manufactures for the world. In the main, the British people know what they once were, but not what they have now become, or what they will be in the future. In a comparatively short space of time, they have lost two forms of national identity which have yet to be replaced. Perhaps more than at any other time in its long history, Britain is faced with the urgent need to define the nature of its society, to define the true nature of the democracy to which it claims to be committed, to define in more precise terms the values which are, and are not, negotiable, and to discriminate between 'what is good and evil, what is public and what is private, and what is primary and what is secondary'.

No society can proceed on the simple assumption that evil will be recognized when it arises. The Chinese who deposed Chiang Kai Shek and his regime may have done so because they identified him as evil: not all of them did so because they viewed Mao Tse Tung as good or less evil. A people who cannot define the basic principles on which they are united are left only with the many things on which they are divided. Politically, economically and socially the issues which divide British society are relatively clear. Far less clear, however, are the core principles capable of binding the nation together as a unified and indivisible entity. There is no bill of human rights against which the individual can test what freedom government permits with the degree of freedom the individual is entitled to expect. In the absence of established rights, the personal freedom of the individual becomes a concession: to be granted or withheld at the whim of government. Before the nature of social relationships are understood, as they apply between one individual and another, the individual and the community, and the community and the state, there must be some common agreement on the importance of the individual. Since there is no defined common agreement in Britain about the importance and rights of the individual, it is not surprising that other social relationships are increasingly difficult to understand.

The British ship of state is yawing dangerously among the hidden reefs of the political extremes. So unpredictable are its movements, it is becoming increasingly difficult for crew and passengers to determine either course or destination as dissenting helmsmen squabble to get their hands on the tiller. Politically, Northern Ireland is separated from the British mainland by a gulf wider than the Irish Sea. There are obvious signs of disaffection with central government appearing in Scotland and Wales. Local and central government authorities appear in many instances to be in a state of permanent conflict with each other. Elected to deal with local matters, local politicians are increasingly involving themselves in national issues far beyond their electoral mandate, while central government interferes more in local affairs. The process of government is increasingly moving away from consultation and compromise. In place of consensus there is militant action and confrontation. In the absence of political self-restraint, the individual looks in vain for a constitutional safety net to ensure that temporary custodianship of the nation's governing process is never mistaken for an electoral carte blanche to jettison moderation.

The gross disparity between vast wealth and breadline poverty remains as evident, abrasive and divisive as ever. The inequalities of wealth between one individual and another have always existed and will probably continue to exist. These inequalities are now becoming more apparent in a national context, in the distribution of the nation's wealth. These divisions separate North from South, one region from another region, urban centres from suburban areas of the same city; perhaps more significantly, they separate the newly devastated centres of industry from the lush life still to be found at the centres of financial manipulation. Policies which are at least questionable on economic grounds are being pursued regardless of the degree of social despair, hardship or unrest they cause. There appears to be a political assumption that economics can be practised in a social vacuum. Instead of the social lottery they really are, economics are being represented as an exact science.

Manic economist surgeons have taken hold of a hacksaw to cure Britain of the internationally common, economic cold. When the patient asks what is to replace what is being discarded, the surgeons cannot answer. When it is pointed out that the patient may die from shock and loss of blood, the surgeons smile reassuringly, pat the patient on the head and answer firmly: 'The patient will not die, only parts of the patient will die'. They say only that the remainder will be healthy, viable and free from the economic cold. Increasingly, responsible elements of every shade of political opinion are questioning whether the British economy is in the hands of surgeons or butchers.

When the economics of a rational society are handled in such an irrational manner, only tension and disorder can result. The virtues of running the nation's finances on the same basis as that of a sound, responsibly managed household are preached. At the same time, no importance is attached to the apparent incongruity of paying sums in the region of £30,000 in redundancy payments to make a worker unemployed. While that is happening, similar amounts cannot be found to repair crumbling roads, deteriorating railways and decaying inner city areas. The wealth generated by the discovery of North Sea oil, which was to have promoted an economic revival in the United Kingdom, is used instead to fund about half the nation's unemployment bill. The national household capital asset, which the prudent housekeeper would have invested in improving the home in anticipation of less affluent times to come, is being frittered away on consumer products. Many of the profligate sons of the desert, the Sheiks of Arabia, have taken the oil riches of the desert, changed the oil into money, and the money into armaments, airconditioned limousines and gambling chips in the world's casinos. The deserts great resources have been turned into an arms dump where rusting military hardware is planted in preference to trees. Using the same logic, British economists have taken the wealth from the North Sea, invested it in the creation of an army of unemployed – who in time may become unemployable – and planted them in the desert of Britain's industrial wastelands. Only in madness can the irrational be made to appear rational.

In economics, as in every other field of human relations, the crucial question for society is what are the fundamental rights of the individual, if any? If there is one thing which economists can agree on, it will be that a nation's wealth is always finite. The only 'right' which the individual in British society has to share in that wealth is the right to acquire. Since there are no limits to how much of the nation's finite wealth any individual may acquire, there are no limits to how little may be left available for the remainder. In an industrial society where there is full employment, a society where the opportunity to work is open to all, and a society where the acquisition of wealth is related to individual human effort, it is at least arguable that the work dynamic will establish the individual's right to share in the wealth available and dictate the upper and lower limits of what that share will be. None of these things now applies to British society. It may be that they never applied.

Britain is no longer an industrial society with full employment where the opportunity to work is there for all to enjoy; the acquisition and creation of wealth are less related to human effort than ever before.

Very few members of the British public seriously believe that advancing technology, applied without restraint, will ever allow a return to such conditions. British society now has to contend with the problem of satisfying the economic aspirations of unquantifiable numbers of people who are surplus to the production and wealth creation requirements of society and who have neither a claim to any part of society's wealth nor a right to work so that they may claim a share of that wealth. If a society refuses to acknowledge the individual's legal right to a defined minimum share of society's wealth, and also denies or fails to provide the individual with the legal means to acquire a share, can society then argue that every individual has a responsibility to its laws?

The stability of any democratic society depends on the justice of its laws. In a civilized democratic society the justice of laws is judged by their effectiveness as a means of balancing individual rights with individual responsibilities. It is inequitable for society to impose responsibilities on an individual without conferring corresponding rights. If the state's laws do not clearly recognize and enforce the individual's right to basic minimum wealth or the legal means to acquire it, only the enforcement of tyrannical laws can prevent alternative means being sought.

The latterday successors to Marx, Lenin, Trotsky and Stalin offer British society one solution to its economic problems. Right-wing totalitarianism offers another. Both solutions are gaining adherents. The first solution is a denial of individuality and calls for society to be regarded as a collective mass. The second solution pays lip service to the concept of individuality. In effect, however, it affirms the right of those who have to hold; those who can seize, to take; and those who are strong to dictate what will be made available for the weak. The challenge for democratic forces in Britain is to evolve an economic system which recognizes every individual's right to an equitable, minimum share in the nation's wealth: a share which is commensurate with human dignity, and a share which is underwritten by the entire resources of the nation regardless of how wealth may have previously been distributed. The challenge for a free and just democracy is to spell out the economic freedoms and rights of the individual.

Every individual in a democratic society should be free to live with dignity and to acquire wealth. The acquisition of wealth, although recognized as a freedom, is however only a contingent human right. Authoritarian tyranny, by the Left or Right, recognizes neither an individual's rights nor freedoms; a tolerant democracy tries to recognize both. When economic circumstances dictate, however, and democracy has to choose between honouring the individual's right to live with dignity and the freedom of other individuals to acquire wealth, society's choice must be unequivocal. The contingent right to take as much wealth as any individual desires must be sacrificed for the basic right of every individual to live with dignity.

Totalitarianism does not make any contract or agreement with individual citizens; whereas totalitarian authoritarianism decrees, democracy agrees. Democracy proceeds on the assumption that there is an agreement between government and the individual which constitutes a mutually binding contract enforceable by law. An agreement between two parties need not be in writing to be considered binding. There can be no true agreement, however, unless both parties understand what it is that is being agreed; without agreement there is no binding contract. However well drawn up a contract may be, however comprehensive and detailed, it is unlikely adequately to cover every possible contingency in detail. When unforeseen circumstances arise which are not specifically catered for by the conditions in the contract, the question will arise whether the contract is enforceable. When there is no written agreement setting out basic terms and conditions, the agreement is much more open to misinterpretation than the written one.

Between the individual and democracy it is generally accepted that government makes the laws and that the laws will define the conditions on which the relationship will proceed. In the absence of a bill of rights for the individual, however, British democracy tends to operate a social contract which is stronger on obligations, consequences and sanctions as they apply to the individual than to the state and one which is much stronger on the rights, actions and rewards of the state than of the individual. Under the existing contract it is clear that the individual has no absolute right to work and the law is clear that the individual has no right to steal. What the contract is less clear about are the economic rights of the individual who has no work and cannot steal. Can a contract which does not guarantee basic economic rights to the individual to whom work is denied be binding?

Governments, of course, do make payments to the unemployed, the sick, the old and the handicapped. Benefits doled out by governments to individuals are variable, and discretionary and yet it is the basic human right of every individual to have the economic means to live with dignity.

Britain prides itself on the liberty of the individual in society, but as Abraham Lincoln said: 'We all declare for liberty: but in using the same word we do not mean the same thing. With some the word liberty may mean for each man to do as he pleases with himself and the product of his labours; while with others the same word may mean for some men to do as they please with other men and the product of other men's labours. Here are two, not only different, but incompatible things, called by the same name, liberty.' The rights of an individual are similarly capable of incompatible definitions. There must, therefore, be a contract between the state and the individual in a civilized democratic society. On the part of the individual there must be agreement to subordinate some element of personal freedom in order for all to enjoy a degree of personal freedom. On the part of society there must be an acknowledgement that the individual has basic rights which are not capable of being changed by circumstances, conditions or the different perceptions of an elected government.

Individual rights cannot exist unless they are capable of being defined and therefore understood and agreed. Every basic human right which has been defined, understood and mutually agreed can be written down. In law, agreements may be legally enforceable even when not committed to writing. The law, however, also demonstrates that agreements which are unwritten are more open to confusion, misinterpretation and violation. In Britain there is no written contract between individual and state which binds government in the same way that the individual is bound. There is no charter or bill of individual rights which limits the extent to which temporary custodianship of government confers power on an elected political group to redefine basic individual rights, and therefore nothing to stop an extreme left-wing government subordinating the rights of the individual to some artificial and illusory concept of a collective will. There is nothing to stop an extreme right-wing government from creating a society in which those who have, or can acquire, wealth are encouraged to believe that they are entitled to keep what they have, and continue to increase it, without regard for those who neither have wealth nor the legal opportunity to acquire any. Politically and economically, the individual in British society is vulnerable. When the individual is vulnerable, democracy is in danger. Perhaps more than at any other time, the opening years of the 1980s have highlighted just how perilous is the position of British democracy and how imminent the danger.

At the same time that the position of the individual in Britain is threatened by political and economic schisms for want of an agreed contract with the state, the rights of the individual in society are being steadily eroded for want of a social contract. In the nation state there have to be bonds by which individuals are linked to each other. If the state is to survive as a cohesive entity the bonds which hold individuals together must be stronger than the pressure of individual, divisive differences. In a totalitarian society the bonds are forged by a number of individuals uniting to suppress the voices of individual dissent, to intimidate the individual by power or force. Under totalitarianism the bonds are those of imposed conformity. In a democracy, however, the bonds which hold the nation together are forged through an alliance between the individual and the state. The alliance recognizes both the independence and interdependence of each with the other. In exchange for supporting its integrity, the state offers the individual its protection and an equal voice in the governing process. The alliance is both a pact of non-aggression and one of mutual support and respect; it is founded on the principle of a direct relationship between the individual and the state being maintained. The individual elects the government to administer the affairs of state on behalf of each individual. Elected government is the medium through which individual and state conduct their dialogue and the alliance makes no provision for intermediaries. Unfortunately, the alliance is a social theory which is rapidly giving way to a vastly different reality.

The voice of the individual has over the years increasingly been submerged by the stridency of vested interest, collective groups claiming an authority to act as intermediaries between the individual and the infrastructure of community and state government. The principle of free association between individuals is being extended to the point where power blocks are emerging to claim special collective rights never envisaged in the concept of direct relationships between state and individual. Increasingly, factions with vested interests are being formed outside the parliamentary electoral system in British society. Assumptions are being made that particular shared interests merit a degree of social importance, which is calculated by multiplying the numbers who share the interest and considered to exceed the importance of the individual. These assumptions are untenable in a democratic state and can only devalue the individual. As a matter of administrative, social expediency it is obviously proper for government to note collective views expressed by minority groups. The danger arises when, in its concern to reflect minority group views, the state forgets that, in democracy, there is only one relevant minority group: the individual.

Every individual in society is unique and, therefore, each individual is a minority of one, the most vulnerable of all minorities. If the state and the community respect and protect the rights and freedoms of the individual, there can be no oppressed or underprivileged minority in society. It is when attempts are made to extend the rights and freedoms which apply to the individual to encompass collective social groups that serious distortions and tensions arise for both state and individual. Social behaviour which is tolerable from a minority of one, as an expression of individuality and the exercise of personal liberty, may become a form of social repression to others when adopted by collective minorities. Individuals have, by right of free association, the freedom to have their views articulated by a collective voice in a democracy. The voice which speaks for the collective group, however, can claim no greater authority nor right to public recognition than the authority claimed by the minority of one. Any claim to the contrary is founded on the power of numbers, not on reason or on the inherent justice of the cause being espoused.

Blaise Pascal made the point that, 'Unable to make what is just strong, we have made what is strong just'. However true that may have been, an evolving democracy has to hold fast to the principle that the phenomenon identified by Pascal is not inevitable or inescapable. The process can be resisted when it is seen to happen and it can be reversed when it has already happened. Social justice for the individual is social justice for all. More and more, however, the relationship between the individual and the state, and the extent to which individual rights are respected, appear to be determined by membership of special interest pressure groups. There is a tendency to quantify rather than qualify the basic rights of the individual: it is as if individual human rights were social perks to be doled out according to the collective strengths or weaknesses of one section of society in relation to another.

Management and union groups jointly decide the fate of individual workers in industrial affairs. Both sides indulge in ritualistic posturing and stage-managed confrontations which often belie the degree of unanimity they share. In the name of collective bargaining, both sides vie with each other to reach new peaks of dishonesty and obfuscation. Although this is not exclusive to the National Health Service, nowhere is the flagrant disregard for the basic human rights of the individual by collective action more evident.

The NHS was created as a tangible expression of British society's concern to ensure that individuals who were ill, injured or dying were not deprived of their human dignity and not subjected to unnecessary hardship by a lack of means. The service was not conceived as a conditional right or freedom: it was an absolute right limited only by the parameters of financial and technical possibility. No one who is unwilling to work in the Health Service is compelled to do so and anyone who does work in it has a right to leave. It is one of the few areas of social endeavour where concern for the right of the individual (the patient) is paramount, taking precedence over profit and marketplace economics. No individual employee in the NHS would dare claim the 'right' to say that a patient in need of care was to be denied attention. Yet, in recent years, British society has on a number of occasions seen the state stand back while the most basic of individual human rights have been savagely and inhumanly denied to them as a result of strike action. Individual patients, who might possibly have lived if their basic rights had been honoured by society, have died. The collective actions of groups working the Health Service have placed in jeopardy the very lives of patients: actions which, if perpetrated by an individual worker, would have incurred the moral outrage of society, if not legal sanctions.

One of the few genuinely altruistic examples of state machinery has been desecrated by the collective might of a vested interest group exercising power outside the electoral system. If the right of a patient to live is not respected and protected by the state, it becomes increasingly difficult for the individual to know which rights the state is capable of defending on the individual's behalf against the power of vested interests. Len Murray, General Secretary of the TUC, was quoted in 1983 in *The Observer* as having said, 'One of the main things that distinguishes democracies from dictatorships is the right to go on strike'. Is collective strike action a right or a conditional freedom? If it is a right, is it one which, in the Health Service, overrides the right of an individual to life free from unnecessary suffering? Can a democracy accept that the basic human rights an individual is entitled to expect, in the contract between the individual and the state, are subject to the agreement of unofficial groups which were not party to the original contract? If this is the case, the rights of the individual are more fragile than the fundamental principles of democracy make them appear.

The basic issue is not about management, unions or even the Health Service. The issue is, quite simply, the degree of importance society and the state places on the individual. Unless a democratic society attempts to define the basic human rights and the intrinsic value of the individual, the rights of all individuals will always be at the mercy of the perceived priorities of vested interest groups and subject to their influence. In the absence of defined rights, the integrity of the individual cannot be preserved. When individual rights come to be appraised in collective terms they become prizes in a form of social 'Monopoly': prizes which are acquired or denied by the dice.

The collective mentality can only be dangerous for the cohesion of a nation. It opens up social divisions which transfer the loyalty of the individual from the state to other entities. British society is increasingly being made to witness the potential for tyranny by vested interest groups when they engage in civil disobedience and disorder in pursuit of collective aims. More invidious, and ultimately more dangerous, are the many ways in which the collective phenomenon is undermining the position of the individual who relies on the state for protection from tyranny.

When a prostitute freely elects to ply her trade, within the bounds of society's laws, she is exercising her individual right to dispose of her body as she wishes. It is unquestionably a form of tyranny for the state to dictate to the individual on matters of private behaviour, or on how consenting adults should behave with each other. Clearly, a collective group with a mutual interest in furthering the cause of prostitution, for example, has the democratic right to advocate changes in the law through the democratic process. The collective group of prostitutes, however, can only claim the rights in society which are available to the individual: the rights do not multiply in direct relation to the numbers who claim them. If they did, prostitutes might suddenly find that the rights they presently enjoy as individuals far less secure if subjected to the wishes of other elements in society.

In 1982, a collective group of prostitutes in London's King's Cross area took over a church to demand an end to what they identified as police harassment of prostitutes in that area. The activities of prostitutes in King's Cross, the pimps who exploit them, and the crime which stems from prostitution, had turned the area into a social cesspool to the detriment of all who lived or went there. Although it is by no means true that all the social problems in the King's Cross area were attributable to prostitution, it is unquestionable that the prostitutes attracted to the area from all over the country immeasurably added to the problems. Whether prostitution is a symptom or cause of the area's social conditions, it had in itself attracted censure and stretched society's tolerance. Their collective action in seizing a church to publicize their own particular grievances was social tyranny. It amounted to a monstrous intrusion on the individual rights of others to attend church and worship free from interference. There was no conflict of individual rights between the prostitute and the churchgoer; no individual prostitute could have legitimately claimed a right to take the action, and the church members were not infringing any prostitute's rights. The collective action did not establish the rights of individual prostitutes, it denied them. What it established was the power of collective bodies to suspend individual rights to worship.

When prostitutes or homosexuals demand the freedom in society to indulge in their particular form of sexual activity permitted by law, they ask for no more than their due. They claim a basic individual right not to be judged and categorized solely according to their sexual preferences, but to be treated as individuals in their own right. In the same way individuals have the right not to be unfairly discriminated against because of sex or race. Instead of strengthening the individual's claims to basic rights, group activities are now beginning to produce something quite different and socially divisive. What is now emerging are demands for social recognition of collective group rights and views based on nothing more concrete or tangible than sexual preferences, gender or ethnic origin. Increasingly, social movements originally intended to further the cause of individual freedom are being adopted by elements determined to operate them as instruments of power and not merely as mechanisms for advancing the individual who may suffer discrimination.

Social groupings based on shared characteristics almost invariably produce an irreconcilable social paradox: having come together to urge society to treat them as no different from any other individual, they then go on to claim that they are entitled to special recognition because they are different. Within the electoral system, democracy can cope with contradictions of this kind. When this is pursued outside the system it leads to social distortions, with the collective voice drowning the voice of the individual. Artificial issues are made to appear fundamental; and the insignificant differences which separate one individual from another, and the individual from the state and community, are made to appear more important than the things which hold them together.

Captains of industry speak for business, as if business and workers were different entities operating in unrelated spheres. Unions speak for those who are in work, as if they were a different race from the unemployed. Of all the divisions appearing in British society, however, race most spectacularly highlights the dangers of social fragmentation posed by the special-interest group mentality. By recognizing the legitimacy of ethnic minorities to speak, society is denying to every minority of one the dignity of individuality. The state has no contract with ethnic groups, only with each ethnic individual. By accepting other than that, links between individuals of ethnic and indigenous origins have become obscure; links between immigrants and the community strained; and the relationship between ethnic immigrants, the community and the nation distorted.

One problem which Brixton, and similar areas, have posed and society has never satisfactorily resolved is that of defining what 'community' means in a national context. Was there a community in Brixton before the arrival of immigrants and, if so, does that community still exist? If there was, and if it still exists, are there now two communities in Brixton? Or, does the original community remain intact, having simply adapted to the influx of immigrants? If there are two, then one is made up of an indigenous population and the other is mainly West Indian. No provision is made for the two communities to be represented on a pro rata basis on Lambeth council or in national government. There are no visible differences in the social conditions between one community and the other. The right of one local community to absorb itself into another by a process of territorial expansion, unaccompanied by adjustments to boundaries and electoral procedures, is not one which is generally recognized in Britain. Yet, if two distinct communities exist in Brixton, it is being created by the territorial expansion of one community at the expense of the contraction of the other. All there is left to distinguish one community from the other are ethnic origins, colour, creed and cultural differences.

Any deprivation experienced in Brixton in terms of housing, education, employment, amenities and material possessions is as equally shared as it is elsewhere in Britain, and the degree of deprivation does not differ significantly from that in countless other communities in the United Kingdom. What makes Brixton different is the West Indian origin of large numbers of the population, and the individual immigrants of West Indian origin or extraction have formed stronger bonds with each other than they have with the indigenous local community or the national community. The social contract between each individual and the state, where the former undertakes responsibilities in exchange for the latter's guarantee to respect rights, has ceased to function effectively. It may be that the process of alienation was prompted by the state's failure to accord individual West Indians with the economic rights they were entitled to expect: the right to live with dignity. In the absence of any defined minimum level of economic independence for the individual, the state has failed many millions of indigenous citizens in precisely the same way. That is not a situation which can be changed democratically by giving credence to the idea that, collectively, West Indians or any other group have any claim to special recognition. Every West Indian, as a minority of one individual, is relevant: collective West Indian groups have no relevance in the national conscience. To challenge that principle would mean creating far more serious social divisions than exist at present. If Black Power is to be accorded a position of social influence outside the established political and social system, there are also many other groups waiting in the wings who have the numbers, organization and potential collective strength to issue a similar challenge.

The establishment of a West Indian ethnic fortress in the midst of the indigenous Brixton community was unwanted from its inception. It was created without the consent of the community and was actively resisted by some. The influx of unlimited numbers of immigrants into Brixton has reached proportions which now make it difficult for the indigenous population to retain either their community identity or the rights bestowed by their national heritage. In the same way, the collective West Indian voice, issuing from an apparently unassailable ghetto fortress, is denying individual immigrants their right to have their voices heard and to have their social contract with the state enforced. What the British nation is hearing and seeing in Brixton is the relationship between the individual and the state being arbitrarily redefined by unaccredited groups. These unaccredited groups are claiming nonexistent rights: the right to speak on behalf of the individual West Indian in all matters; the right to separate community status by virtue of colour or non-British ethnic origins; and, most sinister of all, the claim to such community rights without responsibilities.

Mugging is not the most prevalent crime in Britain and it forms a minor part of the overall statistics for crime. Opinion in authoritative quarters differs on the relative importance of mugging and street crime as distinct from other forms. There can be no dispute, however, that mugging is a social evil and that it has a significant influence on the degree of stability the public attribute to the community and society they live in. As the nation's capital city and, therefore, the focus of much of the national news media, crime in London has an effect on public views and attitudes far beyond its geographical boundaries. Given the size of London, it is inevitable that crime will be numerically greater than in any other British conurbation. While it may or may not be inevitable, it is also true that some forms of crime are both numerically and disproportionately greater than elsewhere. In relation to virtually every other area in the country this is true of mugging and street crime in Brixton.

In relation to London's population and total geographical area Brixton is comparatively insignificant; yet figures released by the Metropolitan Police in 1982 showed that about 10 per cent of all muggings in London were being committed in the Brixton area. The vast majority, according to the evidence available, were committed by members of the West Indian ethnic community. The information was not revelationary: it was no more than the police had been pointing out for years, and it was no more than the indigenous population of Brixton had known for years and tried in vain to impart to the authorities who refused to let their private disquiet ruffle their patrician public complacency.

There can be no other major issue in society where so many of the nation's moral, intellectual and political leaders so blatantly abdicated their responsibilities to provide public guidance. On no other major social issue have so many public figures and academics refused to say publicly what they privately believed. For over a decade social forces had been fusing in Brixton to create a timebomb. Responsible moderate elements in society allowed themselves to be intimidated by two extremes: the high-flown rhetoric of social concern expressed, most often, by those far removed from the day to day problem, on the one hand; and the prejudice of racial bigots, on the other hand. Many expressed no opinion in public in case the opinion be misrepresented as support for one or other of the extremes. Information, privately regarded as factual, was not made public in case it proved unpalatable. Terrified of allowing harsh reality to intrude into idyllic fantasies of interracial harmony, the rights of thousands of individuals, white and black, were cynically and sometimes brutally sacrificed in Brixton. Instead of British democracy emerging as a society dedicated to truth and committed to open debate, social tolerance, which should be a strength, came to be portrayed as weakness and impotence. The state reneged on its responsibilities to the individual in society for fear of offending an unaccredited West Indian voice which had no mandate to speak for individual West Indians, and which tyrannized them no less than others in the community.

The real question posed by Brixton is not whether there exists one community or two: it is whether any community exists there which can claim recognition as a legitimate entity. For years, community leadership failed in Brixton although, in the aftermath of the 1981 riots and the Scarman Report, strenuous efforts are now being made to alter the situation. The reason community leadership failed was that the problem it confronted was not a community problem; it was a national problem foisted onto the Brixton community by successive governments refusing to take responsibility for their own actions. The national debate which periodically surfaces in Britain about immigration numbers, racial discrimination and Britain as a multiracial society can never be resolved until it is openly acknowledged that there are a number of absolute truths which, when applied indiscriminately, prove to be directly contradictory to each other.

If the number of non-caucasian immigrants were to be instantly doubled in the United Kingdom, under certain conditions no threat would be posed to the identity of the British people or to the integrity and cohesion of the nation. The vast majority of the British people are not strongly influenced in their personal attitudes by individual characteristics of race or colour much more than by other individual physical characteristics. There is no evidence to suggest that the British people, who have absorbed waves of immigrants over the centuries, have any aversion to living in a multiracial British society. If the existing non-caucasian population was immediately doubled or even quadrupled, it would still amount to little more than one person in ten of the British population. The threat to the stability of British society does not come from the total numbers of non-caucasian immigrants, from the racial attitudes of the majority of the British people, or from the reluctance of the indigenous population to live in a multiracial British society. The threat arises from the distribution of the numbers involved.

On acceptance, the state undertakes to provide every immigrant with the same rights as every other citizen; the immigrant accepts in return the same degree of responsibility as every other citizen. Immigrants are entitled to no less, but no more, than the least affluent of the native public. That means the immigrant may be entitled to very little. West Indian immigrants, however, were attracted to Britain by high expectations of material reward which contrasted with the poverty of their background. They found themselves in a society where high expectations were encouraged, where enormous material success was achieved by some, and, yet, one in which their more modest expectations remained unfulfilled. Not having the same cultural affinity with the state as the indigenous population, they had not been conditioned to understand inequalities in distribution of wealth. One consequence of this has been for some of them to transfer their allegiance from the state to each other. The process is perfectly understandable, but the question is how long will the process continue and how far can it be taken before it becomes an unacceptable threat to the rest of society.

While it is true that the vast majority of the British people are not strongly influenced by racial or colour prejudice, it is also true that the vast majority of the British people are not personally affected by immigration or immigrants. It is true that Britain has absorbed waves of immigrants in the past, and that there is no significant aversion on the part of the majority of the British public to living in a multiracial British society. It is also true, however, that the majority of the British public is not involved in the absorption process to any significant extent, and what is emerging in affected areas is not an integrated multiracial society, but self-proclaimed communities which, through unaccredited voices, are demanding separatist recognition. What some of these voices are advocating is not integration but disintegration of the British state. While it is true that a proportion of one immigrant to ten of the indigenous population is not a major threat to the national identity, that is a ratio which has no relevance to the reality: for huge numbers of the British public the ratio is more like one immigrant to one thousand of the indigenous population, while for significant numbers of the indigenous population, living in highly sensitive inner-city areas like Brixton, the ratio which has direct relevance to their social, economic and cultural environment is much, much higher.

The uninvolved majority of the British public has for too long been allowed to shirk its responsibility for providing the social conditions which would enable the theory of socially harmonious multiracial integration to become a practical reality. The majority has sought to shed its responsibilities by placing them on communities like Brixton on the absurd premise that what might be possible for a nation to cope with would equally be possible for local communities. The riots of 1981 should have demonstrated beyond all doubt how illfounded this belief was. The same riots should have provided another lesson which seems to have been ignored: if the major cities of Britain are destabilized, then so is the country as a whole. Brixton, in common with other inner-city areas, has two problems which, although interrelated, are not identical: material, social and economic deprivation generally shared, and a community divided by ethnic and cultural differences.

Many now recognize that greater investment and material improvements to Britain's inner cities and areas of urban decay are national priorities. This recognition is not always expressed in the allocation of resources. At a time of general economic constraint, it may be difficult to sustain even the existing degree of priority. In themselves, however, financially realistic material improvements will not resolve the ethnic and cultural collective differences in Brixton as long as the indigenous population demand the individual right to live according to the mores of a British community and West Indians demand the collective right to live according to the mores of a West Indian society. What Brixton demonstrates is that the unrestrained territorial expansion of high numbers of any ethnic group, geographically concentrated, who unite around the characteristics which set them apart, is the conceptual antithesis of an integrated multiracial society. Every individual West Indian has the right to retain an affinity with the cultural heritage of the West Indies providing it is not inimical to the cultural heritage of the adopted society. When collective West Indian groups demand territorial sovereignty and a collective voice in local or national affairs, their demands become a unilateral declaration of independence from the state which threatens the constitutional position of every other individual in society.

Any social and economic initiatives, undertaken in areas like Brixton, which shy away from compassionate measures to disperse the concentrated ethnicity of the areas far wider than at present will merely be tinkering with the symptoms of the problem and leaving the core untouched. Ethnic groups must recognize that their individuality is more important than their collective ethnic identity. To forge individual links with the wider British public is more important than forging ethnic links with each other. Integration into the national community offers immigrants a more certain, lasting security than collective independence in ghetto fortresses. Unless all these things are accepted by immigrants and indigenous public alike, the internal security of British democracy will be in considerable jeopardy, and the rights and freedoms of every individual in all parts of the nation threatened. If all this is to be achieved, it must be with the active co-operation and participation of the vast parts of British society which have hitherto been uninvolved in the immigration process. With government assistance, British communities far removed from the areas where ethnic groups have been concentrated in the past must make provision to attract members of the ethnic groups. Although, hopefully, altruistic concern for the wellbeing of those affected should be the most persuasive influence in the process, there are other factors which may be more compelling. Not least of these is self-preservation.

All the 1981 riots took place in areas of economic deprivation, all with heavy immigrant concentrations, and in all cases black youth played a predominant part. The riots, however localized, proved that local community resources could not deal with the fundamental causes and national resources were required to deal with the effects. One section of British society which drew its own conclusions, and acted on them, was the police service. They responded by implementing policies which will affect police relations with the public far beyond the areas immediately affected by rioting, areas which are unconnected with immigrant ethnic unrest. The policies demonstrate how vulnerable the rights of the individual in society are when state institutions are forced to respond to the collective action of small groups who place collective rights above individual rights.

Much of the blame for the breakdown in law and order in Brixton, as in other areas, which culminated in street rioting was attached to the policing of the area. To some extent the blame was justified. A number of unique factors have dictated that the Metropolitan Police, as an entity, have traditionally been less responsive to the specific needs of the many varied communities in London than other forces for the communities in their areas. No other force in the country has had to balance the same degree of national and local responsibilities. With 26,000 officers, the Met is not only the largest force, it is the only one accountable directly to the Home Secretary and unaccountable to the elected representatives of the 7,000,000 Londoners it polices. In the absence of any other formation structured to undertake national responsibilities, the force has served as the nearest thing in Britain to a national police.

The sheer size of the force made it difficult to manage effectively. A cumbersome, bloated and over-centralized management structure created grossly overstaffed ranks in which promotion, without commensurate responsibility, became an end in itself. Externally, the force exercised enormous corporate authority and power over the public without being directly responsible to them. Internally, individual responsibility for management decisions hovered around an intricate, tangled web of command with the predictable consequence that it did not come to rest anywhere. It was, at the same time, over-managed in detail and under-managed in terms of direct managerial responsibility. Efforts inside the force to reorganize and restructure the internal mechanism tacitly reflected what the police would never publicly concede: the probability that no police force can perform satisfactorily the dual function of serving local communities and national interests. The Metropolitan Police was unquestionably mismanaged; it may have been mismanaged because, as a corporate entity, it was unmanageable. All of these issues had a direct bearing on policing and events in Brixton.

There was a strong sense of anti-black prejudice in the police. This prejudice was openly expressed in police circles in sentiments which had much in common with the fascism of the National Front, with which numbers of officers openly identified their sympathies. Hundreds of West Indian individuals were physically and mentally brutalized by direct violence, verbal abuse and manufactured evidence. This sort of conduct was not typical of the vast majority of the British police service. It was not even wholly typical of the vast majority of Metropolitan Police officers; and it may not have been typical of the majority of operational Met officers. All that was cold comfort to the West Indians concerned, however, since it was only a very small minority of the British police, a minority of the Metropolitan Police, and, probably, a minority of operational Met officers who were constantly engaged in policing large numbers of West Indians heavily concentrated in particular areas. It was also that same minority of police who saw the visible disintegration and disorientation of indigenous communities unable to retain their identities in the face of the immigrant influx.

With considerable justice, elected local authority representatives pointed out that Brixton was being destabilized by an unacceptable level of muggings, street crimes and lawlessness. They pointed out that they were impotent and could not be held responsible for the failures of a police force, which was beyond their sphere of influence, operating policies and policing strategies and tactics with which they were not in agreement. The police, with equal justice, pointed out that they were not policing a single community with an integrated structure. They were being asked to police two separate groups. The police pointed out that they could not possibly police a community adequately by conventional means when a significant element of the immigrant population withheld its consent – an element which spoke through the voices of self-elected or obscure sectional interest representatives. This element shielded muggers and other criminals within its ranks from the process of law and condemned as fascist and excessive the police measures to combat street crime, but was not prepared unreservedly to condemn the imposition of violent tyranny by their own young people on the old, weak and solitary individuals in the community.

The Brixton syndrome, reinforced by events in Bristol, Liverpool and Manchester, highlighted a number of issues with profound implications for the long-term security of Britain. The relationship between an ethnic immigrant group, and the mass of the indigenous national population, in an integrated multiracial society, is not a union of two independent and sovereign peoples. Neither is it a treaty between two separate communities each with a group voice in national or community affairs. The only collective voice which can have any validity in a democracy is the one which emerges from the electoral system through the ballot-box, since that is the one voice which is not individually exclusive. Increasingly, however, even the voice of the electorate is being distorted by the growing influence of society's new dominant interest groups. More and more the individual is devalued as political power becomes a dutch auction, to be traded and negotiated by groups who have a vested interest in exaggerating characteristic differences among individuals and creating divisions, rather than stressing the common interest of maintaining society's solidarity. This ignores the maxim that for every action there is an equal and opposite reaction. It is a maxim that militant, vested interest groups loudly proclaiming their differences, and the relative social importance of these differences, should remember.

When any group claims special rights through collective strength, they do so at their peril. There are in society many who consider prostitution a social evil, homosexuality a pernicious and contagious social disease which threatens to corrupt the nation's youth, militant feminism a vehicle for female inadequates, trades unions and managements instruments of social repression and minority governments uncertain institutions through which to conduct the nation's affairs. It is the basic tolerance of the many in society which has permitted the collective voices free expression. It would be wrong to assume, however, that there has been no reaction. Collective voices are becoming more dominant. Collective rights are subverting individual rights: characteristic group differences are becoming easier to identify with than the social links which bind the individual in a direct relationship to the state structure; and increasingly individuals are having to rally to what holds the national community apart rather than to what should hold it together. The individual, who should be of primary importance in a democracy, is being relegated to a secondary position and state institutions are being deployed to defend one collective interest against another.

In reaction to the 1981 race riot, the police service throughout the country moved rapidly from basic strategies founded on the idea of community policing by public consent to contingent strategies for policing without consent. Whereas formerly the police had relied on preventing large-scale civil disorder with low profile policing and, on the occasions when disorder did take place, limiting and containing the violence, the police added a new dimension to their response capability. Throughout the country, police forces have been trained, or are being trained, in new riot control techniques and equipped. Police armouries have been expanded to include vizored helmets, protective clothing, riot shields, CS gas and riot guns. Mobile inter-force reserve formations have been created to move into potential troublespots at short notice. New tactics have been formulated around the deployment of this form of riot response. With the additional equipment available and the new contingency plans, the police service is logistically more capable of reacting immediately and more positively, with greater force than ever before to any threatened disorder wherever the threat arises.

This does not necessarily mean that policing with public consent is at an end. It does not mean that there will no longer be attempts made to contain the possibility of violence. It does not mean that the police will always resort to overwhelming force as a first resort. It is true that the officers trained for riot control are ordinary police officers, the same officers who perform beat duties in the community. It is also true, however, that not all of the officers present will be from the community where disorder is threatened. In the same way, it is also true that when riot equipment is readily available, and officers have been trained to use it, it becomes increasingly more difficult to resist using the overwhelming force available as an early, if not a first, option. With considerable justice it will be argued that a disturbance should not be allowed to escalate into a riot before using the available equipment to quell it. It will be argued that officers should not be placed in unnecessary danger by holding back, and risking injury. Some argue that anti-riot equipment and dispersal tactics are most effective when applied before a riot takes place, before things have got out of hand.

To many of the British public, all these things sound perfectly acceptable when they are considered in the context of street riots and ghetto fortresses. That is only part of the story, however, since the tactics evolved and the equipment made available are not exclusively designed or intended to be used in these circumstances. The same professional considerations which are applicable under those conditions must, per-force, be applied to other circumstances where there is a possibility of serious public disorder and consequential police injuries. Looked at in that light, it can be seen that the new measures may have far wider and more profound implications for the whole of British society.

The 1960s saw major demonstrations against the Vietnam war turn into full-scale riots in London's Grosvenor Square and Red Lion Square. Similarly, in the 1970s, protests against deaths in Ulster, during what had become known as 'Bloody Sunday', turned into a full-scale riot when thousands of demonstrators attempted to force their way through police cordons from Whitehall into Downing Street: a full-scale riot at the centre of British government. In all of those riots the police relied on containment. As a matter of policy police arrested only when it was considered unavoidable, 'snatch' squads were not used, and direct police force was deliberately kept low key and minimal. In the course of these riots the Metropolitan Police suffered hundred of casualties. At the time there were no organized groups of officers who were specially trained in anti-riot procedures who could recognize the tactics of forceful escalation. Now that officers and commanders have been trained and equipped, it seems less likely that the police will be prepared to sustain the same attrition rate. It even seems less likely that they will be prepared to take the same degree of risk before full-scale rioting actually breaks out.

To officers taking part, the distinction between civil disturbance, or disorder, and rioting will often seem too fine to be operationally relevant. Protesters may be engaged in what they consider to be legitimate civil protest; strikers may be engaged in what they consider to be a trade dispute; and the unemployed masses may be demonstrating to draw attention to their inability to maintain individual human dignity for lack of economic rights. To the police charged with maintaining order, protesters, strikers or unemployed will not appear any less threatening because they are black or white or both. The police will not be influenced by the legitimacy of the cause espoused or by the failure of the state to honour its obligations to the individual. The police will respond to the immediate situation they are confronting and, sooner or later, the temptation to respond with all the force available will prove irresistible. When force is applied in those circumstances, it will be indiscriminately applied to violent and non-violent alike. A police force and officers who are seen to impose indiscriminate force on innocent and guilty members of the public in a community are unlikely to be welcomed into the community: they may remain in the community but they will not be of the community.

Perhaps none of this would matter quite so much if it could be shown to be necessary as a result of the race riots for the police to adopt tougher anti-riot tactics with a greater defensive and offensive armoury. Perhaps it would not matter so much if the new armoury could achieve an overall reduction in riot violence; and perhaps it would not matter quite so much if the new equipment and anti-riot measures marked police limits. In reality, of course, all of those things do matter because none of them is true.

Despite the horrendous spectacles witnessed by the British people during the 1981 riots, and the appalling numbers of police officers injured, these events did not prove beyond any doubt that it was necessary to increase significantly the anti-riot armoury. What the riots proved was that whatever had passed for community policing in the affected areas had failed, and failed in areas where the community had disintegrated long before any rioting had taken place. What the riots also proved was that many of the police commanders on the spot, even when they had overwhelming police resources at their disposal, lacked the resolve, professional competence and leadership qualities to deploy their resources rapidly and to maximum effect. Instead, the police officers were lined up like ninepins to take their turn at being hit by whatever could be thrown at them by delinquent children and a lawless rabble. The magnificent fortitude, resilience, and courage displayed by the ordinary police officers was a tribute to their dedication to duty. This could not, and should not, disguise how supremely irrelevant were their 'thin blue lines' or the Cardigan and Raglan-like qualities displayed by some of their commanders. What, above all, the riots proved was that the centres of ethnic immigration in Britain posed special internal security problems which could not be solved solely by police action.

There is no reliable evidence to show that increased police powers, more equipment and weapons, or more force in riots will reduce damage, violence or injury. There is ample evidence, however, to show that they can and often do lead to more damage, more sustained violence, and more numerous and serious injuries. Whatever marginal gains may accrue from increased police powers and more forceful policing, there is ample evidence to show that this will be more than offset by the alienation of new sections of the public. Particular situations will be misjudged by the police, errors will be made and what were intended to be measures of last resort will, inexorably, become measures of first resort. The public had dramatic confirmation of this principle in operation during the opening months of 1983. The police, with the exception of those who are permanently armed for specific duties, are in theory issued with arms to protect their own and the lives of others who are in immediate danger of death or serious injury. When the practice of issuing guns started to become more or less routine in London, it was generally understood and accepted that the criterion of danger was that it be recognizably imminent. Guns were never intended to be issued as a means to keep an officer's own fears at bay since fear is not always linked to the reality of particular situations. How things had changed was brought home to the public in 1983 when they learned of an unarmed and innocent Stephen Waldorf shot by mistake in a London street. In the hunt for David Martin, the man Waldorf had been mistaken for, Londoners read about a tube train drawing into an underground station to be met by police officers lined up on the platform pointing guns at the passengers. The public learned about armed police raids in the West Midlands in which innocent elderly people and children had been held at gunpoint by police who had either received misleading information or had raided the wrong addresses. All these incidents had one thing in common: the police could see no imminent danger since there was no actual danger present; the only lives put at risk were those of the innocent individuals who had police guns trained on them. Guns which were always intended to be measures of last resort have now quite frequently become measures of first resort. Despite far more widespread issuing of police arms, the evidence all shows that armed criminal violence in society is escalating. Only blind faith can suggest riot violence will be diminished by a more powerful community police armoury.

The new contingency plans for dealing with serious public disorder and the additional equipment supplied to British police forces do not mark the limits beyond which the police will not be permitted to go. There is a whole array of technology available which can be deployed, technology which will be deployed if security salesmen have their way. There are water cannon, plastic bullets and dyes; batons; implements which can give electric shocks; chemicals which can induce nausea, and soundbeams which can cause acute pain and discomfort. They have one common feature: they cannot discriminate between guilty and innocent. Any major public order strategy the police form around this technology is doomed to failure in a democracy or democracy itself is doomed. The strategy is founded on the misconception that the police can inflict pain or discomfort on significant numbers of the community without suffering a backlash of revulsion which will ultimately prove to be counter-productive. Police who are identified by significant numbers of a community as oppressive cannot be regarded as a community police.

More fundamental, however, is the underlying social problem of how the basic rights of every individual in society are being undermined by the claims of special and dominant interest groups in society. Having submerged their individuality into a collective ethnic group identity, immigrants have emerged as a dominant interest group capable of distorting national priorities. Attempts to meet the aspirations of ethnic immigrant groups can only be successful at the expense of sacrificing the legitimate social aspirations of other individuals who are equally deserving. The 1981 riots, which focused attention on the genuine grievances of immigrants in the inner-city ghettos, also identified the potential threat they posed to the internal security of the nation. As a direct result of this, the entire British police service upgraded its strategic and tactical potential for responding more aggressively to major civil disturbances. In theory the police still intend to respond with disciplined restraint and pursue policies of containment: in practice, the temptation to apply the more forceful measures available will become increasingly difficult to resist. Only the most naive can imagine that any one can be trained to react aggressively only when confronted by rioters and act with restraint in other sensitive situations where there may be equal personal danger. Any increased police aggression will not apply merely to ethnic minority groups, but to every individual in British society and will be reflected in relations between police and public throughout the nation.

It would be a serious underestimation of the gravity of the situation to assume that only the police have been affected by the racially based riots of 1981. The thin-trees element of private security, described in the previous chapter, has responded in predictable fashion to the new opportunities for commercial profit from the visions of an apocalyptic future suggested by the riots. An article published in the *Security Gazette* in October 1981, by Frank Pegg, illustrates some interesting features of social interaction: how the actions of one dominant interest in society prompt a reaction from another and how the rights of the individual are crushed in the process. As chief executive of a commercial security hardware company, Frank Pegg comments extensively on matters of security and reflects widely-held views within the industry. The article, entitled 'The Changing Face of Retail Security', opened with statistics and other information indicating increasing crime levels and trends suggesting increased social violence in the future unless rapid action was taken. Making the point that the police now had more 'protective equipment' than ever before, and expressing the hope that the use of 'aggressive policing tactics' could be avoided, in a clear reference to the riots earlier in the year, Pegg continued, 'The chief security officer, whose responsibility it is to look after the equipment and profit of his employer, must now consider looting, street aggravation [?] and arson as some of his future battles. This will need new methods of training, both for the chief security officer or store detective and for other security personnel including factory guards.'

Setting aside the question of how enthusiastically security officers would greet the prospect of doing battle with looters, street 'aggravators' and arsonists, no attempt was made to place the riots, which by implication were being used to support the theme of the article, into any relevant context. No attempt was made to balance the message by reference to the localized nature of the riots in terms of ethnic group participation. Retailers from the Hebrides to Portland Bill, from John O'Groats to Lands End, were supposed to be under threat from shoplifting, employee theft and a society plunging headlong into criminal anarchy. Salvation of the retail industry lay in the hands of security officers and 'loss prevention executives'. Confronting the forces of ungodliness the white knights of the commercial private security industry would raise the barricades of metal shutters, sensors detecting breaking glass, and burglar alarms, loop alarms, real and simulated CCTV, portable alarms and panic buttons linked to police stations or private control stations.

Measures apparently have to be implemented to control employee theft at cash points walk-through metal sensors to prevent employee theft of tools; security barriers to increase control and access systems. Pegg quotes research which shows that 70 per cent of all employees interviewed had stolen from their employer or given unauthorized discounts – surprising when it is related to only 2 per cent losses in retail.

Pointing to a 'tragic increase in juvenile crime', Pegg quotes a Home Office study showing that 'upwards of a quarter of a million children may be playing truant in any one day'. 'What' asks Pegg, 'are these children doing?' Pegg of course provided his own answer: 'Obviously, they are vandalizing, they are stealing from cars, thieving from retail stores, etc.'

One might be forgiven for suggesting that 250,000-plus vandalizing, thieving shoplifters is more than even the technologically aware 'loss prevention executive' can contend with when added to looters, 'aggravators' and arsonists. Not so, says Pegg. 'He will need to be a new breed of man; he will need more skilled training; he will need to understand EPOS, EFTS, computerization, bar coding, etc.' What will set the 'new breed of man' apart from his 'old breed' predecessors and contemporaries is that he will 'understand the new sophisticated technology that will be available to him'. This will make a considerable difference for, as Pegg makes clear, 'Closed circuit television will be married with other forms of technology into complete automated systems. They will accomplish a multiplicity of jobs and this will free the security executive to do more creative security – CCTV will become his eyes.' Granted that CCTV eyes can go places that human eyes cannot, they have nevertheless been around for a long time without making any significant impact on crime. Pegg continues: 'The microprocessor, which will analyse the information received from the various sensors and will issue commands, will be the brains of the security officer.' In reality the 'new breed of man' with the CCTV eyes and microprocessor brain is actually well known to the mass of the British people. In the popular television series, *Dr Who*, the breed was known as Daleks; others have been known as robots, automatons, Cruise or SS20 missiles. In case this sophisticated apparatus proves insufficient, Pegg's company (in the same issue) advertises 'observation mirrors' – two-way mirrors.

Pegg enjoys a high reputation as an authoritative voice in the private security industry. His technical expertise is no doubt beyond question and his company well respected. In many ways his is a voice of moderation and responsibility in an industry in which many are irresponsible, charlatans trading on public fears for personal gain. With far less justification than the police service, who are at least to some extent answerable for their corporate conduct, the private security industry is a dominant interest, unaccredited social group which is exercising a quite disproportionate influence in shaping the future of British society. The thin-trees element of the industry sees no natural beauty in the forest; in the same way, they see no merit in holding individual rights of freedom and privacy more precious than their own sterile vision of a society where the human is subordinated to the machine. John Davys' article in *The Observer*, in which he described his interview with Professor Joseph Weizenbaum in the Department of Computer Science at MIT, ended with an interesting anecdote and two crucial questions: 'A friend driving me to the airport, hearing I was going to see Weizenbaum, described a scene she had witnessed that day in a supermarket. A customer was in dispute with a girl operating an electronic till. "It must be right," said the girl. "The machine is smarter than I am." The girl at the next till turned to her fiercely and said: "If you think that, you're dead." Which girl should we see as our hope for the future? Weizenbaum has no doubt of the answer. Do we?'

If the same question were put to the security industry, it too would have no doubt about the answer. The answer, however, would not be Professor Weizenbaum's. The question British society must ask itself before it is too late is which one is it prepared to accept? The future dignity, rights and freedoms of the individual will be determined by society's decision.

US President James Madison, addressing the Virginia Convention in 1788, said: 'I believe there are more instances of the abridgement of freedom of the people by gradual and silent encroachments of those in power than by violent and sudden usurpations.' In the opening years of the 1980s the insidious process of encroachmnent on individual rights has gathered momentum. Microprocessing, computerized and surveillance technology threatens the privacy of the individual as never before. The application of this technology without adequate safeguards against abuse by government institutions, law enforcement agencies, secret security agencies, industrial and commercial interests, is gradually coalescing to deny individual privacy or confidentiality. In a society in which personal confidentiality is not respected, there can be little trust either between individuals or between the individual and the state. Relationships under threat include those between doctor and patient, minister and parishioner, journalist and source, and shop and customer. Paradoxically, while technology makes wholesale breaches of personal privacy, it produces the opposite effect in relation to public institutions, cloaking what should be public knowledge in an impenetrable privacy. Attitudes in the all-pervasive private security industry crystallize the individual's position; if the mass of the public do not insist on privacy, no individual is entitled to receive it.

In the opening months of 1983 the Police and Criminal Evidence Bill was considered by the Standing Committee of the House of Commons. Among other things the Bill proposed major extensions of police powers to stop, question, search and detain. Proposals in the Bill provoked considerable opposition among the Law Lords. Considerable unease was created by the lack of time to consider the full implications of the wide-ranging proposals. One of Britain's most emminent Law Lords, a former Lord Justice of Appeal, Lord Salmon voiced general concern in comments made to London's evening newspaper, *The Standard*, in March 1983: 'I think that there is a danger that this Bill brings Britain closer to being a police state.' Describing it as 'shocking and monstrous', he went on, 'What is being proposed in the Bill has never been allowed in common law and looking at this Bill I don't even think it could be redrafted.' ... and ... 'The Bill is going through much more quickly than a Bill normally would.'

Defending one of the proposals in the Bill, to extend the time anyone can be detained in police custody without being charged beyond 36 hours, a senior police officer pointed out that only about 4 per cent of persons currently arrested would be affected by the proposed provision. This represents 20-22,000 people. Enacting the Bill as proposed, moreover, would not merely result in an increase – the numbers would multiply. Without cast-iron safeguards, the proposed powers would be extended by operational police officers far beyond the limits envisaged by legislators. The police tend to ignore the implied spirit of powers they are given: they look to the letter of the law. Once the substance of new powers has been digested in police training schools, thousands of police and detective minds are directed away from the central core towards the periphery. There at the dark edges, where black and white merge into indeterminate grey, questions about what the law intends give way to questions of what the law will allow. In practice, police officers will see themselves no more bound by the new words of 'the book' than they were by the old.

There are some signs that society is finally recognizing the dangers of a policing which has become detached from the community and that the bulk of social crime is community based and can only be effectively contained by police and citizens in the community working in concert. For this to work the police have to belong to and identify with the community. It means communities have to reclaim their police service from the control of chief constables to a greater extent than large amalgamated police forces currently allow. This will require a major restructuring of the police service. In any major reconstruction, however, there has to be a true reflection of policing realities; there are policing responsibilities which are not related to specific communities. There are a whole range of responsibilities for protecting the monarchy, parliament, and the institutions of state, to provide a defence against terrorism, organized crime which crosses national and international boundaries, and acts of subversion. In the main, these national responsibilities are not only beyond the capacity of community policing resources, they are incompatible with the community police function.

Events in 1981 in Brixton and other inner-city areas have shown that law and order in some communities can break down. These events demonstrated that occasions may arise when the state must step in to defend individual rights in a community. Unless, therefore, the state maintains a policing capability independent of community resources, it cannot adequately shoulder its responsibilities. Sooner rather than later, society will have to confront the long-standing anomaly of its attitudes to 'blue collar' and 'white collar' crime. Conventional policing, as a means of preventing fraudulent and corrupt practices, is virtually impotent. Although it is generally acknowledged that the financial implications of fraud and corruption transcend 'blue collar' crime in financial terms, the totally inadequate resources applied to investigation is a national scandal. Unless the state creates a coherent investigative apparatus capable of investigating and exposing this form of criminal activity, it is a scandal which will continue. In the absence of a directorate of public investigations with the independence and professional expertise to investigate allegations of serious institutional or public misconduct, public confidence will continue to be undermined by scandals in the police, security services and other bodies. There have to be strict limits on the extent to which institutions of an open government are allowed to operate in secrecy. In a society in which there is a reluctance to reveal institutional affairs, and there are no independent means to examine, there can be no public accountability. The secrecy surrounding the security forces illustrates the social problem. The security services and Special Branch protect the public from enemies they refuse to identify: enemies, therefore, who cannot be recognized by the public, the potential victims.

There are few signs that the public recognize the dangers of a ubiquitous private security industry establishing its own mores in society. Yet it seems self-evident both at national and community levels that there can never be any satisfactory rationalization of policing until much of what is now considered 'private' is brought into the public domain. The resources of society are currently being squandered by the failure to co-ordinate the peacekeeping and crime-fighting efforts of private security and police. The lack of public control over the private security industry, in addition, is permitting it to apply technological remedies to problems which are not capable of technological solutions and, in the process, is changing the face of British society. To allow private security indiscriminately to apply security technology is to allow Neanderthal man to run amok with a laser gun. At the heart of the problem is something which is fundamental to society: the question of the extent to which government, local and national, is committed to fulfilling its obligations to ensure the safety and wellbeing of its citizens.

More and more private citizens and organizations are having to seek redress for crime from commercial insurance companies. Insurance companies are increasingly defining the conditions for the social environment which will determine whether or not they will provide cover for the individual. Aesthetic and environmental considerations play no part in an insurance company's commercial judgment: 'Thin trees – high foliage' is much more financially attractive. This is fair enough since insurance companies cannot pay out more than they receive and their commercial risk has to be minimized; insurance companies naturally promote as many precautions as possible, regardless of the wider implications for the general good. If this means imposing on society a massive security apparatus and a technological nightmare, so be it. In this process, however, where is the state's commitment and obligation to the individual?

In Britain, the state pays compensation for property damaged during riots and to individuals physically injured as a result of criminal attack. If the underlying principle were to be extended to include other forms of loss as a result of crime, and the state were looked to for compensation in the first instance, much could be achieved in returning responsibility where it belongs. At least communities would have a voice in the choice of trees and foliage preferred.

British society's roots appear to have become detached from their democratic foundations. Public lip service is paid by government to democratic principles privately treated as untenable: the human is being allowed to become subservient to the machine; collectivity is superseding individuality; and the individual's links between the community and the state are being eroded. There is a need to rediscover what it is that holds all the elements of a democratic state together in preference to being obsessed with all that divides them. There is a case to be made for a Bill of Individual Rights which is at least as strong as bills designed to place constraints on freedom: a new Magna Carta. A Charter which sets out in positive terms the elementary rights of the individual which are to be held inviolable: unequivocal rights which cannot be sacrificed by government in the interests of convenience or expediency and which cannot be compromised by dominant interest factions even though their presssure may not be unlawful. Britain is already under the shadow of Big Brother and will continue to be for some years to come. If it is to emerge from that shadow with a free society intact, there is an urgent need to discriminate between the jargon and the substance of democracy.

# Index

## A

Accountability, 54–5, 69, 76
Atoron Cameras, 165
Agnew, Spiro, 17, 146–7
Aims of Industry, 110
Ainsworth, Joe, 146–7
Alderson, John, 55–6, 143
Alphabet —
   Security technology, 168
Anderton, James:
   importance of views, 71
   obedience, 69–70
   records, 144
   security industry, 168, 171
   use of views by
      left, 116–18, 120
   view of society, 68–75
Angleton, James, 85
Anti-Nazi Movement, 106
Anti-Nuclear Movement, 106
Arnold, Bruce, 146–7

## B

'Baby-sitter', 85, 87–8
Binoculars, 158–9
'Bloody Sunday'
   (Whitehall riot), 206
Blunt, Anthony, 88–9, 109
Boateng, Paul, 56
Boyle, Andrew, 88–9, 91
Britain, stability of, 11–20
British Communist
   Party, 105, 108–9
British Leyland, 110
British Security Industry
   Association, 168–70
Brixton, 27–8, 114–16, 197–206
'Bugs' (miniature
   transmitters), 159–165
Burgess, Guy, 88–9, 109

## C

Cabal, 70–1, 118–19
Calder, Lord Ritchie, 137–8, 142
Cambridge Apostles, 90–1
Campbell, Duncan, 131–3
Castro, Fidel, 106
CCTV, 166, 182–5, 210, 211
Censorship, 24–6
Chiang Kai Shek, 138–9, 187
Chief Constables, 52, 69, 71–2
CID, 39–40, 59–64, 92–4
Civil Defence, 118–19
Civil Rights Movement, 106
Committee for a Workers
   International, 108
Community Policing, 55
*Computer* magazine, 131
Computers:
   false programmes, 127
   incorporating
      themselves, 127–8
   information
      surveillance, 130–47
   Weizenbaum, Professor, 212
Connor, Steven, 131–3
'Countryman'
   Investigation, 40–1, 59, 63
Crime Prevention, 65–8
Criminal Law, 44–8
Criminal Records, 139–43
Crown Agents, 175–6
Customs & Excise, 65, 83–4

## D

*Daily Express,* 52
Data Protection (Lindop)
   Committee, 132, 138
Davy, John, 127–8, 212
Debray, Regis, 111
Democracy, 30–1
Diplock, Lord Justice, 81

Director of Public
  Prosecutions, 40-1
Doherty, Sean, 146-7
Driberg, Tom
  (Lord Bradwell), 89, 98
Drugs, 83-4, 86-7

**E**
Education, 23-4
Eire:
  Littlejohn brothers, 82-3, 86
  threat from Ulster, 29, 114
Electronic Directional
  Transmitter, 157-8
Electronic Handkerchief, 166
Electronic Stethoscope, 162
Enemies of Britain, 77

**F**
Fianna Fail, 146-7
Fifth Column, 96-7
Finnelly, James R., 182
Fluency Committee, 90
Foco, 116
Food mountains, 20
Foot, Michael, 103-4, 123-4
Foreign & Commonwealth
  Office, 83
Fraud:
  inadequate
    investigation, 59-62
  social costs, 176-7
Freedom of Information Act, 95

**G**
Gay Liberation Front, 106
Government Communications
  HQ, 91
Greater London Council:
  left wing putsch, 113
  Police committee, 55-6
*Guardian, The,* 179-80
Guevara, Che, 106, 114
Griffiths, Eldon, 52
Group 4 (security company), 170

**H**
Hambledon, Arthur, 40-1
Hand, Learned (United States

Judge), 95, 131, 136
Haughey, Charles, 146-7
Havers, Sir Michael, 40-1
Heath, Edward, 96, 102
Hertzen, Alexander, 103-4, 108
Hollis, Sir Roger, 80, 90, 98-99

**I**
IFSSEC (security
  conference), 68-75, 169
Independent Television (ITV), 84
Infinity Transmitters, 165
Information (computer
  surveillance), 130-47
Insurance Companies, 215
Internal Security — military, 117
International Marxist
  Group, 108-9
Interrogation Methods, 41-4
*In the Office of Constable,* 40
IRA, 82-3, 86-7, 93-4
Iranian Embassy, 184
Irish (living in Britain), 29
*Irish Independent,* 146-7
Investigation, 59-62, 213

**J**
Joint Intelligence Committee, 80
Joint Warfare Establishment, 121
Journalists, 20, 24-7

**K**
KGB, 80, 85, 96-9
King, Cecil, 119-20
Kings Cross, 196
Kipling, Rudyard, 133
Kitson, Lt. Gen. Sir Frank, 120-2

**L**
Labour Party, 109, 111-13
Ladbroke Casino
  Prosecution, 141
Laser Beams, 164, 214
Liberty, 9-10, 30-1
'Liffygate', 146-*7*
Lincoln, Abraham, 9-10, 30
Littlejohn,
  brothers, 82-3, 85-6, 94
Livingstone, Kenneth, 15, 113

Lloyds Insurance — London, 61
Long, Leo, 89
'Low Intensity Operations'
    (Frank Kitson), 120-1
Lyalin, Oleg, 96

**M**
McCann, James, 83
McLaughlin, Patrick, 146-7
MacLean, Donald, 88-91, 109
Macmillan, Harold, 98
Madison, James, 212
Malpractice, 44-5
Manchester, 26-8
Mao Tse-tung, 106, 114, 139, 187
Mark, Sir Robert, 39-45, 52, 68-9
Marks,
    Dennis Howard, 83-4, 85-7, 94
Marsden, Graham, 58
Massachusetts Institute of
    Technology, 127, 212
Mass Media, 22
Marxism:
    fear of, 73
    groupings, activities, 108-12
    strategies, tactics, 100-22
'Media Man', 22
Meritocracy, 70
Mervyn-Jones, J, 58
MI5, 79-99, 131-3
MI6, 79-99
Microphones, bugging, 159-65
*Militant,* 113
Militants, 16, 108
Militant Tendency, 56, 112-3
Military/Staff College, 117-22
Ministry of Truth —
    (Orwell), 24, 127-8, 212
Minolta camera, 165
Minox cameras, 165
Mitchell, Graham, 80, 90
Mitchell, John, 146-7
Mock Trials, 43
Mountbatten, Lord Louis, 119-20
'Mugging', 115-6, 198-9
Murray, Len, 195

**N**
National Health Service, 194-5
National 'interest', 70-1, 118-9
National Police College, 71

National Police Force, 55-7, 71-2
*New Statesman,* 131-3
Nixon, Richard, 17, 127, 146-7
Norwood Green, 183

**O**
*Observer, The,* 103-4, 127-8, 211
Orwell, George, 20-1, 50, 74

**P**
Parliamentary Labour
    Party, 112-3
Pascal, Blaise, 32-3, 73, 194
Peach, Blair, 42
Pegg, Frank, 210-11
Philby, Kim, 88-91, 109
Pincher, Chapman, 88, 90-1, 97
Police:
    accountability and
        scrutiny, 33-4
    arms, riot equipment/
        tactics, 205-9
    authority and anti-authority, 34
    attitudes to Special
        Branch, 69-70, 92-4
    chief constable
        autonomy, 34, 52, 69, 71-2
    community policing,
        John Alderson, 55-6
    complaints procedures, 39-40
    corruption and
        'Countryman', 39-41, 59,
                                63, 69,
    drugs and former allies, 36
    end of silent service, 70
    interchange and
        specialists, 58-67
    interrogation
        methods, 41-4, 49-50
    James Anderton, views, 68-75
    legal niceties, Sir Robert Mark's
        views on, 45-9, 39-45, 52,
                                68-9
    malpractice, dual
        standards, 36-47
    powers and constraints, 35
    race relations
        Brixton, 197-200, 204-8
    records, 132, 134-44
    recruitment base, 52-3
    riots, confrontation,

race, 28, 202–7
saboteurs, 97
Scarman report, 200
servant-master
  relationship, 33
Special
  Branch, 79–99, 132, 136, 143
stations, centres of first
  resort, 48
stop, search, arrest,
  detain, 48–50
surveillance, 183–5
the institution, 32–7
unofficial weapons, 41–3
Polygraph, 166
Powell, Enoch, 26
Prime, Geoffrey, 91–2
Private Security
  industry, 168–82, 210–12
Prostitutes, 195–6
Psychological Stress
  Evaluator, 166
Psychological Warfare, 121
Publicity Experts, 20–3


**R**
Race, 26–8, 197–207
Records, 132–43, 145–6
Regional Commissioners (Civil
  Defence), 118–9
'Rifle' Microphone, 163–4
Right Wing Reaction, 116–22
Riots, 26–8, 199–209
Rollei cameras, 165
Rosewell, Roger, 110


**S**
Salmon, Lord (former
  Lord Justice), 213
Scargill, Arthur, 21
Scarman, Lord, 200
Scotland, 29–30, 188
SDP/Liberal Alliance, 15–16
Securicor, 169–70, 179
*Security Gazette*, 182, 210
Security Services, 76–99
Secrecy, 79
Sennheiser, 163
Sensory Deprivation, 49–50
Shoplifting Bag, 182
Silone, Ignazio, 103, 108

Sinn Fein, 92–4
Sociologists 22–4
*Socialist Press* 110
Socialist Workers Party, 108–110
Special
  Branch, 69, 70, 79–99, 92–4
*Spectator, The* 146–7
'Spike Mike' 162–3
*Standard, The* 213
St. Johnstone, Col. Sir Eric, 71–2
*Sunday Times* 182
Surveillance:
  computer technology 130–47
  conventional 151–7
  technical 157–67


**T**
Tawney, R.H., 103
Teachers, 20, 23–4
Technological Elite, 19–21
Telephone taps, 164–5
Terpil, Frank, 84–5, 87–8, 94
Thatcher, Margaret, 14, 15, 24
Thomas, Anthony, 84–5, 87–8
Thornett, Alan, 110
TINA, 16
Totalitarianism, 31, 50–1, 68–75,
                    100, 213
Toxteth, 26–8
Tube Microphones, 162
Traffic, 64–8
Trotskyite Groups, 108
Trotsky, Leon, 105, 108


**U**
Ulster, 29, 114, 188
Unemployment, 14–15
United Kingdom Land
  Forces, 118, 120–2
United
  States, 17, 29, 95, 127, 146–7


**V**
Voice Stress Analyser, 166


**W**
Wall, Pat, 56
Wales, 29–30, 188
Watergate, 146

West, Nigel, 88–9, 90
Whitelaw, William, 59
Wilson, Sir Harold, 98
Wilson, Peter, 121
Wilson, Edward, 84
Womens Rights Movement, 106
Workers Socialist
  League, 108–10
Workers Revolutionary
Party, 108–9

**Y**
Yashica cameras, 165

**Z**
Zuckerman, Lord, 119